Impressions of The Seine

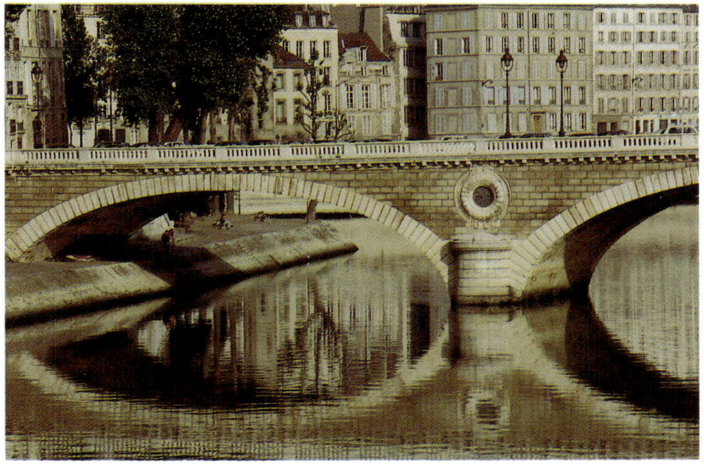

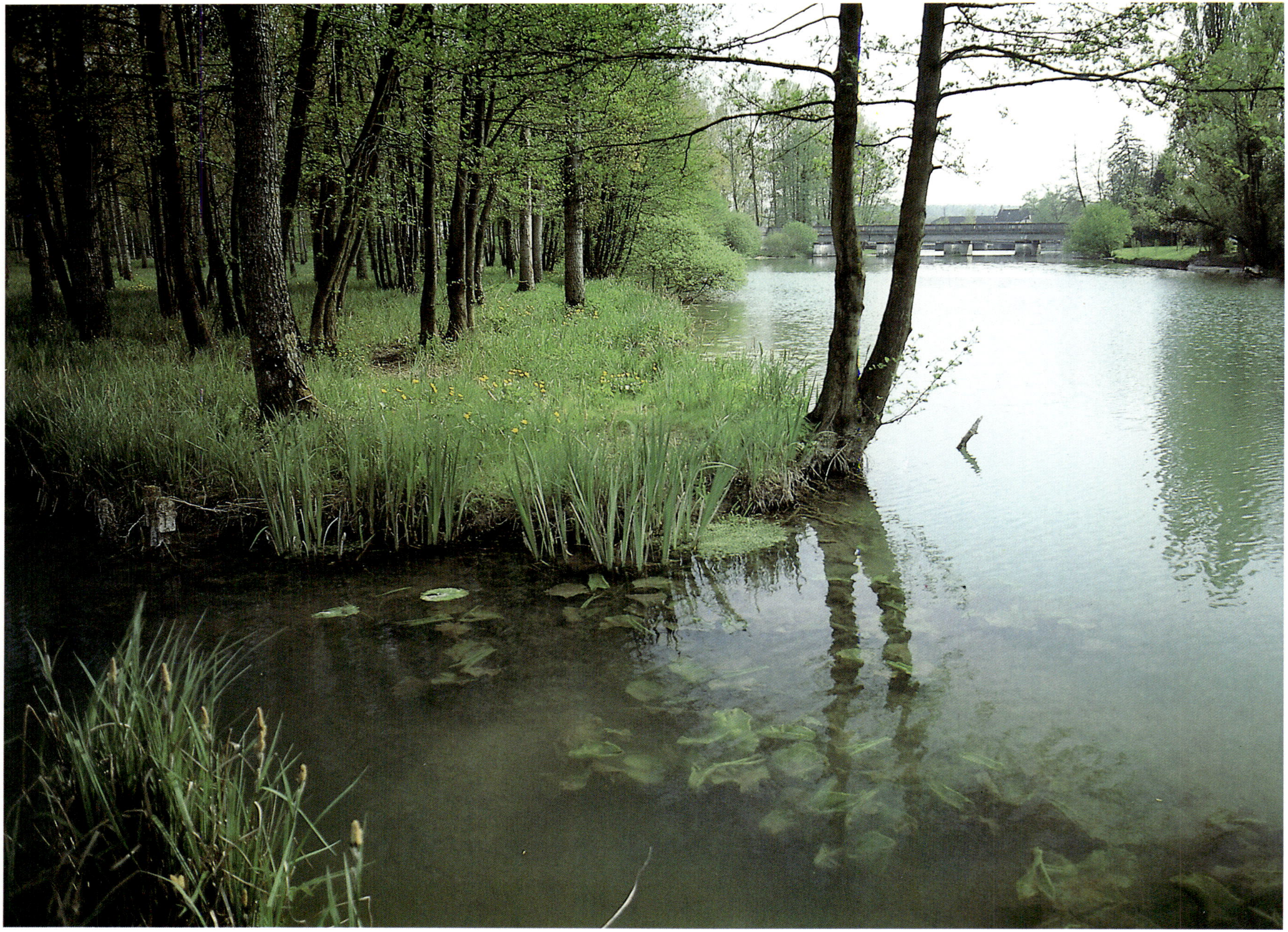

Fouchères, Champagne

IMPRESSIONS OF THE SEINE

PHOTOGRAPHS BY CAREY MORE
TEXT BY JULIAN MORE

PAVILION

For Manon

First published in Great Britain in 1991 by
PAVILION BOOKS LIMITED
196 Shaftesbury Avenue, London WC2H 8JL

Designed by Bernard Higton

A CIP catalogue record for this book is
available from the British Library

ISBN 1 85145 3725
10 9 8 7 5 4 3 2 1

Printed and bound in Italy
by New Interlitho, Milan

CONTENTS

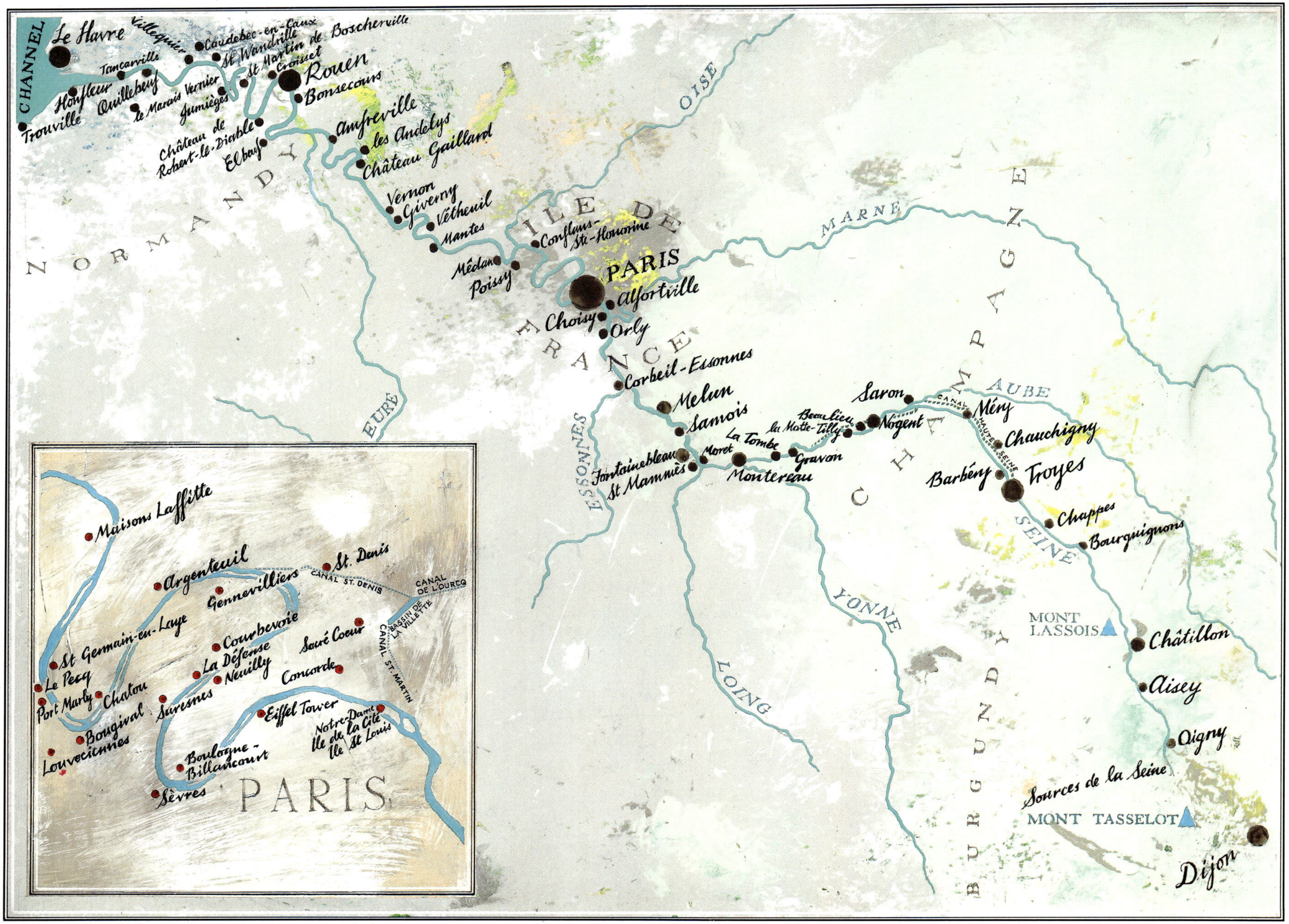

CHANNEL
Le Havre
Villequier
Caudebec-en-Caux
St Wandrille
St Martin de Boscherville
Tancarville
Croisset
Rouen
Honfleur
Quillebeuf
Le Marais Vernier
Jumièges
Bonsecours
Trouville
Château de Robert-le-Diable
Elbeuf
Amfreville
les Andelys
Château Gaillard
N O R M A N D Y
Vernon
Giverny
Vétheuil
Mantes
Médan
Poissy
Conflans-Ste-Honorine
I L E D E F R A N C E
PARIS
Alfortville
Choisy
Orly
Corbeil-Essonnes
Melun
Samois
Fontainebleau
St Mammès
Moret
La Tombe
Montereau
Gravon
Beaulieu
La Motte-Tilly
Nogent
Saron
CANAL
Méry
Chauchigny
HAUTE SEINE
Barbéry
Troyes
Chappes
Bourguignons
C H A M P A G N E
OISE
MARNE
AUBE
EURE
ESSONNES
YONNE
LOING
SEINE
MONT LASSOIS
Châtillon
Aisey
Oigny
Sources de la Seine
MONT TASSELOT
B U R G U N D Y
Dijon
Maisons Laffitte
Argenteuil
St. Denis
CANAL ST. DENIS
CANAL DE L'OURCQ
Gennevilliers
BASSIN DE LA VILLETTE
CANAL ST. MARTIN
St Germain-en-Laye
Courbevoie
Sacré Coeur
Le Pecq
La Défense
Neuilly
Concorde
Port Marly
Chatou
Suresnes
Eiffel Tower
Bougival
Notre-Dame
Ile de la Cité
Ile St Louis
Louveciennes
Boulogne-Billancourt
Sèvres
PARIS

PART I

THE SOURCE TO PARIS

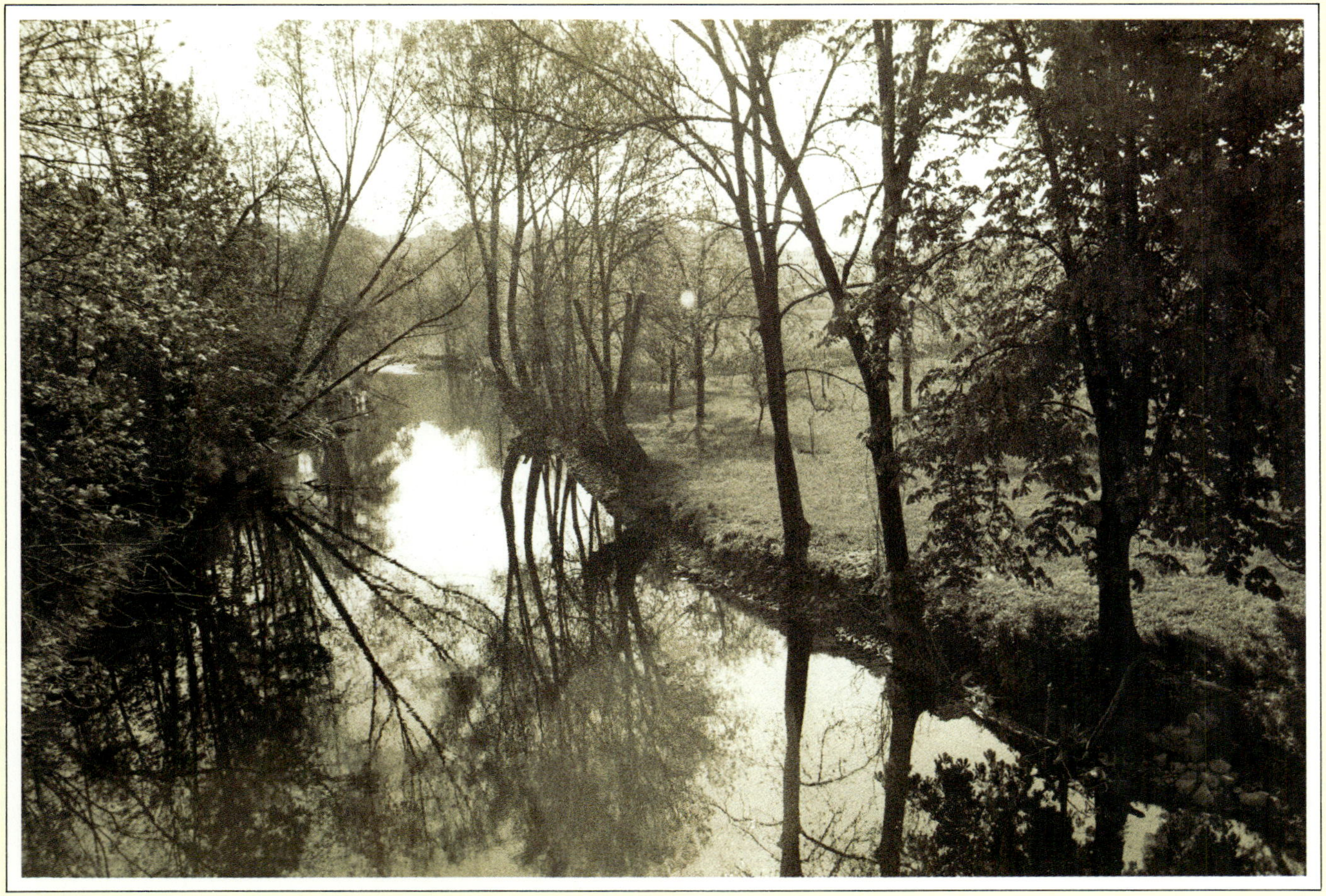

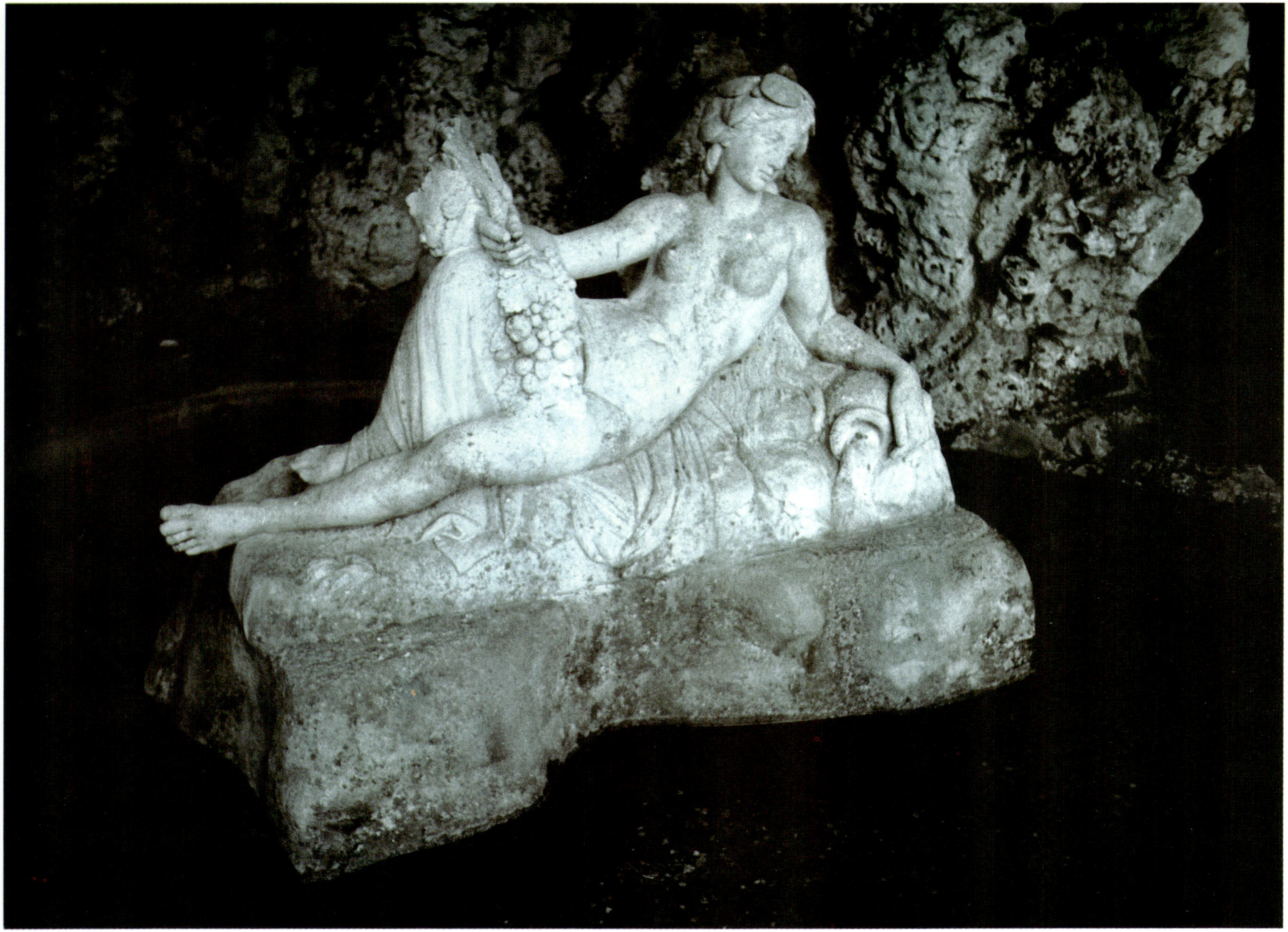

Goddess Sequana, Source of the Seine

SEQUANA'S SPRING

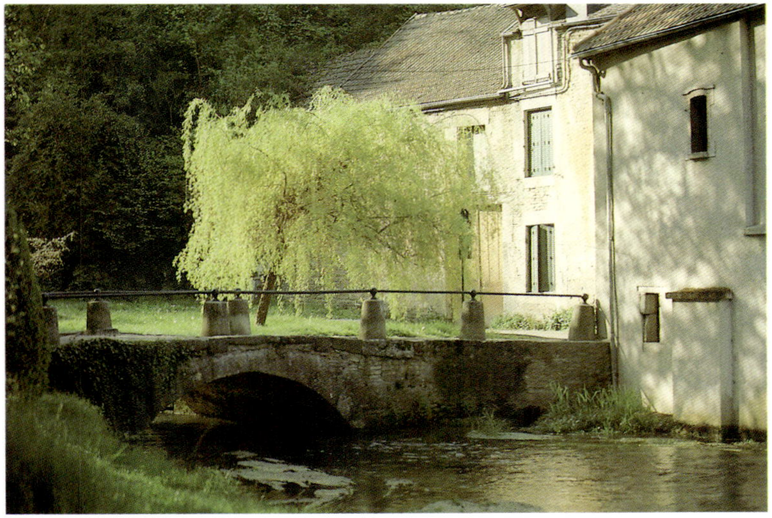

It was like being present at an unusually tranquil birth. Very feminine: the goddess Sequana, La Seine. The sound of the Seine beginning was a burbling beneath a statue of the goddess, who gazed down upon the water like a proud mother just delivered of a bouncing river.

We watched the infant Seine begin her 481-mile journey from Burgundy to the sea. As the seagull flies, Mont Tasselot is only 248 miles from the river's mouth. And starting comparatively low – 1,540 feet above sea level – her growth is slow, her progress devious. What a mazy motion goes into that meandering! The Gallo-Roman goddess Sequana's name comes from the Celtic *squan*, meaning serpentine. Sequoine (in French) lost her 'quo' if not her status and was contracted to Seine.

A little way downstream of this grotto were found the ruins of a Roman Temple, a pagan shrine whose water had healing properties and where votive offerings were made to the goddess Sequana. One can see ex-votos representing the ailment of the person to be healed on display at the nearby archaeological museum of Dijon. The nymph-goddess has such a benign face, I would be tempted, even today, to offer an ex-voto for the commonest of colds.

The nymph's statue was installed by Baron Haussmann in

CHÂTILLON-SUR-SEINE

1867; it was Paris's way of staking a claim to this patch of Burgundy, where the capital has installed a peaceful, bosky garden around its river's source. The Baron's mind was sensibly not just concerned with his spanking new boulevards and sewers; he showed due respect for the river, too. Napoleon said, 'Le Havre, Rouen and Paris are one city, of which the Seine is the main street.' And the river reached its zenith of importance in the nineteenth century – to Impressionist painters and coal-bargees alike.

But, to us, it was as yet a mere trickle of peat-stream clarity, winding from shade to sunlight, in miniature evoking the chiaroscuro beloved of the Impressionists. Looking down on a toy stone bridge carrying a toy footpath over the toy river, I thought of another bridge far, far downstream – Monet's railway bridge at Argenteuil.

Much water would flow under many bridges before we reached that one. We left the enchanted garden to its nymph, and followed the stream into *La France Profonde*, that deep, lost countryside of beauty and melancholy. I inhaled heady wafts of manure and the last wood fires of spring.

At Oigny, the source was already a four-and-a-half-hour hike behind us. A romantic, dilapidated Burgundian château loomed from forest shade. *Chef d'oeuvre en péril*, with no state grant to save it. It looked totally deserted. Moss tufts sprouted from the roof, yet the arched entrance was piled high with logs. To warm whom? Perhaps the owner had died before the winter, and no one had noticed.

In a chain of sleepy villages-sur-Seine, tiled-roof *lavoirs* take the Monday wash; they are basins of cut stone with the Seine's water diverted to provide a constant flow. Aisey-sur-Seine's ancient watermill by the weir had seen better days. As had two local fishermen. When asked by me, the foolish foreigner, 'How's the fishing?' they gave the sharp reply 'Go and see for yourself!' A conversation stopper, if ever there was one.

To fishermen and water gypsies and river folk of all kinds, the Seine has always been *la rivière* and not *la fleuve*. Semantically, this gives her a more intimate cognomen – the stream as opposed to the river. And at her first town, Châtillon-sur-Seine, she is still little more than a stream.

River fish would feature pleasurably in our Seine-side meals – long lunches on a terrace with a view recalling Renoir. As yet the river was too small for that. But even at the dullish Brasserie Europa, Châtillon, we were served crayfish, their tails tickled with crisp white Bourgogne Aligoté, young wine for a young river. They were, in fact, part of a cream sauce accompanying a Burgundian chicken. With French fries on the side. No calorie-counting here. This was Burgundy at its most traditional.

Other old-fashioned pleasures were to be enjoyed at the Hôtel Sylvia, Châtillon. I had one of those mansarded top-floor rooms with flowery wallpaper and big springy bed for afternoon love-making and a douche with red linoleum. The room overlooked a rose-filled garden. 'You can come back any time at night,' Madame Perrin assured us. 'We never lock up.' I told her how lucky she was, in these days of security by killer alsatian (who eats *grandmère* instead of the burglar), to live in such an honest town as Châtillon, but I'd got her wrong. 'What would be the point of locking up?' she added with the philosophy of Voltaire. 'Thieves would break in, anyway.' None did, however, and we were treated to a breakfast of buttery croissants and home-made strawberry jam in a private room full of bibelots.

An after-breakfast walk took us to La Douix, the Seine's first tributary and what surely must be the world's shortest river. Less

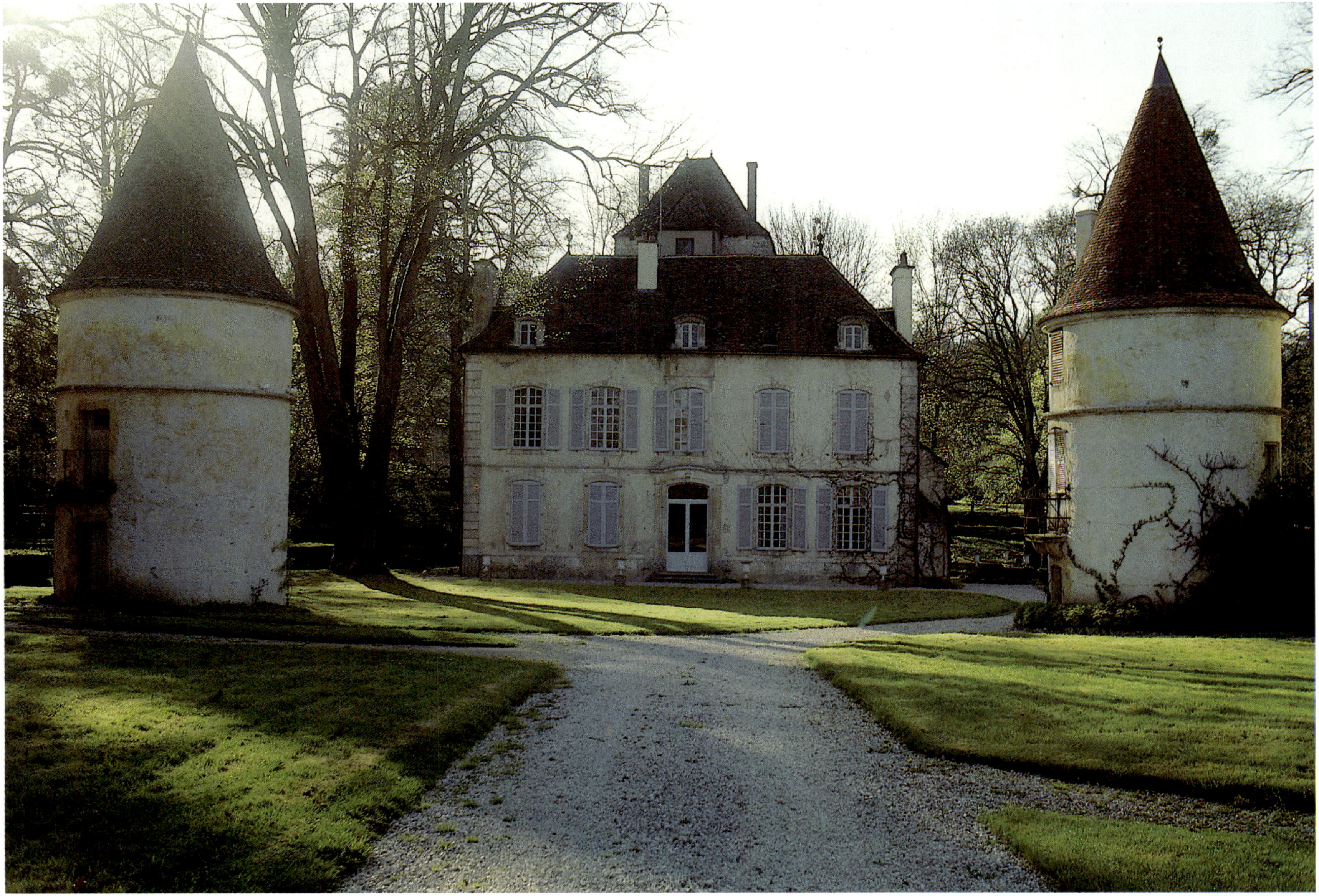

BURGUNDIAN CHÂTEAU, QUEMIGNY-SUR-SEINE

than a hundred yards from the confluence, La Douix springs from a wooded limestone cliff on the Old Town's right bank. Gushing up to 3,000 litres a second, it reminded me of La Fontaine-de-Vaucluse, that torrent in Provence; it is, in fact, called a vauclusian spring even in Burgundy. The dry, impoverished soil of the Langres plateau absorbs water through its calcareous crust, and a whole network of underground streams penetrates the deep clay. When several come together, they emerge as waterfalls like the mightily rushing Douix which, determined to assert itself in its short course before joining the Seine, bubbles noisily past weeping willows and senior citizens on park benches.

Falling rapidly from the hills of Burgundy, the Seine widened as we approached Champagne. The first Seine-side village of Champagne was named, strangely, Bourguignons – 'Burgundians'. Perhaps a few traitors preferred Champagne's wine to their own home-grown burgundy and had therefore moved to appreciate the rival grape: at Les Riseys, a rare *vin rosé* grown along the river in the most southerly champagne vineyards.

Above the weir of Bourguignons, the stream flowed calmly, then came torrenting beside a disused lock. I stood on a creaky, rotting wooden bridge, fascinated by the unaccustomed ferocity of the water. Not a bridge to linger on, specially with that swirling maelstrom beneath. Wiser than I, fishermen in calmer water downstream were safely fishing from a plastic boat; others, on the village's meadowy waterfront, barbecued trout by their caravans. The smell was too mouthwatering, and we dashed in search of lunch – never easy to find in *La France Profonde*, if you leave it much after one o'clock.

Pizzas prevailed. It was our first meal in Champagne, but Roederer Cristal was not on the wine list.

Champagne is flat. I can think of no *mot* more *juste*. Since its descent from the Burgundian hills to the plain, the Seine is now at 525 feet above sea level – not very high, with the whole of Champagne, Ile-de-France and Normandy to cross before reaching the English Channel. Slowed down by the gentler slope, it begins to meander through Chappes, and Clérey, and Verrières.

A dormitory river with private waterfronts, as we approach Troyes. Neat roads lead to the bourgeois villas of notaries and dentists and glove-manufacturers. Down Rue de la Plage, ending at a sandy little beach beneath poplar trees heavy with mistletoe, we fall among two louche lads who have captured a crow and are trying to get it into a sack. Is crow, I wondered, a regional speciality?

Sinister, this reach of the river. The suburbs of Troyes are Simenon country. Oh, yes, there's the nice municipal walk by the river near the Léon Blum 1930s Mairie and Rue Jean-Jacques Rousseau at St-Julien-les-Villas. But what goes on in those gingerbread villas with their savagely pointed roofs? The reek of respectability has a mildewed mustiness about it – something nasty in turreted attics. Who dropped whom in the river after some family feud about inheritance? Inspector Maigret is expected any moment.

Or am I thinking not of Simenon but Maupassant?

'I saw another boat and we hailed it. The man in it joined his efforts to ours; then little by little my anchor yielded. It rose, but slowly, slowly, and loaded with a considerable weight. At last we saw a black shape, and we pulled it to my side:

It was the body of an old woman who had a huge stone round her neck.' (Guy de Maupassant: *On the Water)*

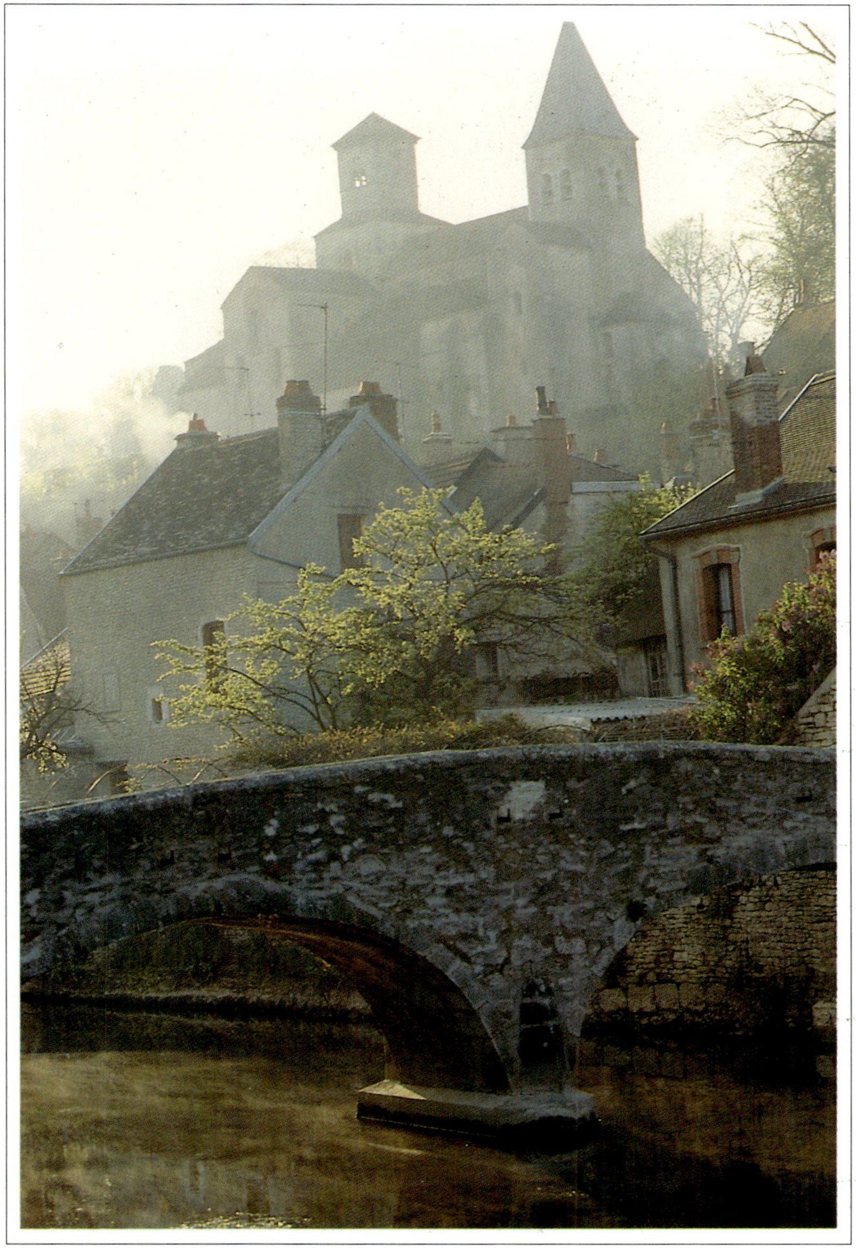

Old Town, Châtillon-sur-Seine

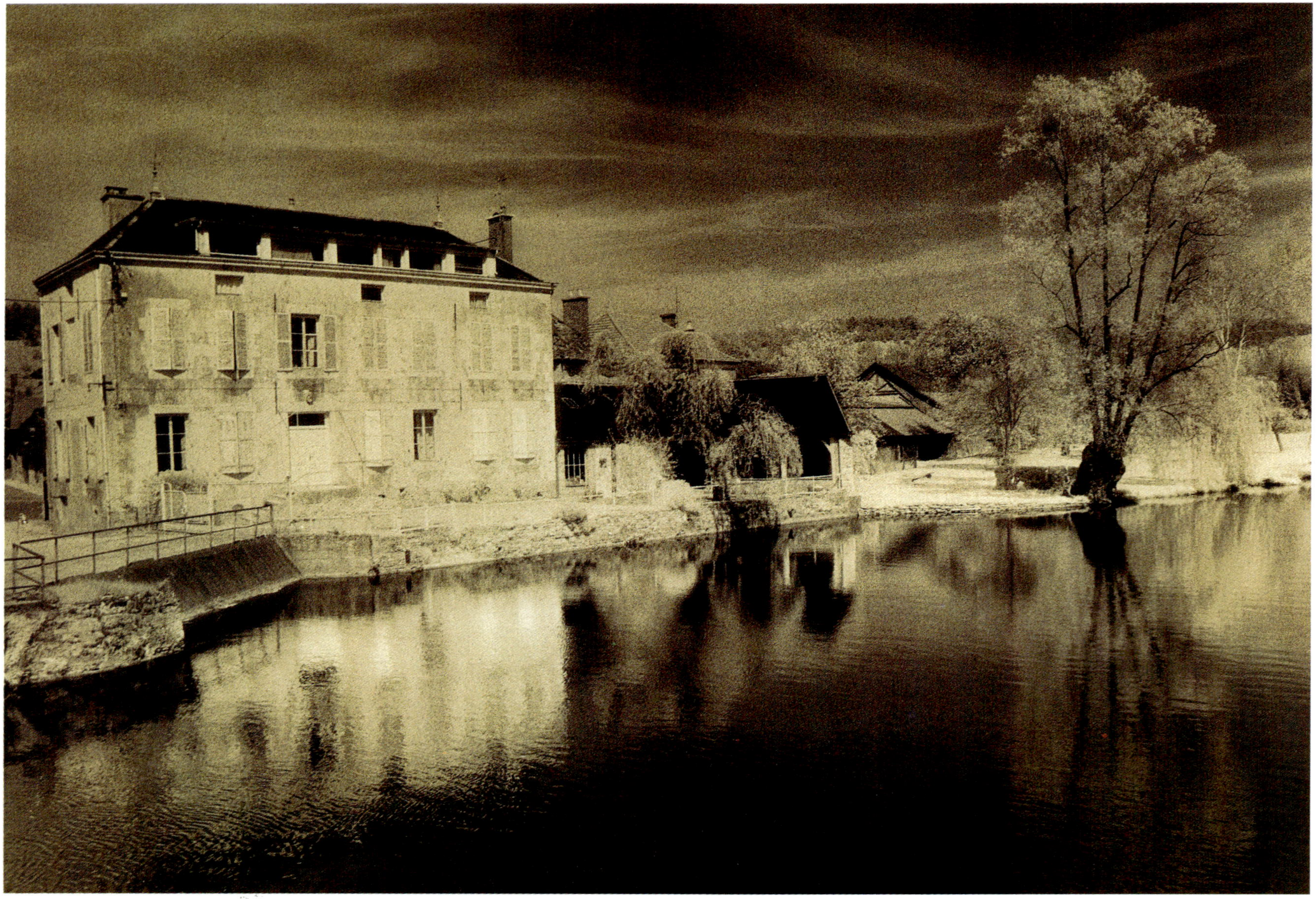

Bourguignons

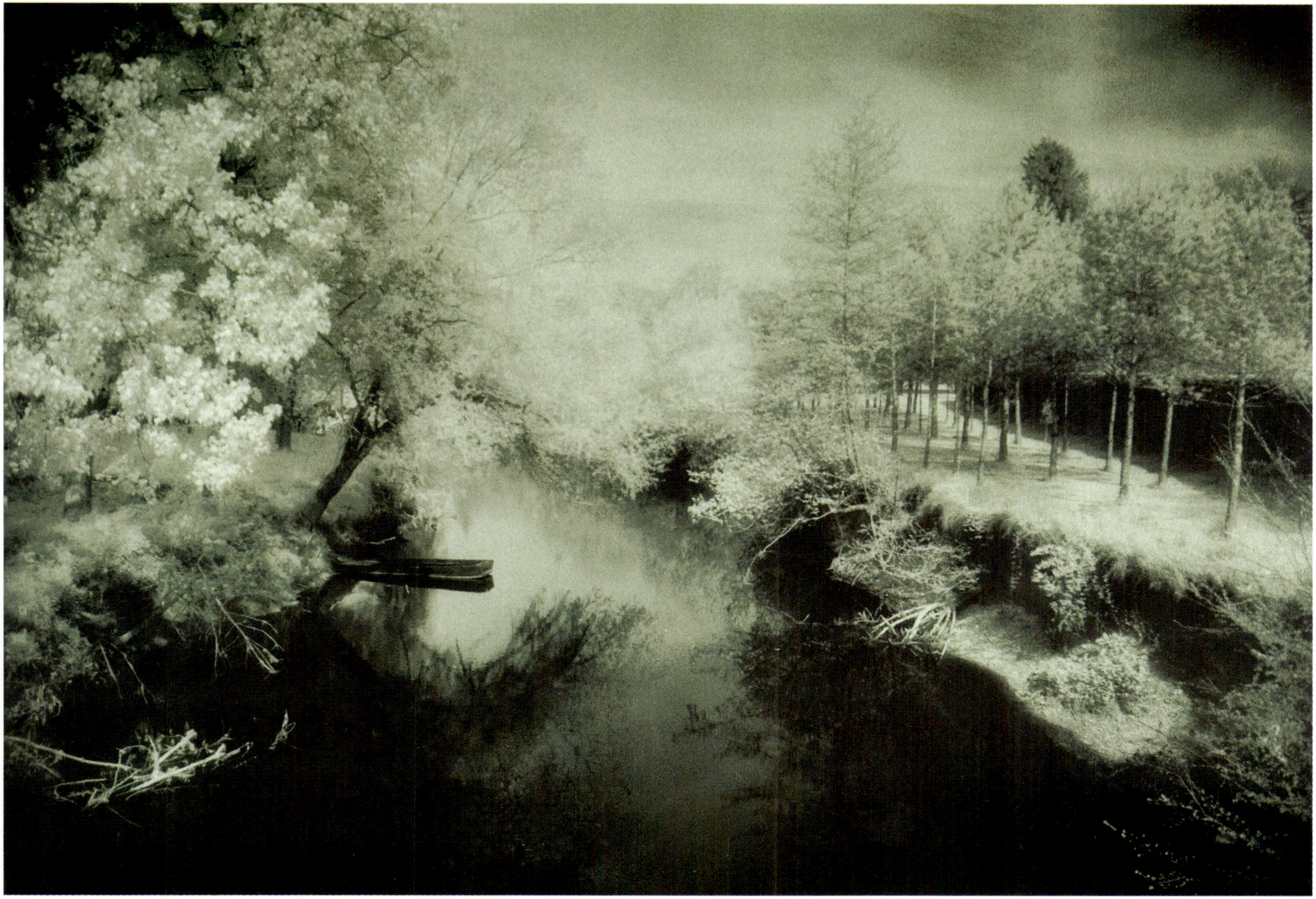

CLÉREY

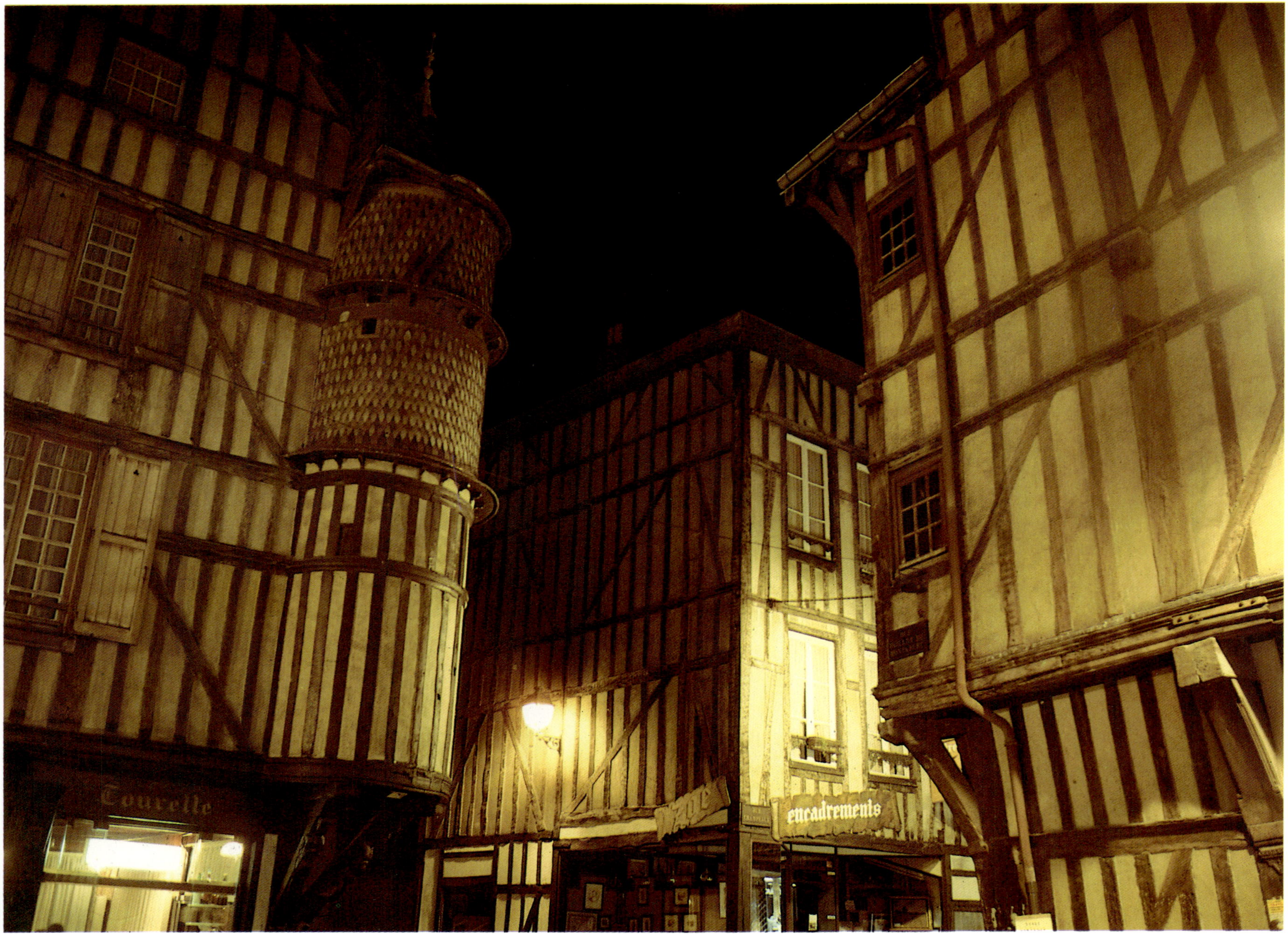

Tour d'Orfèvre, Troyes

Champagne Cork City

At the Préfecture de Police, early morning sunshine bathed the official room. Sinister imaginings in the suburbs of Troyes were quickly forgotten. And Pierre Stefan, the kindly Chef de la Direction de la Protection Civile, made numerous telephone calls on our behalf. Châteaux not open to the public immediately became open to us; permits would be granted to photograph nuclear power stations. '*Il faut jouer le piston*,' he winked. And clout he used.

From M. Stefan's room, if it weren't for the circus of revving cars and hissing trucks and apoplectic, whistle-blowing gendarmes, you could hear the splash of three fine fountains in the Bassin de la Préfecture. Now an ornamental lake in the city centre, it is fed from the Seine which bounds the old town's north-eastern perimeter.

Old Troyes is appropriately shaped like a champagne cork. The course of the Seine forms the cork's misshapen top, and it is pleasant to walk from the petrol fumes of Place de Vauldry to the whiff of new-mown grass along a chestnut-shaded, riverside promenade. We turned into the old town, following a disused canal – one of the many featuring in Troyes' sub-Venetian history. Within sound of the cathedral's bells, these narrow, stagnant waters and rotting warehouses and abandoned workshops are a ghost-neighbourhood of past artisanal prosperity dependent upon water.

In the Middle Ages, Troyes was renowned for its trade fairs, founded by the poet-knight, Prince Thibaut. It wasn't just costume drama and 'Sire' every other word; despite the jousting and spit-roasting and Gallic gallimaufry, these fairs attracted serious traders from all over France, bringing their produce by flat-bottomed boat through the already important inland waterway system.

The river, too, brought far-reaching results to the very centre of town – now a superbly floodlit pedestrian precinct. Results not immediately obvious from the medieval half-timbering of the Tour d'Orfèvre and the fairy-tale gables of Ruelle des Chats, an alley so narrow that cats can jump across it from house to house. How, I wondered, did all that timber get there before trucks and railways? Then it struck me: by Seine. Floated down from the forests of Burgundy.

Timbered building meant frequent fires – and Troyes needed Seine water to put them out. On one famous occasion, it did not. The Emperor Napoleon, passing through Troyes, remembered a horrible hotel he'd stayed at on a visit before his fame, and gave the order: 'Burn the fleapit down!' And the firemen stayed home.

Over the years, the Seine has served tanneries, mills, hosiery factories. From a riverside slaughterhouse comes the tripe which plays such a large part in the manufacture of the Troyes speciality, *andouillette*.

Can one canonize a sausage? I fear not. Or the clergy of Troyes would certainly have done so. Long ago, in the Wars of Religion, *andouillettes* saved the city. Or so goes the legend. Protestant Huguenots had invaded the city, intent on capturing

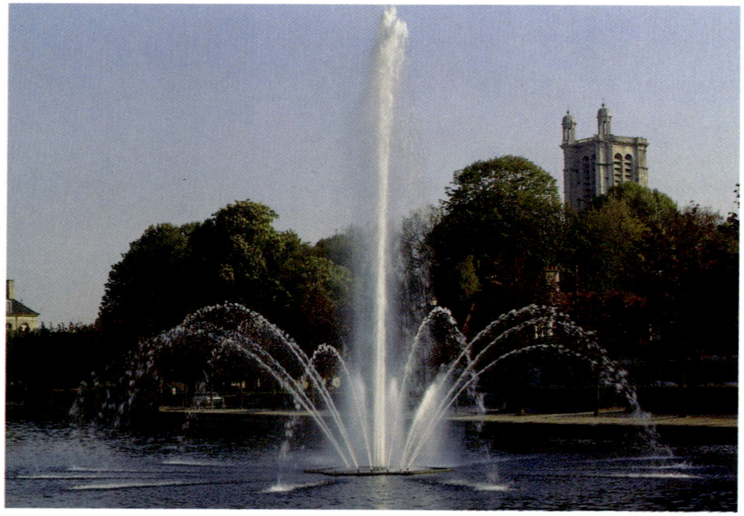

BASSIN DE LA PRÉFECTURE, TROYES

the eleven-year-old Catholic governor, Claude de Guise, who had taken refuge in a cathedral tower. Waylaid by the delicious aroma of sausages in the quarter near the cathedral, the Huguenot soldiers got into such an orgy of *andouillettes* that they forgot they were supposed to be capturing the governor; and Catholic forces surprised and massacred them in mid-guzzle.

I was slightly put off *andouillettes* by this cautionary tale. Tasty they may be, but we settled for fish at the Hostellerie de Pont-Ste-Marie, a romantic riverside inn on the city's outskirts. Bream in a scampi sauce, and fresh salmon with sorrel. There was also a delicious local smoked lamb's tongue as a starter, a by-product recipe of Troyes' once thriving wool industry.

From eating fish to looking at fishermen: *The Line Fishers* by pointillist painter Georges Seurat. Just one of the Seine pictures at the magnificent Museum of Modern Art in the former Archbishop's Palace. It was like a preview of places I was later to visit: *Countryside at Chatou* by Vlaminck, *Rouen Quayside* by Dufy, *The Seine seen from the Quai des Grands Augustins* by Marquet – a wintry view of Paris, this – and *Honfleur* by one of the estuary's most loyal painters, Otto Friesz. Art, near its source of inspiration, speaks louder to the heart. And though the best champagne vineyards were far from Troyes, we left the Champagne Cork City feeling pleasantly high.

Nineteenth-century art lives on for all to enjoy, but its industrial revolution wonders are now unwanted relics.

The Canal de la Haute-Seine is one of them – a long, dead straight waterway, begun at the turn of the eighteenth century to take boats the shallow Seine could not. I imagined 150-ton barges, groaning with cereals from the granaries; a constant coming-and-going of water transport between Troyes and Paris. Now, not a commercial craft disturbs the eerie stillness. These are the days of barge convoys of two thousand tons, with powerful motor pushers. And the towpath of the old canal is left to fishermen and horseback riders.

Above Troyes, the Seine flows at thirty cubic metres a second. Below, with chalk soil draining her water, she's slowed down at the height of summer to two cubic metres a second. But she doesn't seem too fussed about it. Lazily she serpents, splits into branches, makes islands, joins together again, wanders off into the countryside, leaving ponds and marshland in her wake.

A house by the Seine can be quite a hazard. You may wake up – after a long sleep – to find your house on an island.

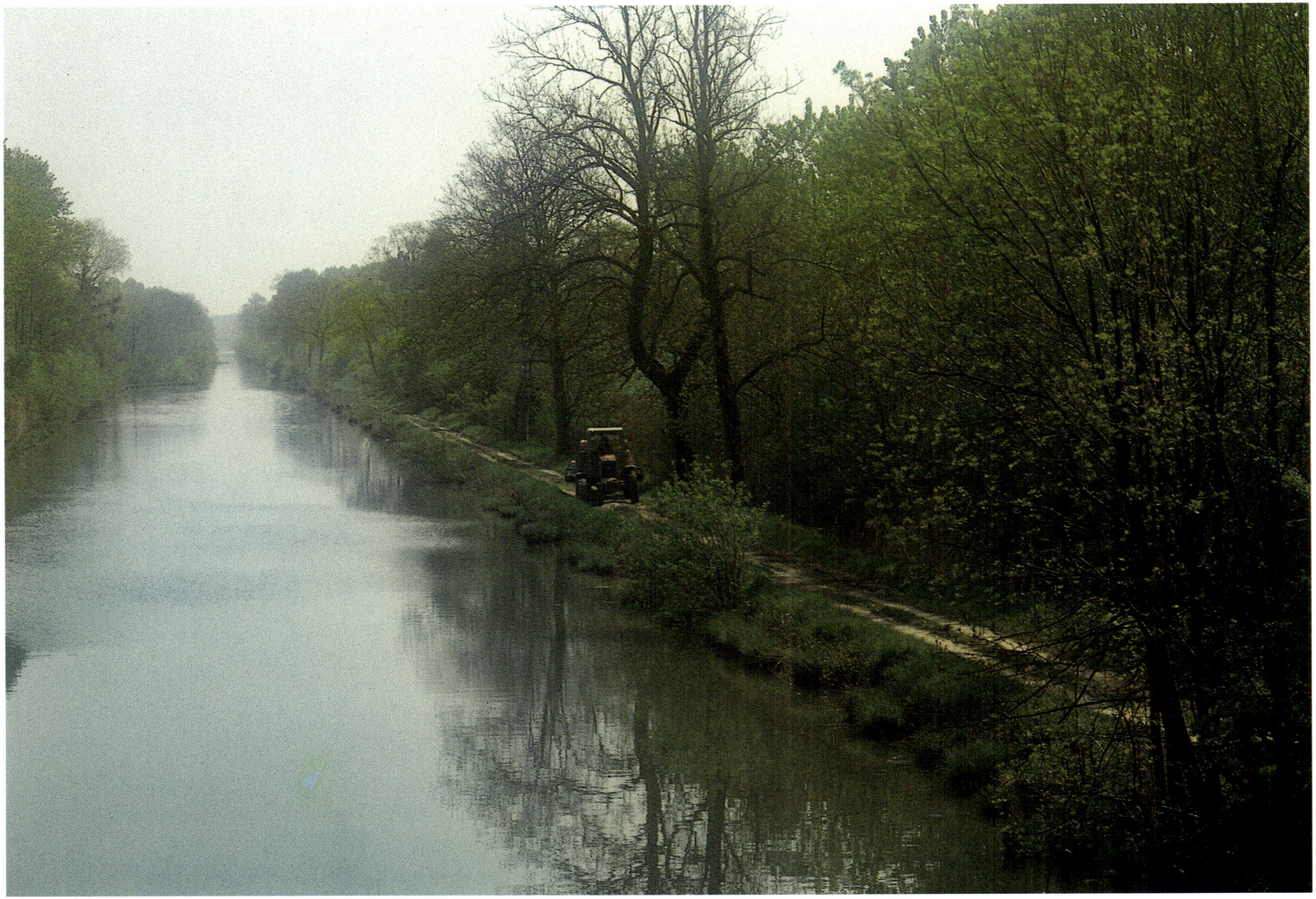

CANAL DE LA HAUTE-SEINE

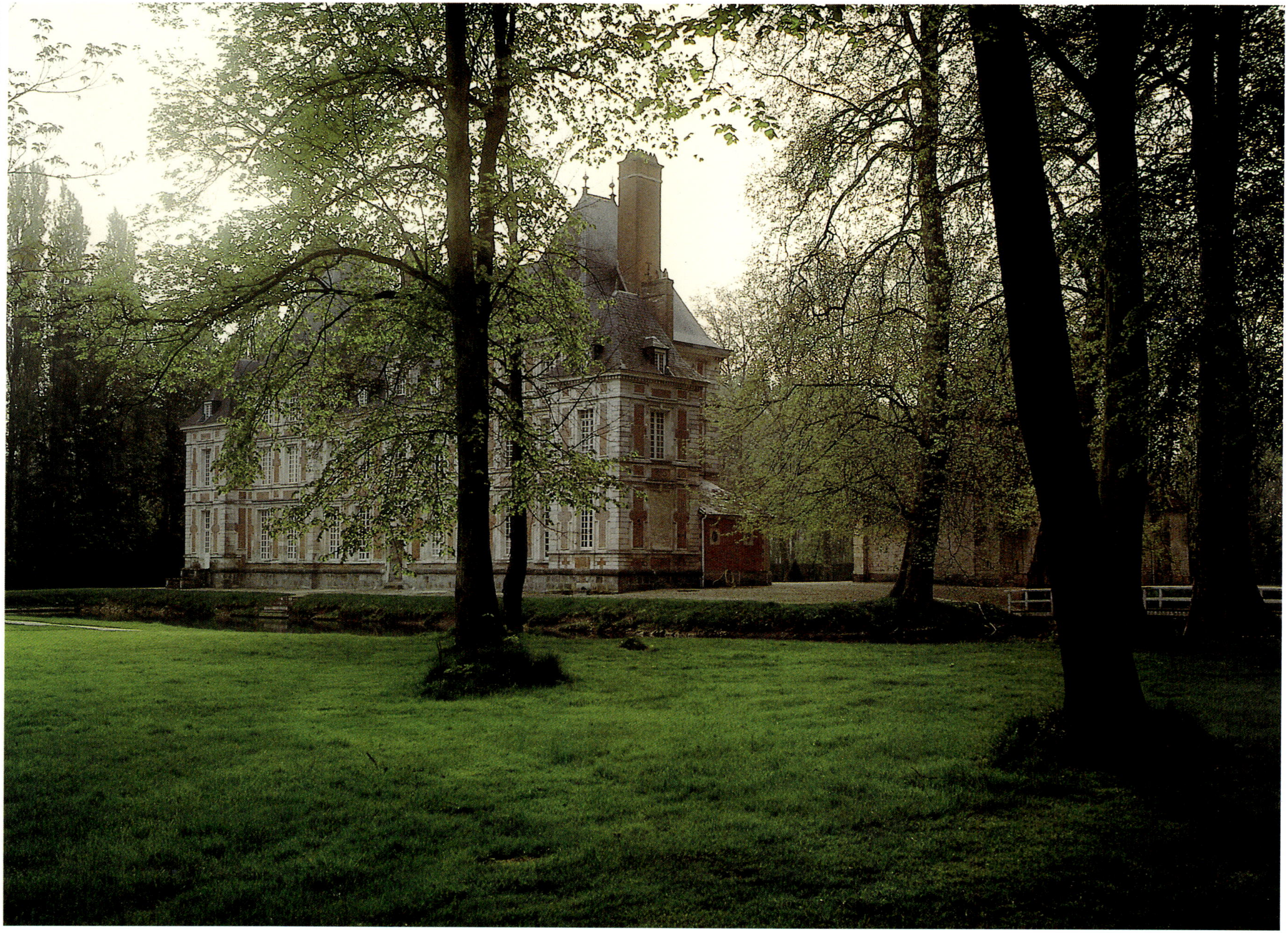

Château Barbéry

Two Riverside Chateaux

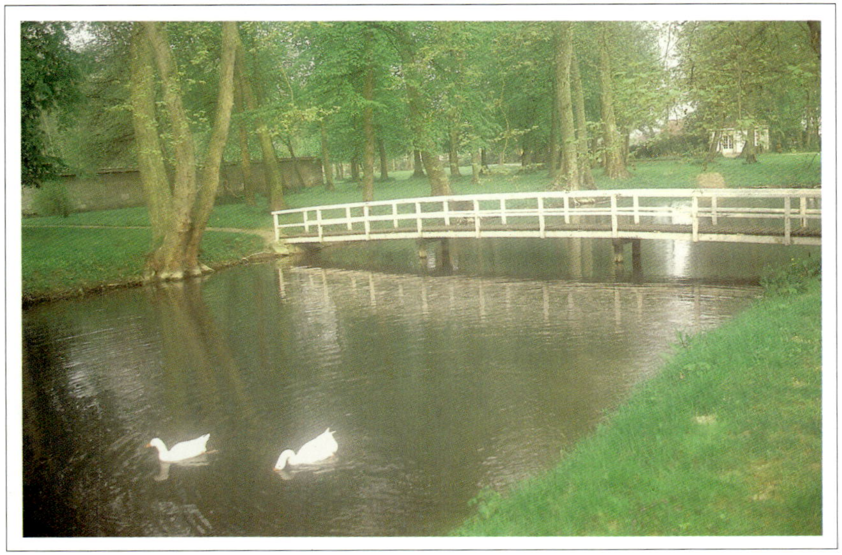

MOAT, BARBÉRY

'Beware,' said Madame Cuny, 'those swans are dangerous.' I had seen no sign CYGNES MECHANTS at the gates of Château Barbéry, privately owned by a married couple – both Troyes cardiologists. But I took her word for it.

The restoration bills were enough to give them their own heart-attacks. Madame le Docteur was off duty from the hospital today, but assured us she had to keep working to pay for it. Her husband had completely redesigned the formal garden and moat, encouraging ducks and geese and the dangerous swans to give it a lived-in look.

Only two hundred yards from the Seine, a dried-up tributary running through the wood emitted a muddy smell. This, Madame Cuny told us, offended the delicate nose of a previous owner. In any case, he had wanted to pull down the château and build a modern house – the Troyes equivalent of stockbroker Tudor, no doubt, with pretty gabling plus a painted farm-cart on the lawn and a swimming-pool in the moat. 'It would have been a massacre,' said Madame Cuny. 'But luckily he failed to get planning permission, because naturally it is a classified *monument historique*.'

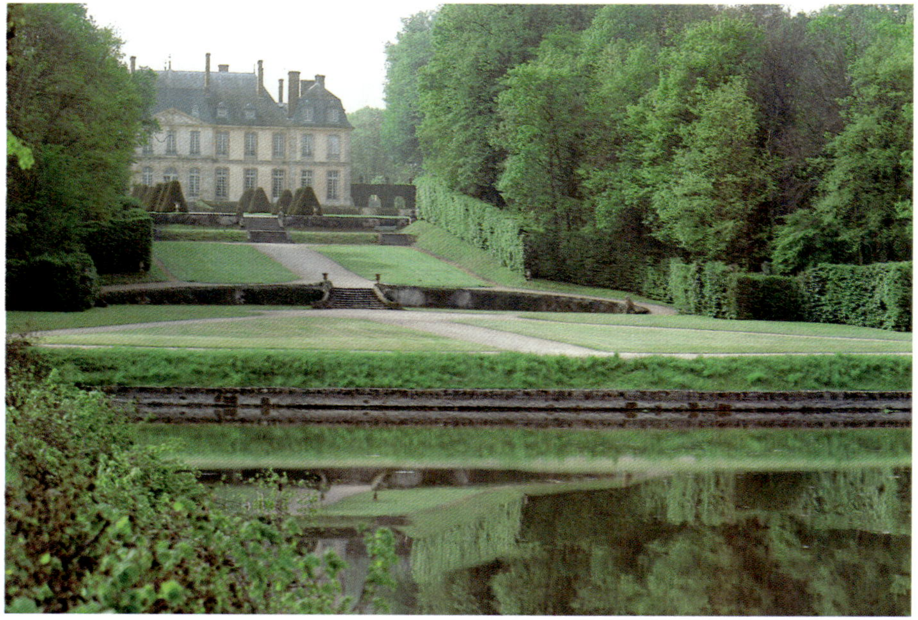

Château de la Motte-Tilly

The owner from whom the Cunys bought was, in Madame Cuny's view, 'an equally ignoble individual'. Married to a rich American woman who had brought in a New York interior decorator, he is alleged to have left telephone bills for the Cunys to pick up, and bankrupt masons and tradespeople ready to kill.

'But the interior decorator was charming,' Madame Cuny assured us. 'A man of extraordinary generosity. He stayed on and helped us with the heating and electricity – all hidden in the walls and floors. Also the furnishing. I think he had fallen in love with the place, like us.'

I wasn't surprised. Barbéry is a gem, pure Louis XIII, built in 1626, symmetrical with conical shrubs mirroring the turrets. It's a narrow house and the main living-rooms face both back and front.

'Quite liveable in, as châteaux go,' the châtelaine-medic bravely declared, ushering us indoors, having pointed out the vast roof reslated this year and the towers to be done next. 'Five bedrooms on the first floor, seven bedrooms on the second. . . .' And so on, up. A cardiologists' conference could have fitted in nicely.

The New York interior decorator's hand was evident in the white brick walls of the drawing-room with wooden panelled doors picked out in yellow; and a small study with Turkish tent effect. At a carved wood eagle lectern, Madame Cuny stopped

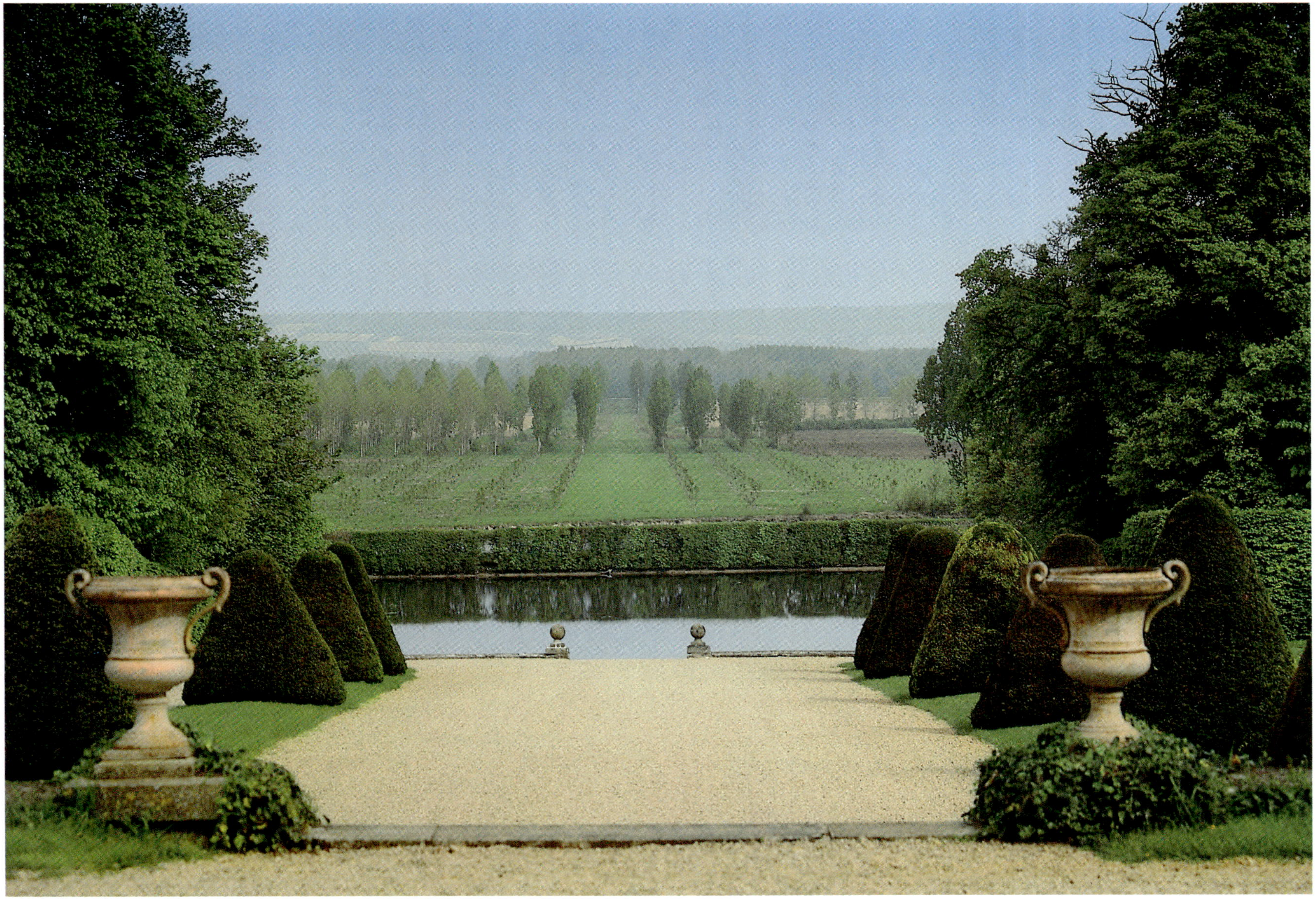

Gardens, La Motte-Tilly

and sighed: 'This was our first antique – we had it on loan from a Normandy dealer for two or three years!'

The Cunys had not always been rich enough to restore a château.

Which is not the case of the late Marquise de Maillé, the distinguished archaeologist and art historian, who died in 1972. Now I am jumping downstream, past Nogent, to include La Motte-Tilly.

It is a most elegant eighteenth-century mansion, with a terrace overlooking the Seine, built in brick and stone with no wood – a luxury in this area poor in natural building materials.

We were shown round La Motte-Tilly by a guide, because it is now a public monument. Evidence of the Marquise's career was charmingly displayed: a Louis XIV bureau, with signed marquetry, where she penned erudite words on the art of the Middle Ages. In the cosy sitting-room where she received guests were leather-bound first editions of Voltaire, Rousseau, and the Fables of La Fontaine.

Less intellectual pursuits at La Motte-Tilly clearly appealed to movie director Milos Forman, when making *Valmont*. It was the perfect location for his version of *Les Liaisons Dangereuses*. Love-seats converted into beds at the drop of a fan. Ground-floor boudoirs were close enough to the dining-room for love-making between courses. *Conversations galantes*, as these mealtime affairs were euphemistically called, were encouraged by mildly erotic prints – a man touching a woman's breasts, which tumble enticingly from her bodice.

But, in spite of this and the young guide's informative and witty commentary, La Motte-Tilly – without its hostess – had a somewhat dead, formal atmosphere. Hedges clipped just so, nothing out of place. And, worse than that, since the château became a national monument open to the public, the very view on to the Seine which was the site's *raison d'être* had been blocked by a high hedge between the ornamental lake and the public road along the river.

Château Barbéry was the home of two hard-working medics; Château de la Motte-Tilly, the legacy of a highly cultivated marquise. In the private one, there's a feeling of love and continuity; in the other, of a beautifully kept museum with the occasional film unit on the rampage through its boudoirs.

Down the lazy river, slowly winding.

Chauchigny. Big white modern mills, strong against the blue sky. Rolling, open countryside of prairie farming, wheat for the mills. A riverside *Graineterie du Moulin*, where grain is sold.

At Méry-sur-Seine – battle-scarred in two world wars – nothing could be less warlike than four punts for hire.

There is much flooding in this country. When the water rises, it swirls round the trees in eddies. Your punt floats over meadows, and below the clear, glassy surface, tall grass waves like corn in the wind. Back on the river's course, you take care not to bash your head on a bridge which seems unnaturally low. And hope to remember that the race gets faster as you near the weir. Till you can't stop. It's safer to shoot duck than the rapids.

Wild duck abound in the poplar forests near the confluence of Seine and Aube. Snipe and woodcock, too. It's a marshy area with petrified trees, tilted and interlaced, like a jumble of spillikins.

We hit upon on the most beautiful village yet – Saron-sur-Aube. Church, barn, manor-house with roofs slanting this way and that, all packed tightly together in a happy accident of non-planning.

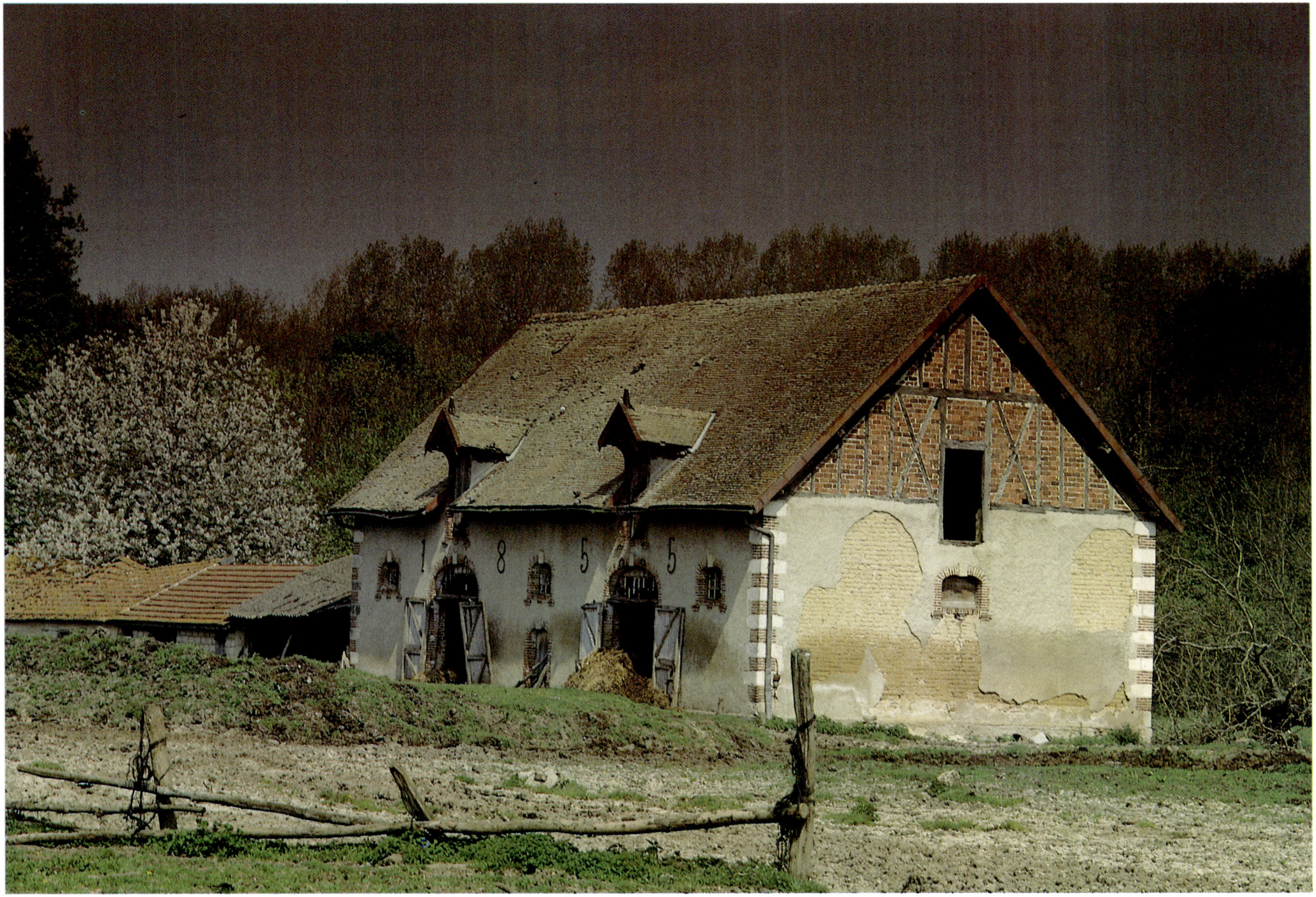

Barn, Sauvage

A GALLO-ROMAN RESTAURANT

There was no sign to it. An old man in Saron pointed vaguely in the direction of the confluence of Seine and Aube, murmuring '*Restaurant de la Plage . . . on y bouffe bien.*' And we found ourselves on a scrubby riverside track which seemed to lead nowhere.

From the jungle by a sandy beach emerged an unpromising shack of a place, and it seemed only too obvious why it kept a low profile. The car park looked like a junk yard. The only people lunching were Monsieur and Madame Gouhier, the owners.

'Did you phone for a reservation?' asked François Gouhier, an earnest young man of intellectual aspect. His tone was polite but suspicious. I said, no, we hadn't. I was sorry, but could he perhaps fit us in? He glanced at the seven empty tables and told us we were most welcome. Some other people evidently had phoned, and later became the only other guests.

Just how bad could the food be?

We needn't have worried. It was simple but excellently cooked. Creamy gratin of fish in a shell, followed by a *bavette* steak with *pleurottes*, mushrooms which grew on elm trees by the river. The other guests seemed suspicious of the weepy name, so François (we were quickly on first name terms) brought a plastic bag of them to prove their provenance.

Eventually, the place's clandestine ambience became clear. François Gouhier, former chef at London's Mayfair Hotel, was only a part-time restaurateur. His restaurant paid for his passion – archaeology. And it also housed his personal collection.

All along the valley of the upper Seine, François told us, artefacts had been found on the sites of ancient settlements. We had already seen the magnificent Treasure of Vix, housed in the Renaissance tower of Châtillon's archaeological museum. Tin from Cornwall, transported up river on its way to Marseilles, went into the bronzes of Greek settlers on the Mediterranean coast in the sixth century BC. And below Mont Lassois, at the village of Vix, was found treasure including a bronze Grecian vase for wine-making, wedding gift from a Greek to a Gallic princess.

'I'm not Châtillon,' François said, modestly. 'But I do have some interesting Gallo-Roman bits and pieces.' He lowered his voice, so that the guests who had questioned his mushrooms should be excluded. 'If you like, I'll show you them after coffee.'

Lunch over, he signalled us to follow him – up a rickety staircase to his holy of holies. It was the kind of chaotic room on which an enthusiast had imposed order not in any way obvious to the outsider.

Lovingly, from battered suitcase and dusty shelf, he revealed his own treasure. Little more than a mile from the Seine, a hunter digging to fix a fox-trap had told François about a pot he'd unearthed, and François went to work. The field turned out to have been a Gallo-Roman burial ground. These were its lamps, pots and glass.

'The rich were buried with glass,' François explained, holding up a glass-encrusted skull, 'the poor with pottery. They were buried with things in their mouths, you see, to pay their passage

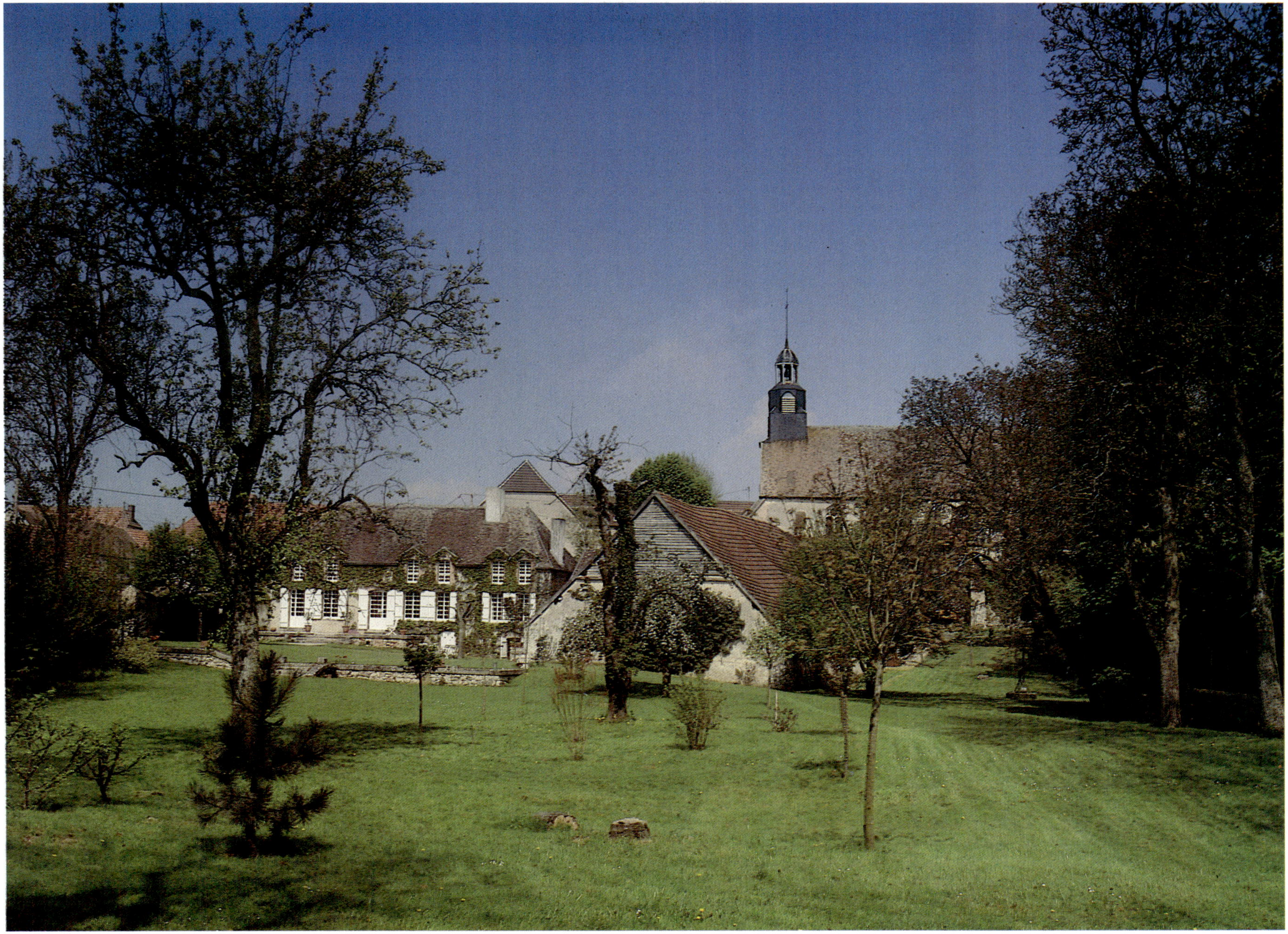

Saron-sur-Aube

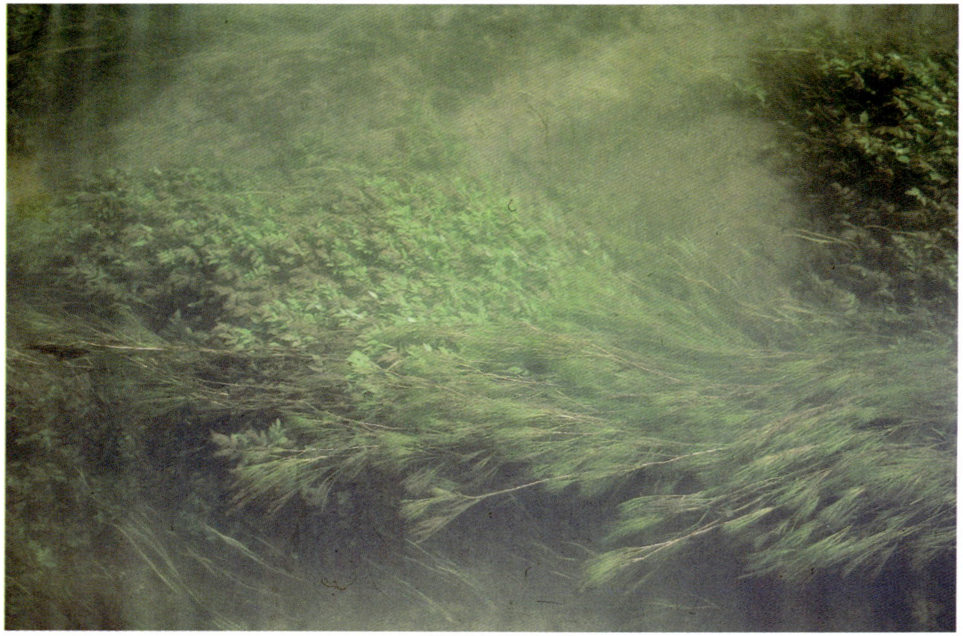

CLEAR WATER AND REEDS, GOMMEVILLE

over to the other side – appropriately enough, crossing the river.' He presented Carey with a couple of nails from a coffin dated circa 500 BC, and continued: 'As water was plentiful in the Seine Valley, people came to live here from earliest times – Neolithic, Gauls, Greeks, Romans, Barbarians, Vikings. . . .'

The collection of François Gouhier included Palaeolithic tools – man's first; a Neanderthal mammoth's tooth, frozen and preserved by the Ice Age; and Merovingian pearl necklaces, buckles and bracelets, belonging to the people of Clovis whose kingdom, at the end of the fifth century, included this part of the Seine and was called Francia.

Privileged to have been let into our reluctant restaurateur's secret, we paid François Gauhier about £12 for our excellent lunch for two, wine and coffin nails included.

La Petite Seine joins up with its wider tributary, the Aube, and becomes La Seine. By the time it reaches Nogent, the stream has become a fully-fledged river – ready for barges and water sportsmen.

A four from Nogent's Rowing Club cut through the water with deft strokes, blades and bodies working as one seemingly effortless entity.

Nogent, part river port and part country town, is nineteenth-century Seine personified. A great mill of rose-pink and grey

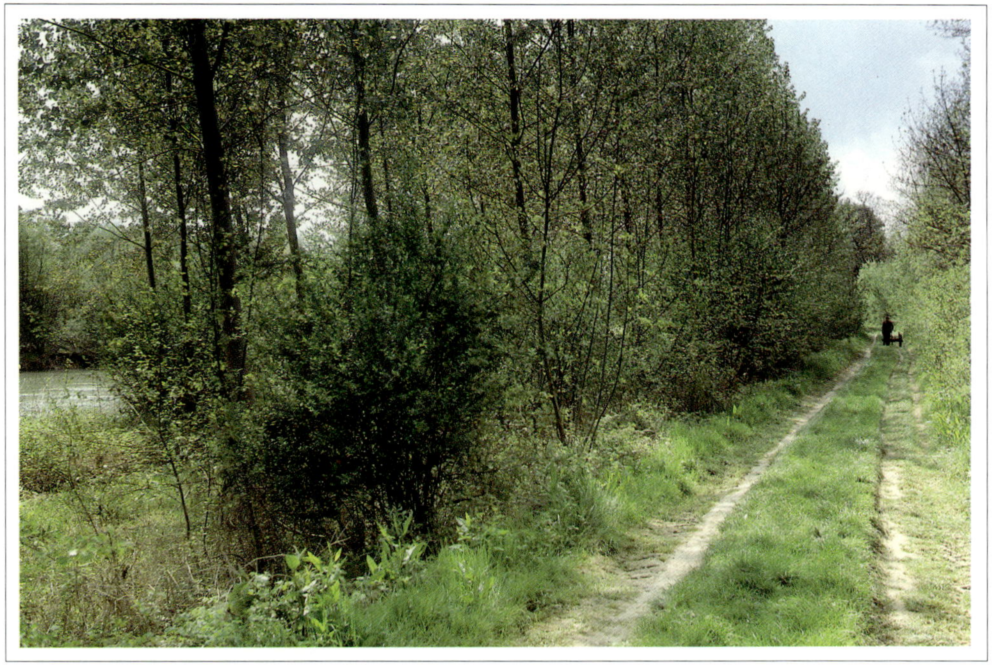

SARON-SUR-AUBE

brick straddles the river like a surreal colossus. Barges load only cereals now, and long forgotten are the salt, wine, vinegar and forage. Along the river banks tall poplars parade, and cool, shady walks can be enjoyed where once horses and men sweated in yoke to a loaded barge.

In *L'Education Sentimentale* Gustave Flaubert evokes the Nogent of 1840 with its lush vegetation and blaze of vivid summer colours.

'They heard the crunch of sand beneath their feet and the murmur of falling water; for the Seine, above Nogent, divides into two branches. At this spot, the one which turns the mill-wheels pours out its excess of water, to rejoin the natural course of the river lower down; and when the bridges approach, you can see, to your right on the other bank, a sloping lawn with a white house above it. On your left, in the meadow, are rows of poplars, and the horizon in front of you is blocked by a curve of the river. It was flat as a mirror; huge insects skated across the calm water. Clumps of reeds and rushes formed its uneven edge; all kinds of plants appeared, sprouting golden buds, letting their yellow bunches hang down, pushing up stems of purplish flowers, shooting green rockets out of nowhere. Water-lilies spread across a cove in the river bank; and a row of old willows hiding man-traps were, on this side of the island, the garden's only defence.'

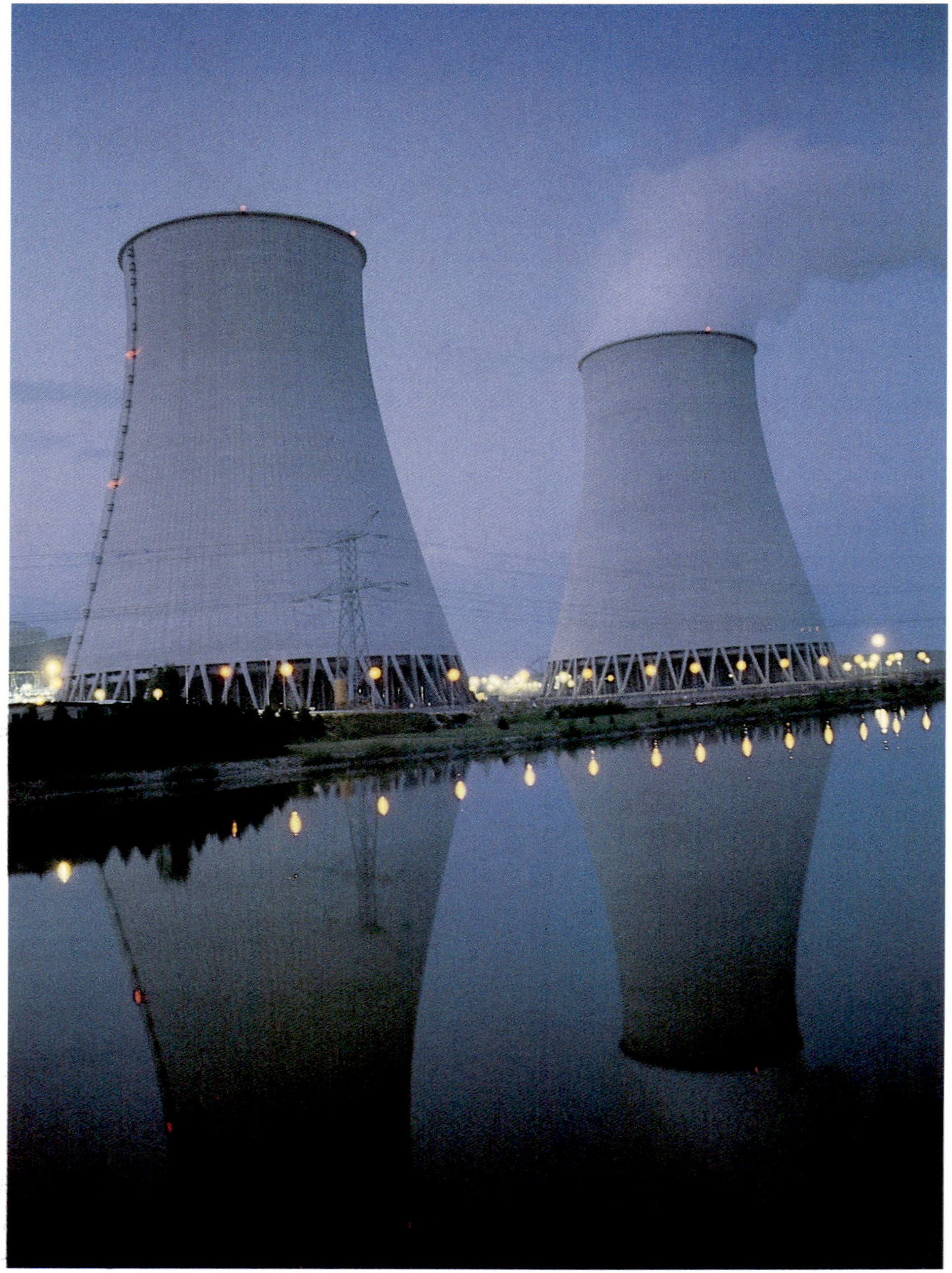

Nuclear power station, Nogent-sur-Seine

A Nuclear Night

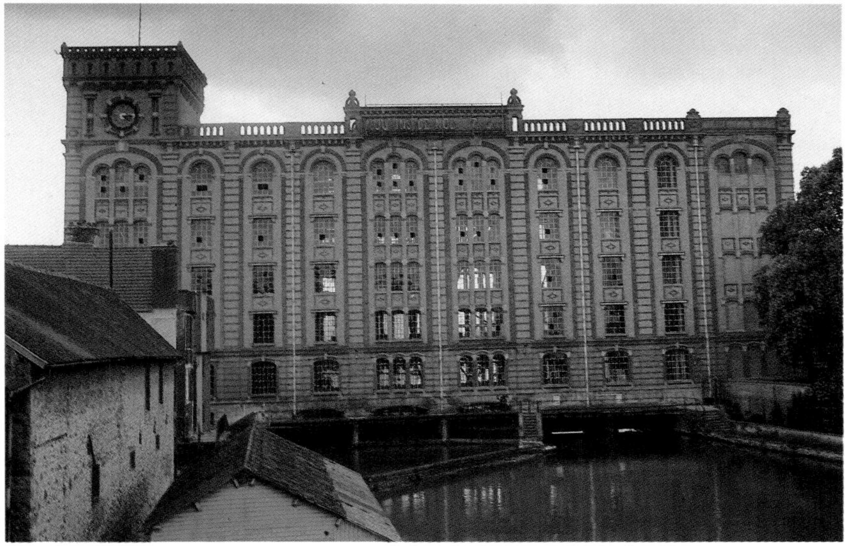

Though they no longer set man-traps, the Nogentais are still obsessed with security – for their Seine-side nuclear power station.

Or so I imagined.

Our visit coincided with hearing the first cuckoo in spring. Reflected in the water were the massive twin cooling towers, and in the woods behind us the cuckoo kept up its dauntless song. Nogent was still combining rurality with industry, it seemed.

We were greeted by not one but two public relations officers. While waiting for our photographic permit and passes, we visited an impressive space-age *expo* of models showing how it all worked. Like children, we pressed buttons, and strings of coloured lights animated turbo alternators and nuclear heaters.

Encouraging info is provided to create public confidence. This centre produces 52 million kilowatts of electricity in twenty hours. If I bicycled non-stop for the same time, I would only produce one miserable kilowatt. So it would take 52 million cyclists pedalling away for nearly a whole day to generate the energy of one *Centrale Nucléaire*.

The Seine was chosen for the site, because its water would

FLOUR MILL, NOGENT-SUR-SEINE

provision the closed-circuit cooling system. But when there's not enough water, heat non-transferable into electricity is evacuated into the atmosphere by means of those white, landmark cooling-towers. Our kind PR friends marked on our map the best spot for a night shot of their floodlit magnificence.

Easier said than found. The road led from a bridge near a gabled Henri IV house to that island Flaubert talks about. We were assured we were going the right way, but the road had a barrier across it, erected by the Service de Navigation who, at this time of the evening, had very sensibly gone home. Our PR friends hadn't told us that. A four-man police patrol stopped us, and asked us our business. Our papers were in order. How, we asked, could we get to the photographic vantage-point? 'Oh, it's only four kilometres,' said a jokey *flic*. 'And a very pretty walk.'

I pointed out we had heavy camera equipment and it was getting dark, but they did not seem much bothered. The PR people were to blame for not appraising the Service de Navigation of our visit, they said, and sped off into the sunset.

Night was falling fast, and the cooling-towers would soon be illuminated. The solution seemed to be to return to the *Centrale Nucléaire*. I had spotted another road, which seemed to head in the right direction. But tall iron gates and serious railings barred it from marauders; we would need security guards to open it.

We flashed our credentials at the guard house. This had all the charm of an airport departure lounge, when an indefinite delay of your flight has been announced.

'Ah, Monsieur,' said the chief security guard, after much discussion with his colleagues, 'Your papers are in order, but. . . .' A sad, sigh. 'That gate. . . .' He tapped his nose wisely. 'I cannot open it without the authority of Monsieur Pasquier.'

Monsieur Pasquier was one of our kindly PR pair. 'Please telephone him,' I requested. 'I think there has been a cock-up.'

The chief security guard went into his office. We waited. He consulted his colleagues. They closed the door. We waited longer. Then the chief security guard came out of his office, and disappeared briskly into the bowels of the guard house where the hot line to Monsieur Pasquier was, no doubt, located.

One of his colleagues – a red-eyed, ferrety barrack-room lawyer – had sprung to our aid. This rigmarole, he said, was ridiculous for a few photographs. 'Henri plays by the rule-book,' he explained, adding with a snort of contempt: 'He calls the President of the French Republic for permission to fart!' Someone was on our side.

A good ten minutes of hot line to the President or Monsieur Pasquier saw Henri back with us at the desk.

'Monsieur Pasquier is out. And I cannot authorize the opening of that gate,' said Henri, with a nod of pleasurable regret. 'It is not Monsieur Pasquier's fault that the Service de Navigation have closed their barrier, and, anyway, his permission would not cover their territory.'

'So where do I take my photograph?' Carey asked.

'From the bridge,' the ferrety man replied. 'It's the best view, anyway.'

So we went to the bridge. The illuminations, Henri promised, would make the cooling-towers beautiful any moment now. We waited forty-seven minutes, during which time heavy water had begun falling from the skies. It was some five hours after meeting Monsieur Pasquier before Carey got her shot.

Bureaucracy can be equally exasperating a long way from the Seine, and in anyone's language. But the French kind has one special quality: find a bureaucrat who shares an interest with

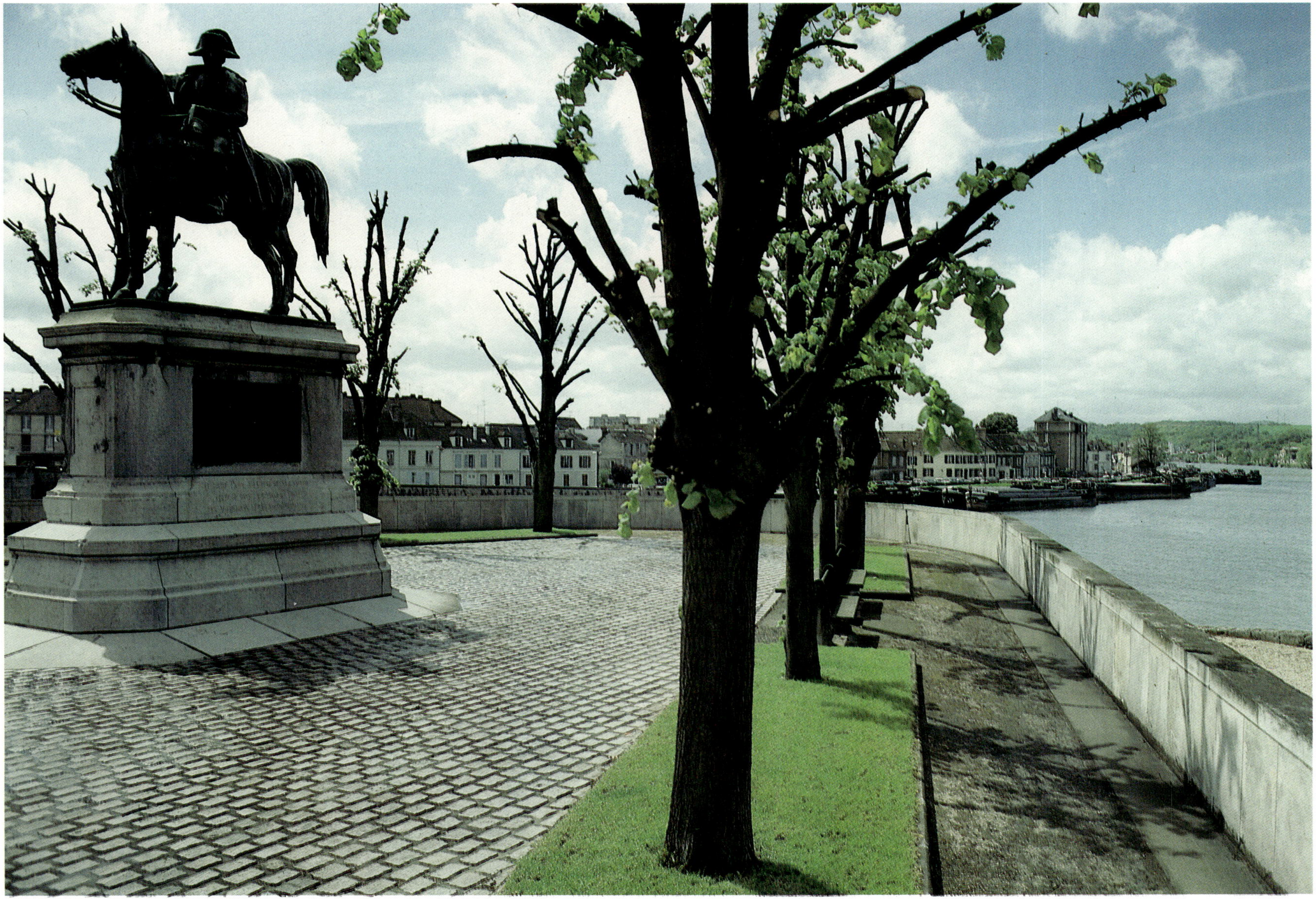

STATUE OF NAPOLÉON I, MONTEREAU-FAUT-YONNE

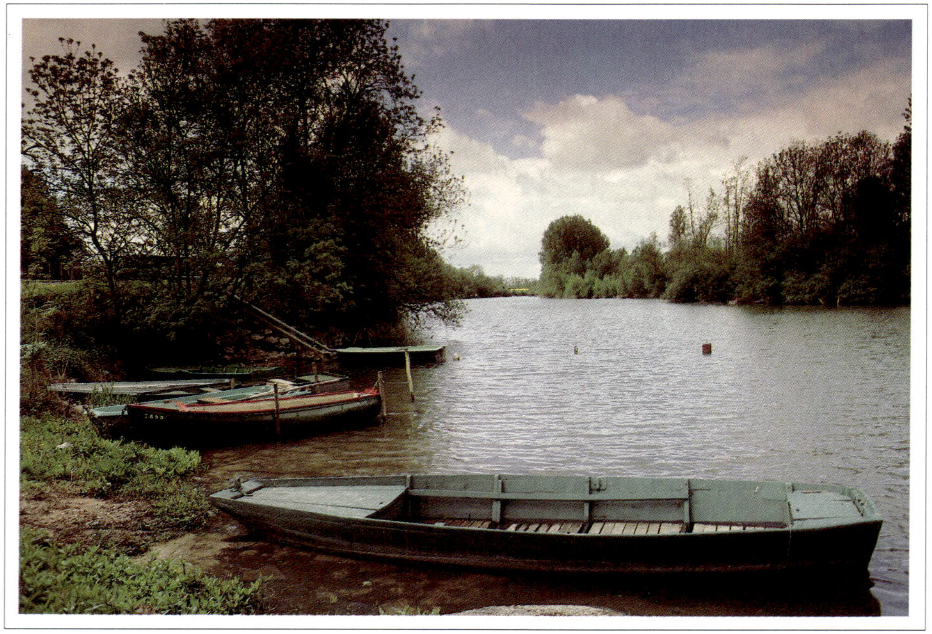

Gravon

you, and red tape snaps. The ferrety security guard who had espoused our cause turned out to be a keen amateur photographer. So when he told us about the bridge's vantage-point, he knew what he was talking about.

It was not the last we saw of him. No sooner were we back at our hotel than Carey found she had lost her purse sometime during that frustrating nuclear night. So, once more back to the guard house. Henri was mercifully off-duty. But the ferrety man had found the purse and as one photographer to another, he was pleased to be of service, and she would find nothing missing. '*C'est normal*,' he said, when Carey thanked him.

Once more, we returned to our hotel – a little country inn, L'Auberge La Grange, on the banks of the Seine at Beaulieu. Not a bed was to be had in Nogent that night: workers from other French nuclear power stations were on a massive goodwill visit.

Our own goodwill, thanks to the helpfulness about Carey's purse, was still just about buoyant. But cheap electricity can cost a packet in patience. Not to mention dead fish.

Since our visit, the Green Party's spies have detected radio-active algae among the river's weed; and the *Nucléaire* is accused of negligence. But the loyal Nogentais claim their renowned pike-fishing is as good as ever. It could become a modern version of Ibsen's *Enemy of the People*: pleased with the business their handsome nuclear power station has brought them, the burghers of Nogent see no pollution and hear no warnings. And the doomwatchers can watch elsewhere.

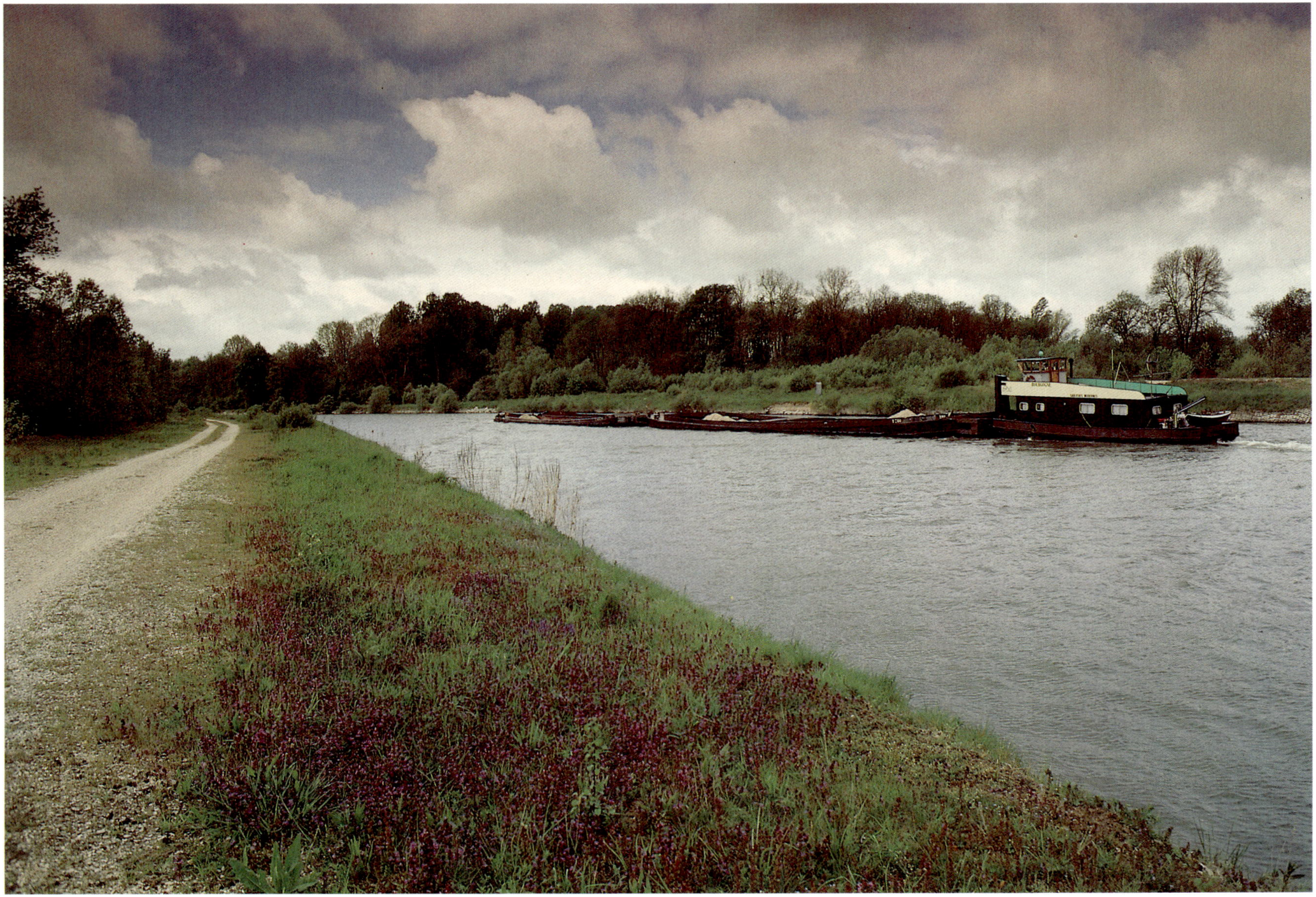

SANDBARGE AND PUSHER, GRAVON

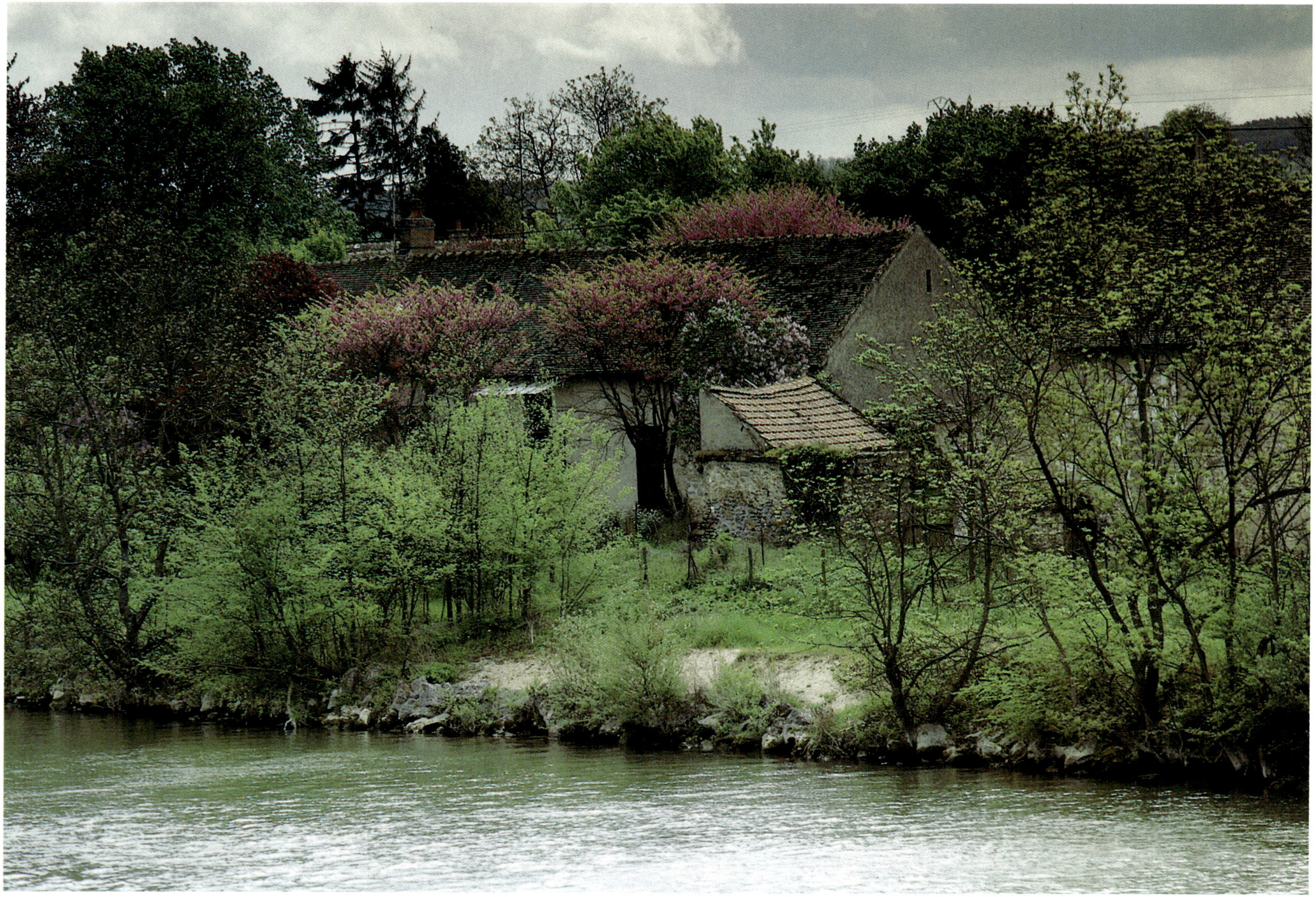

LA TOME, SPRING

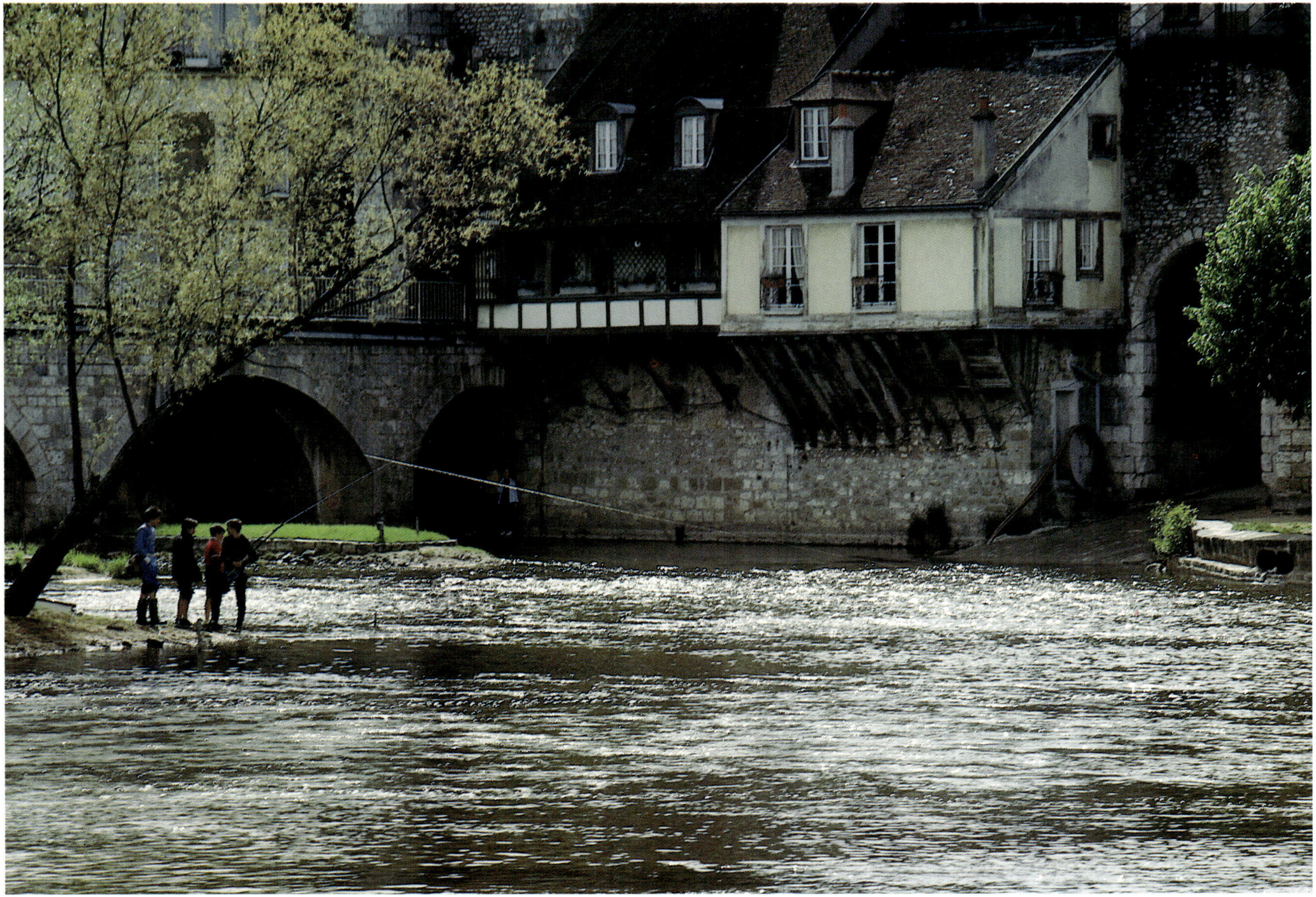

Boys fishing, Moret-sur-Loing

First sign that Paris lies upstream: an island sandworks between Gravon and La Tombe. Three long barges, full of sand, are propelled by their diesel pusher, bound for the capital and its never-ending building boom.

Pleasant surprise. La Tombe belies its name. A beautiful, archetypal one-industry riverside town: flour-mill, church, fine old houses, blossoming orchards and barns coming right down to the river. Then, another country canal bypasses a few small meanders. And another warning: this far upstream, don't expect to get through a lock at lunchtime. The control tower of the lock at Marolles is deserted. Lock-keeping is nice work if you can stay awake. But beware of nostalgia for the good old trades – the Seine had some tough ones. At Montereau, log trains from the Burgundian forests of the Morvan left the Yonne, and joined the Seine for their perilous journey to Paris. Seven rafts of firewood, carrying about ten cubic metres of stacked logs, were floated and formed a convoy. The logger, at the back of each raft, controlled it with a long stick like a punt-pole; up front, the logger's lad, often his own son, would keep watch for hazards.

Day and night, they kept going. And the journey to Paris would take ten days in normal water, up to a month in the low waters of summer. It was common for father and son to be drowned or crushed to death during a raft's sudden disintegration.

Montereau-faut-Yonne was never a quiet town.

Orange high-speed trains hurtle across the Seine on their two-hour dash between Lyons and Paris. Juggernaut trucks are bumper-to-bumper on the bridge spanning the mighty confluence of Yonne and Seine. And that very bridge, in 1419, saw the bloody assassination of the Duke of Burgundy, which led to the Treaty of Troyes, the English King Henry VI becoming King of France, and Joan of Arc's rise and fall – to pot history a little.

Art history – at least, that of the Seine – begins at Moret-sur-Loing, home of the most upstream Impressionist, Alfred Sisley. Not strictly on the Seine, all it takes is a turn to port at the barge harbour of St-Mammès, and we laze a little way up the deliciously leafy, narrow tributary, the Loing, to the medieval stronghold of Moret. *Ça vaut le détour.*

Near the Bateau-Ivre restaurant (hardly ever 'drunk' on these still waters), there are riverside villas with dovecotes and white doves. A mill-house on its island in mid-bridge. Houses with balconies overhanging the river by the Burgundy Gate. And Sisley's house, 19 Rue Montmartre, where he lived the last twenty years of his life and died a pauper. His vision of the Seine at St-Mammès, in pointillist dots of prismatic colour, shows the river as mirror for the sky – with brilliant luminosity.

Moret boasts other distinguished names: Napoleon stayed the night on his way back from Elba; Clemenceau had a house here; and so did François I (where didn't he?).

But medieval Moret lost its royal importance when nearby Fontainebleau took over during the Renaissance. François I replaced all rural vestiges of the hunting-lodge with a magnificent royal palace.

The presence of a great river not far away is reflected in Fontainebleau's vast ornamental lakes, fountains, waterfalls and canals. In the middle of the Carp Pond stands an eighteenth-century island folly, built for intimate luncheons. In Diana's Garden, created for Catherine de Medici, is a fountain of spouting stags and peeing hounds. And, on the Canal du Bréau, a live but camera-shy swan hides its head in its feathers and pretends to be asleep, bored, no doubt, with the endless clicking of tourist Minoltas, as it lays its eight eggs.

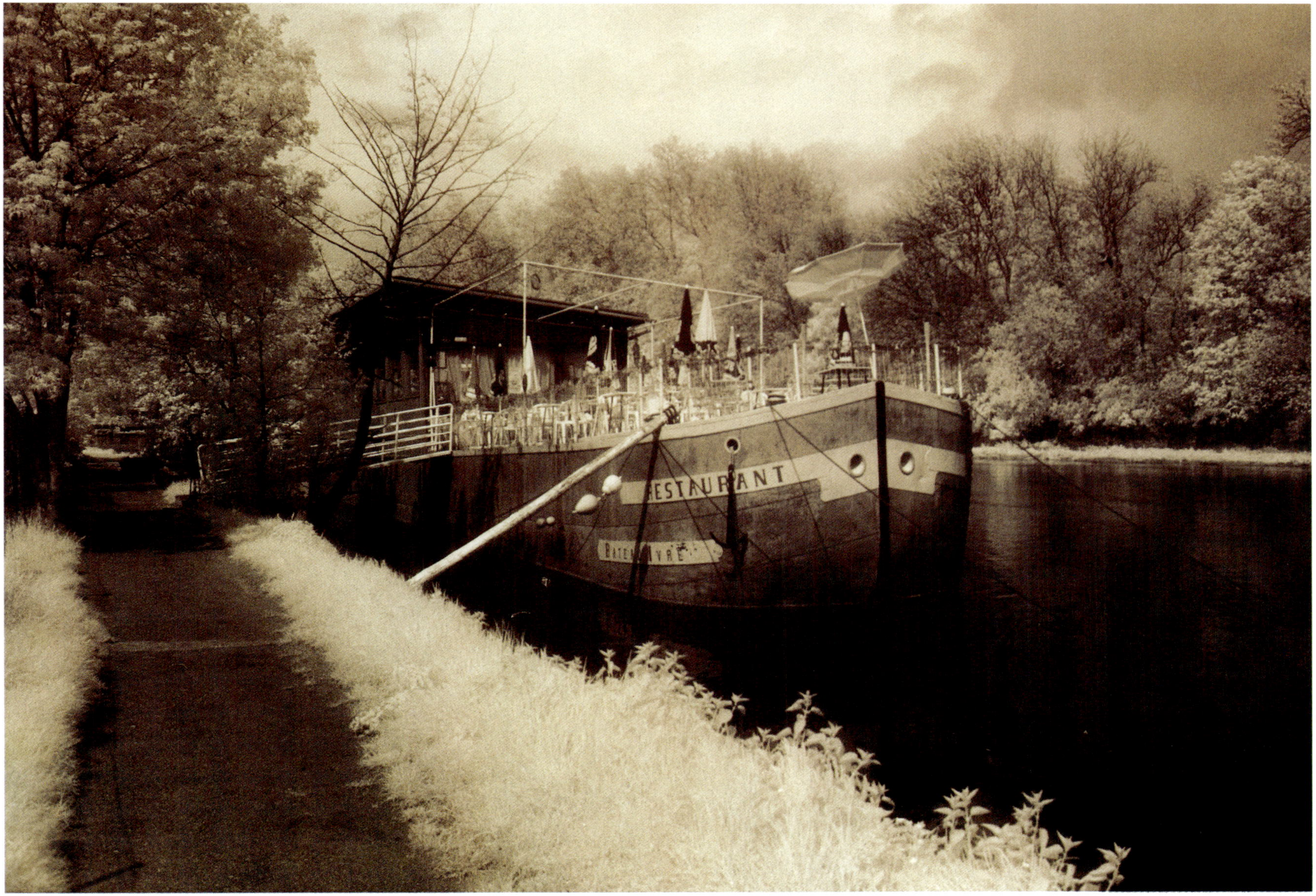

Bateau-Ivre Restaurant, Moret-sur-Loing

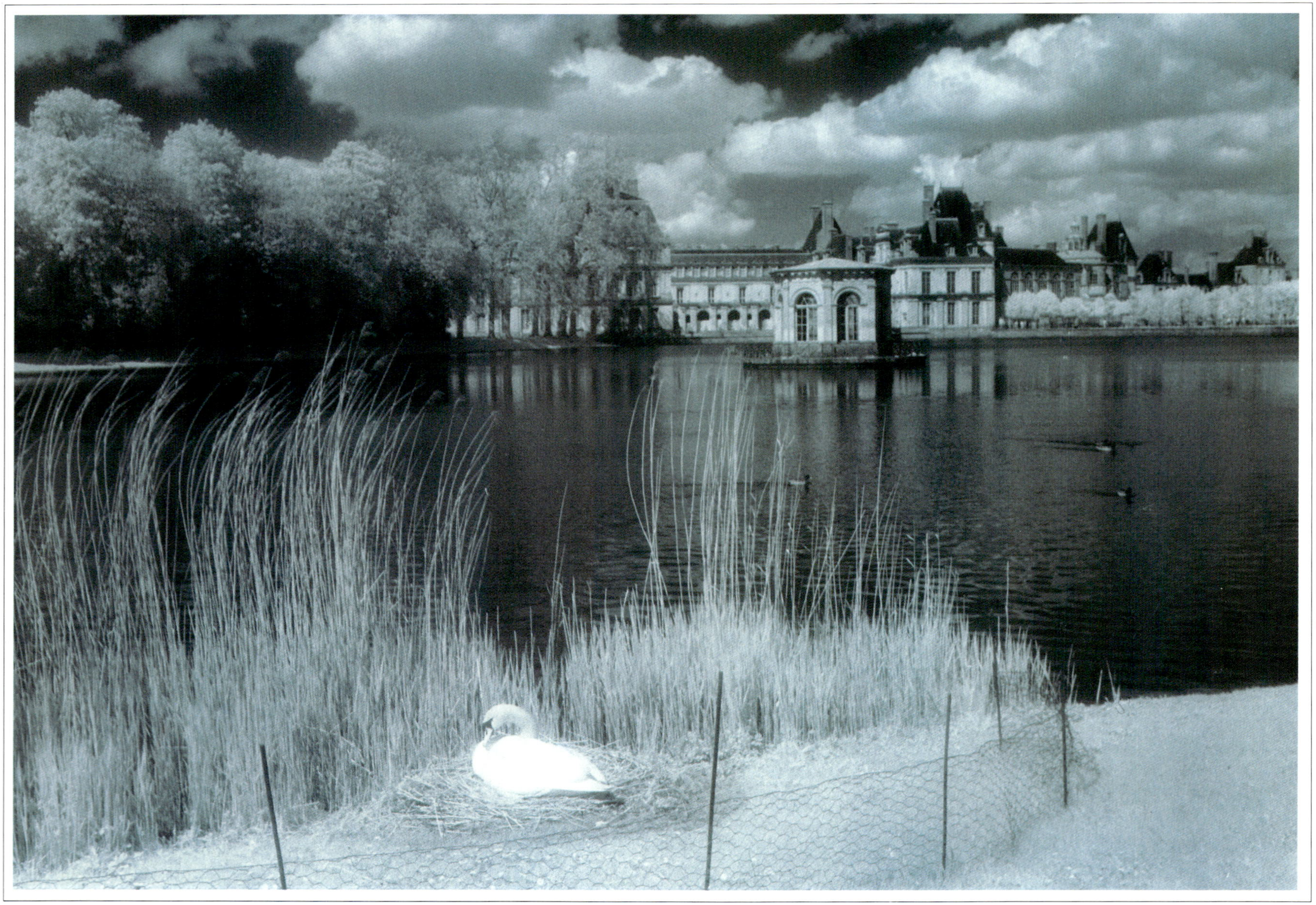

Fontainebleau

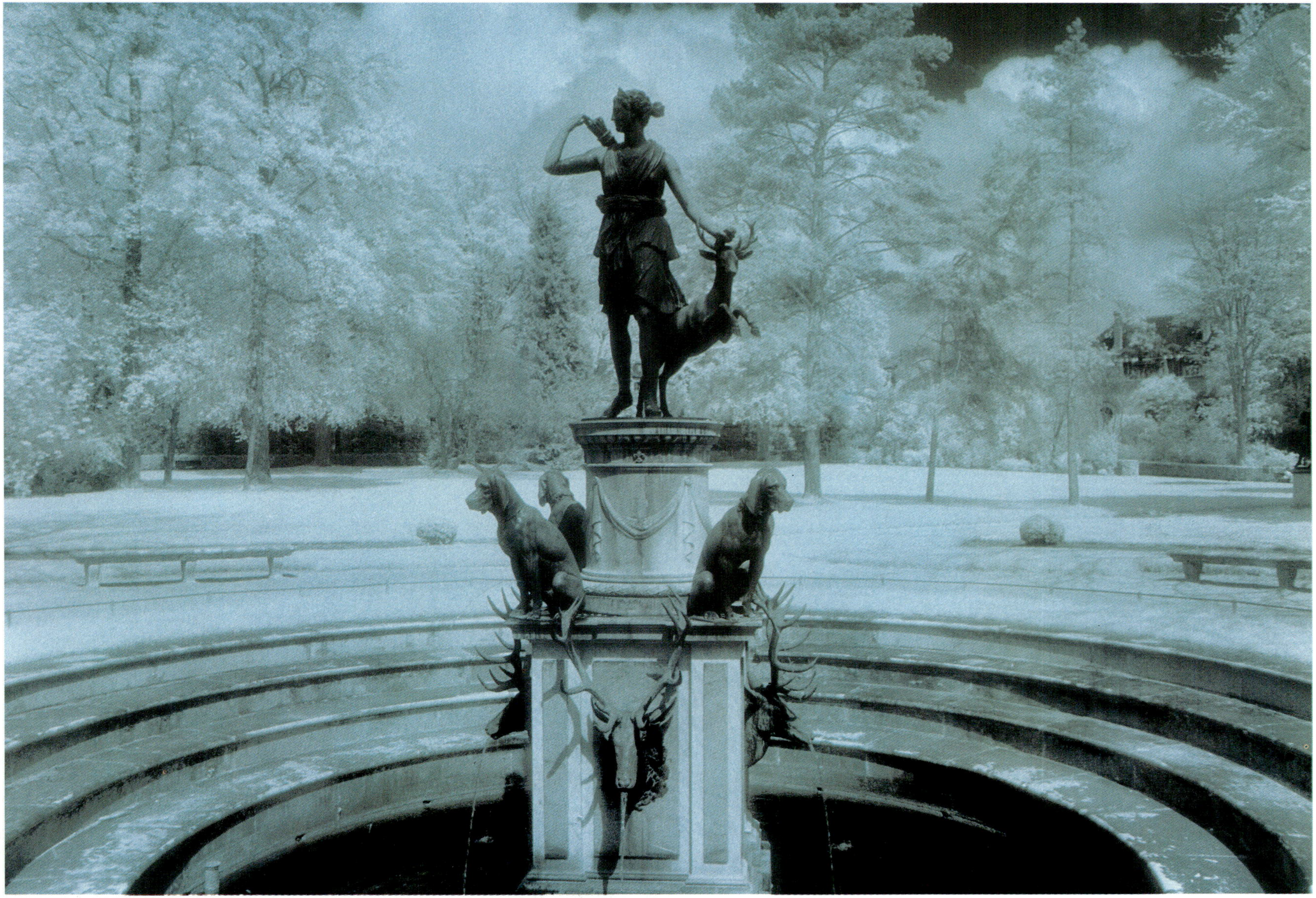

DIANA'S GARDEN, FONTAINEBLEAU

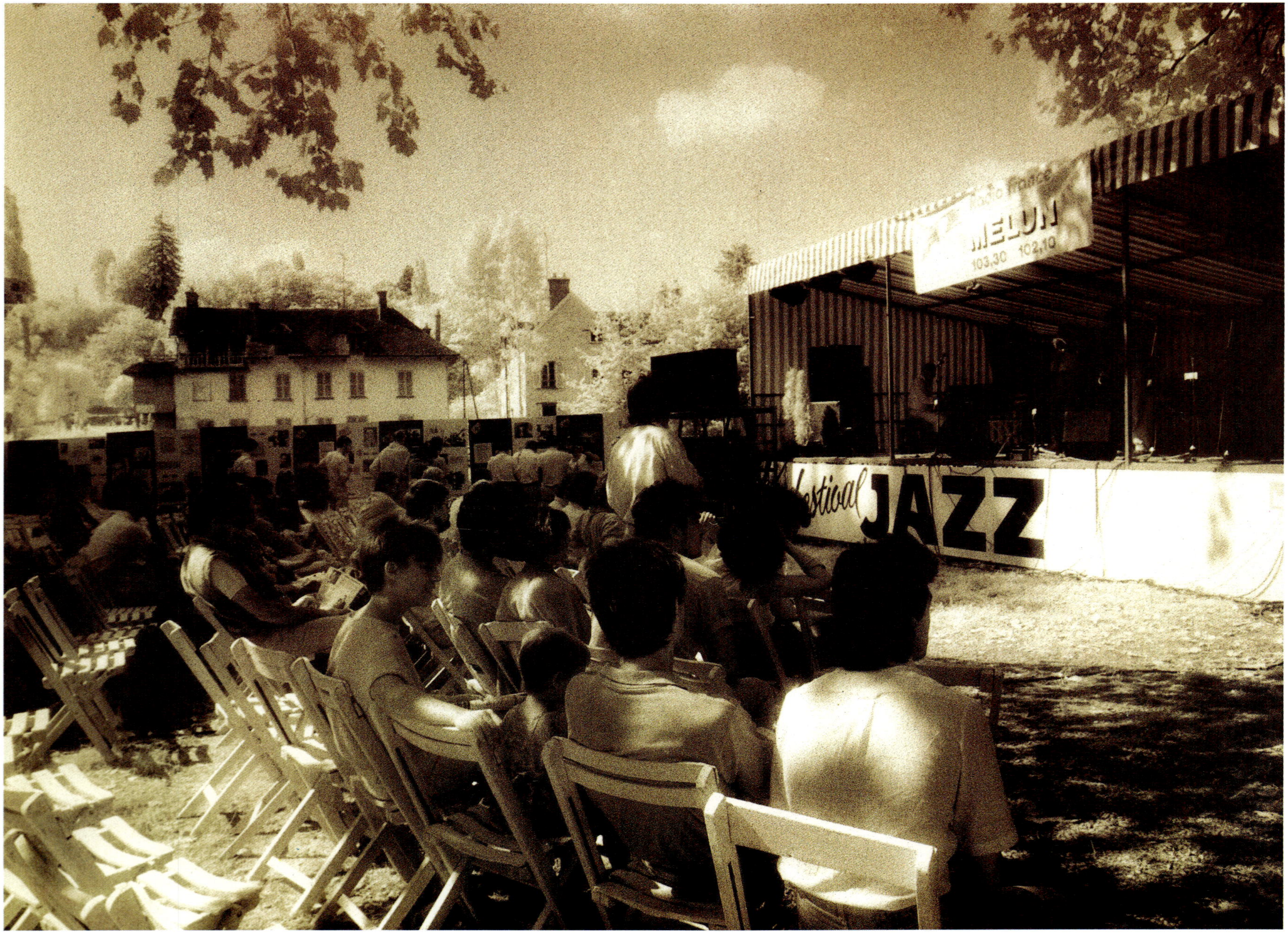

Ile du Berceau, Samois-sur-Seine

JAZZ ON A SUMMER'S RIVER

From the turret of the Tour Dénecourt, rising 426 feet above Samois in the forest of Fontainebleau, I looked across the treetops – all shades of green from dark conifers to bright oaks – away to the sensual, gently sloping trough of the Seine valley.

Here the serpent river took a big, sweeping change of direction from her east-west meandering to a more or less straight run north to Paris. Opulent riverside homes of commuters from Samoreau and Vulaines dotted thickly wooded slopes; and, far in the distance, high-rise Montereau was a white toytown of children's blocks. Even such banal architecture had visual poetry that morning, with wispy clouds bouncing over the treetops towards them. They were the kind of clouds Django Rheinhardt celebrated in 'Nuages'. And the kind of blue sky that evoked Baudelaire's eulogy of music: 'It ploughs the heavens.'

A small plaque on a modest village house at Samois-sur-Seine told us: 'Here lived and died guitarist and composer Django Rheinhardt (1910–1953)'. Three doors down the street was a T-junction with the waterfront, and a bridge led to the Ile du Berceau, where every June a small, lyrical Jazz Festival commemorates Django with two days of spontaneous musical affection. For a musical treat down by the riverside, whether a jazz buff or not, you could not find better than Samois on those two sun-kissed days.

Already, on the quayside across the road from Chez Fernand, three young English musicians were busking 'Jazz Me Blues' in the swing string style of the Hot Club de France – a sound from years before they were born. A pleasing serenade, as we lunched on the terrace in a rustic ambience of ivy, geraniums and shiny copper pans. Stéphane Grappelli would soon be here in person, with Babik Rheinhardt to continue his father's gypsy jazz tradition. But the young Englishmen's violin and guitar and bass now swung out across the Seine, and made all the tastier our hot seafood salad, Barbary duck, Brie (the local cheese), strawberry tart, and Sancerre.

Beneath the overflow of tables along the quayside, feet were tapping. Jazz fans had brought their whole families with them; children were larking about under the red Pelforth umbrellas, mothers grabbing them as they nearly fell into the Seine. The buskers played slow Russian gypsy music that developed into an up-tempo French stomp (Hotcha-corny-a!).

A gin palace draped with golden girls in bikinis swooshed upstream, adding a pah-pahahaaap! of its klaxon to the music. And the crowd swept along, like a New Orleans Street Parade, to the Ile du Berceau.

In keeping with Django's nomadic life-style, it was as though a gypsy camp had been set up for a couple of days on this idyllic island. Django often went missing for more days than that, playing billiards and gambling with his gypsy friends. He kept his money in a wad, never had a bank account. He couldn't read, so never took the Metro because the station names were gibberish to him. But, even with two fingers paralysed, guitar-playing was this thing he did for the sheer joy of it, as easily as we now sat, with the reflected sunlight from the water shimmering on the leaves above our heads, and heard the spirit of Django 'bounding,

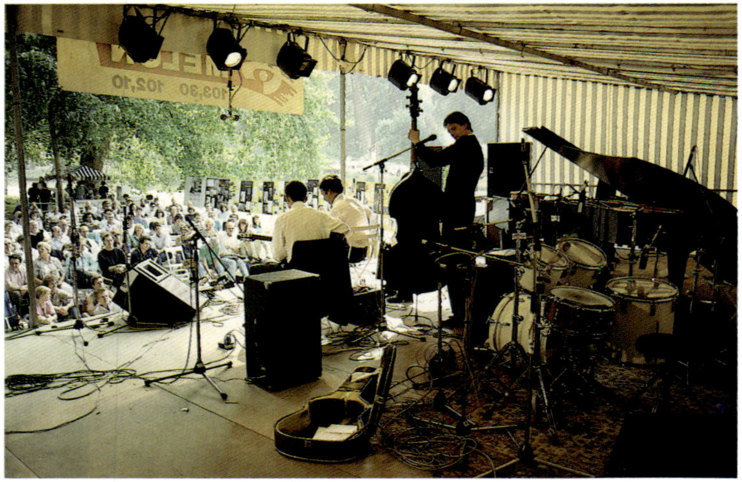

JAZZ FESTIVAL, SAMOIS-SUR-SEINE

going wherever it pleases without ever finding the slightest obstacle to its fantasy. . . .'

There were gypsies in the audience, too. An old man wore a smart double-breasted blue pinstripe jacket with workman's trousers, and a brown felt fedora at a rakish angle on his long, silver-grey hair; the dark woman with him had sleek hair pulled back in a bun, and a full polka-dot skirt.

Sunset and dusk found the island's crowd swollen from a mere handful at the first 'set' of the afternoon to a full house by nightfall. Vendors were doing a brisk trade in tee-shirts with a Jean Cocteau sketch of Django. Lights along the waterfront twinkled on the river, and the heady smoke from charcoal-grilled brochettes wafted through the trees. The current band was playing 'Crépuscule', a romantic Django tune, its arpeggios rising and falling like fountains and cascades.

'Excuse me, M'sieur,' a tourist asked. 'When does Django Rheinhardt himself play?'

The tourist had seen the banner *Festival du Jazz Django Rheinhardt* and expected the great man at least to put in an appearance. Django would have liked that. In fact, he also died as he would have liked – while fishing by the Seine.

Every man has a homeland with its memories of childhood, and there he hopes to spend his last days. But I have none, therefore I have chosen Valvins.

Not the gypsy in Django's soul speaking, but – on the opposite side of the river – the symbolist poet Stéphane Mallarmé a century ago. He describes the bridge at Valvins, where he had a cottage, as 'like a verandah to my house'.

Further downstream towards Melun, the crazy kitsch homes begin, the epitome of Seine Flamboyant. No one seems to live in them. Guard dogs race along behind high fences, barking death by rabies at us. A dilapidated, haunted house worthy of Disneyland flaunts wooden balconies, turrets, curlicues, higgledy-piggledy ballustrades, and a glass conservatory with smashed windows and a tangle of weeds that could turn nasty.

A tree stands surrealistically in the river, strayed there from the forest of Rougeau.

Deep country with beautiful orchards continues between Melun and Morsang. Then, at Corbeil-Essonnes, a metamorphosis begins. On first glance, a country town, with the Essonnes river discreetly joining the Seine from a tunnel near the quayside Mairie and flour-mill. A barge is unloading wheat. Silos and sandworks abound. An active, prosperous town, on the face of it.

But a fisherman tells us differently. 'My parents were from over there – Left Bank people. But my wife's parents were from over

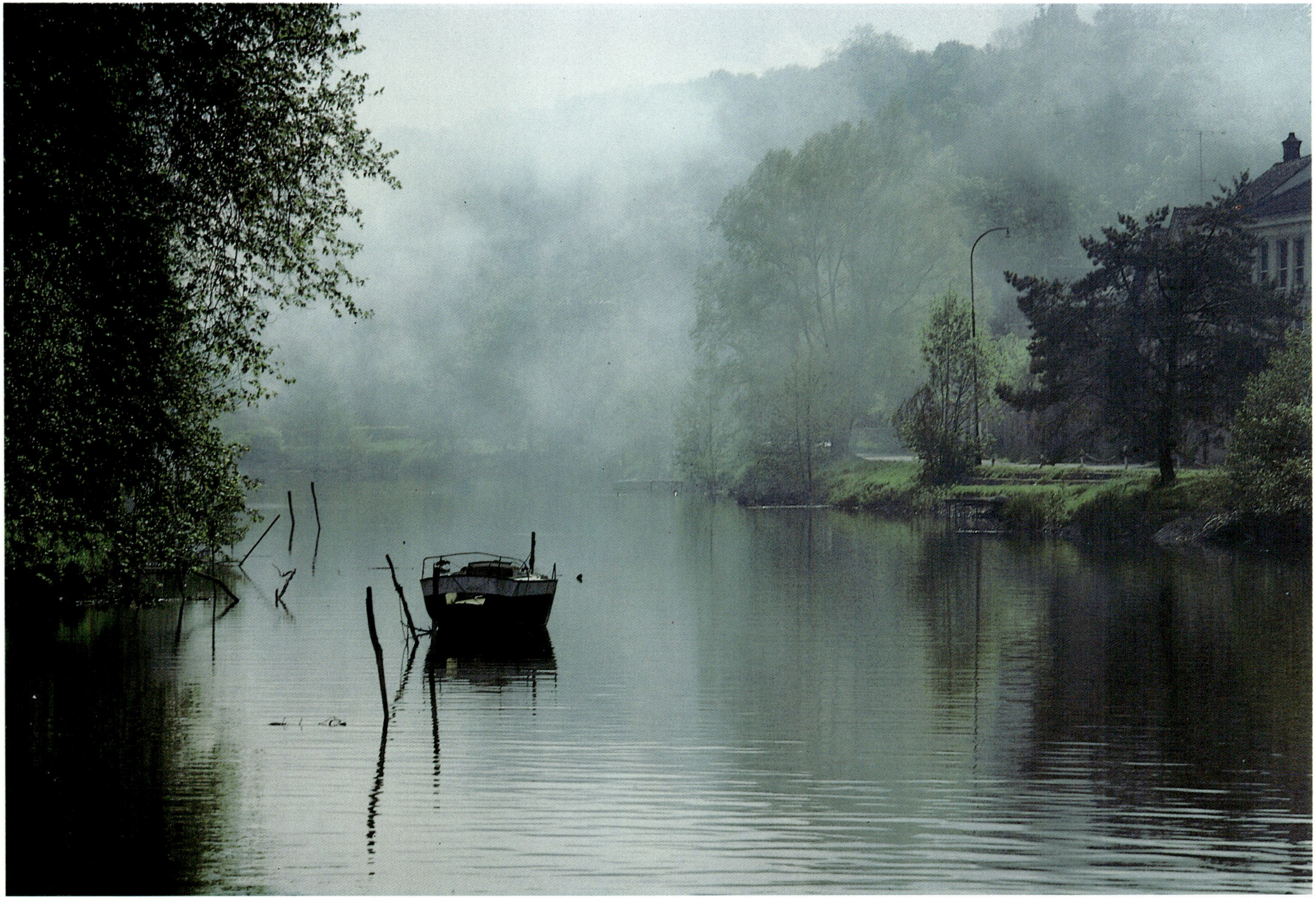

Samois-sur-Seine

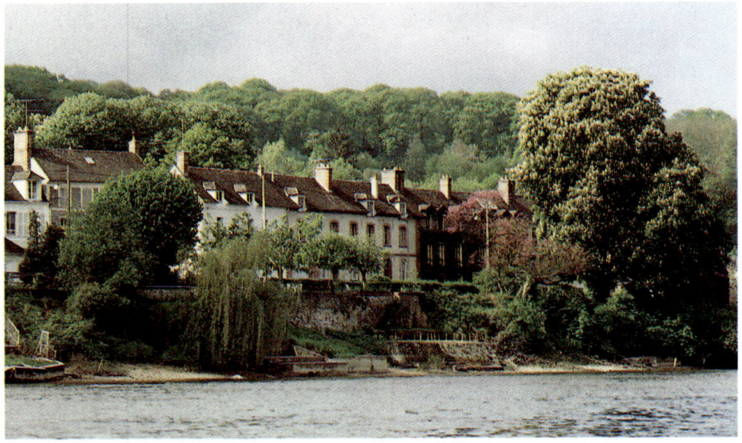

THOMERY

here – Right Bank people. This was the old quarter – the Right Bank was the right bank in those days. Everyone used to know each other. But now. . . .' A hand left his fishing-rod and waved contemptuously in the direction of nowhere in particular. 'Now, M'sieur, there's the Industrial Zone people – commuting from Paris by autoroute and rail, taking our jobs. . . .'

A familiar story: the town over-expanded in boom years. Along the river bank, the pasta factory closed last year; the slaughter-house closed because new building had taken the farmland; and the printing works, which twenty years ago employed 2,700 workers, now had only 300. The riverside was dead. It was all light industry in the Industrial Zone nowadays – and Parisian workers!

'Must be better for fishing,' I suggested. 'Less pollution.'

The angry angler lets up on his tale of woe, as he lands a handsome bream. 'Count your blessings,' he says, adding with impeccable French logic: 'No industry, no industrial waste.'

At Soisy-sur-Seine, neat dormitory houses and sailing dinghies. Above us a Pan-Am jumbo lumbers across the river in its landing approach to Paris-Orly. Choisy-le-Roi, despite the smog hanging over its new pink bridge, has a charming riverside walk with little nineteenth-century brick houses – all balconies and verandahs and globe lamps. Behind the peaceful strand, a busy street clogged with fuming trucks, and pavements full of black immigrant workers returning from the hypermarket. Through blossoming wisteria, a view of Monoprix across the river.

As eastern Paris approaches, the Seine's run-down reaches give it an apocalyptic look – warehouses with smashed windows, bridges collapsing, unused barges rusting. A sick river. But showing determined signs of survival.

A rare barge enters the lock near the Pont de Vitry. The bargee takes the opportunity to wash his jolly red Renault 5, carried aft on the barge. Cosmopolitan Paris. At Alfortville, an amphitheatre overlooks the river, with the Restaurant Cappadoce nearby for the Turkish population. And across the river, by steps as precipitous as a Mayan temple's, is a smelly, beat-up boatyard – Le Port à l'Anglais, the Parisians call it.

Well, it doesn't quite look like Poole Harbour. But certainly *anglais* is the limpid, Turneresque vision of the confluence of Seine and Marne in early morning mist. Curiously romantic, as every few seconds commuter trains move mysteriously across a distant bridge, and our barge with the jolly red Renault catches up with us and turns to starboard, headed up the Marne to Alsace.

We have arrived at the gates of Paris.

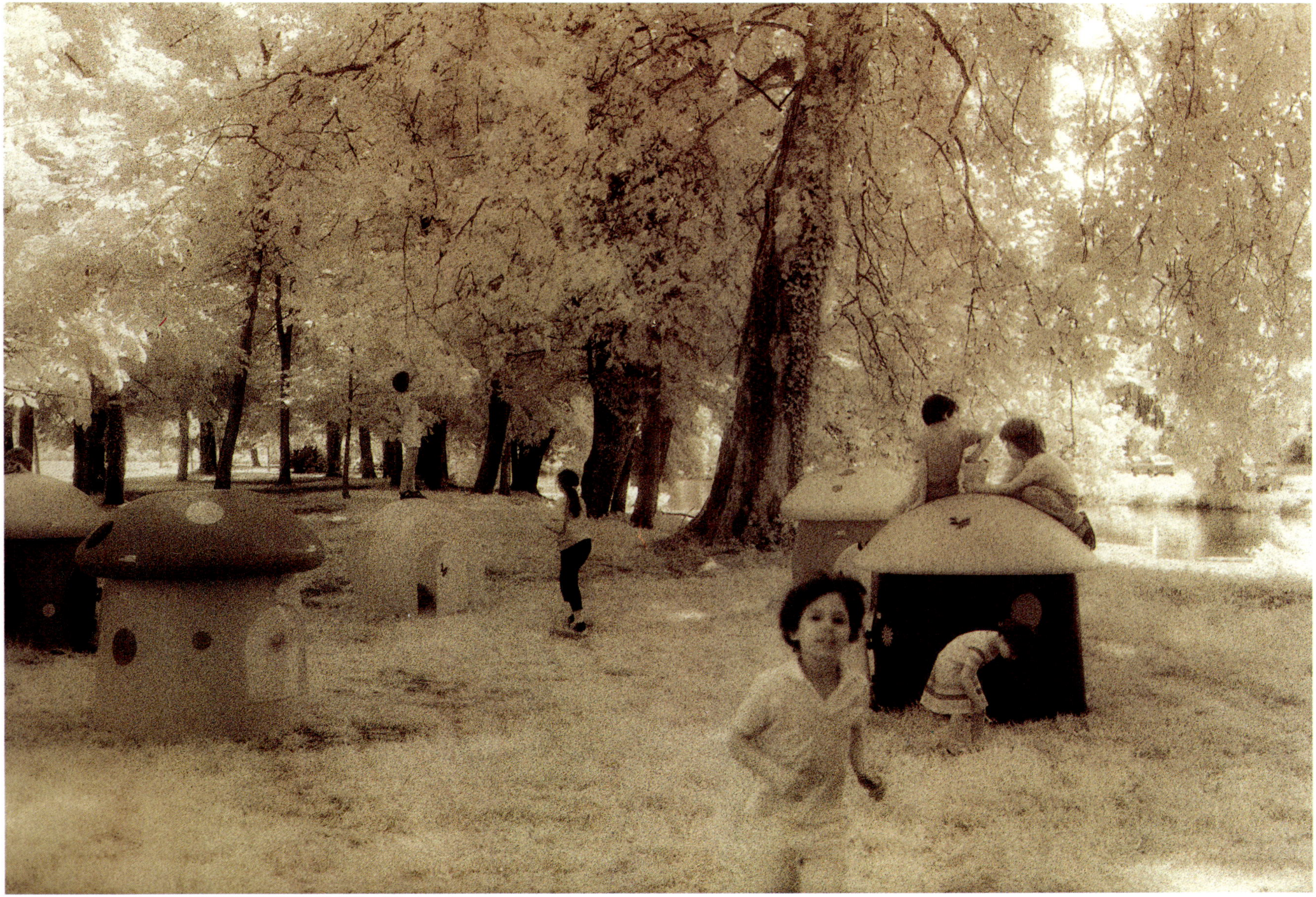

Children's playground, Samois-sur-Seine

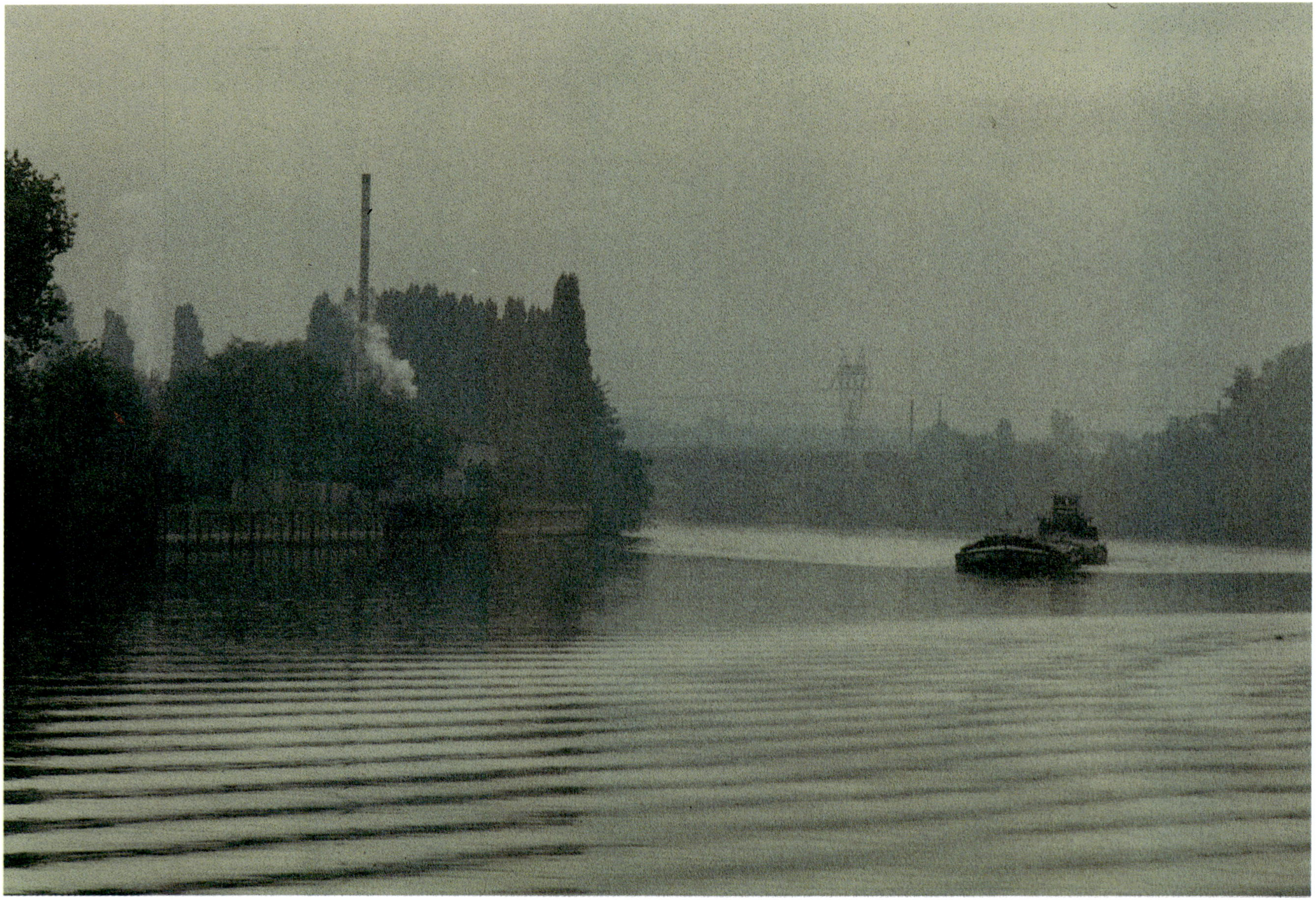

Choisy-le-Roi

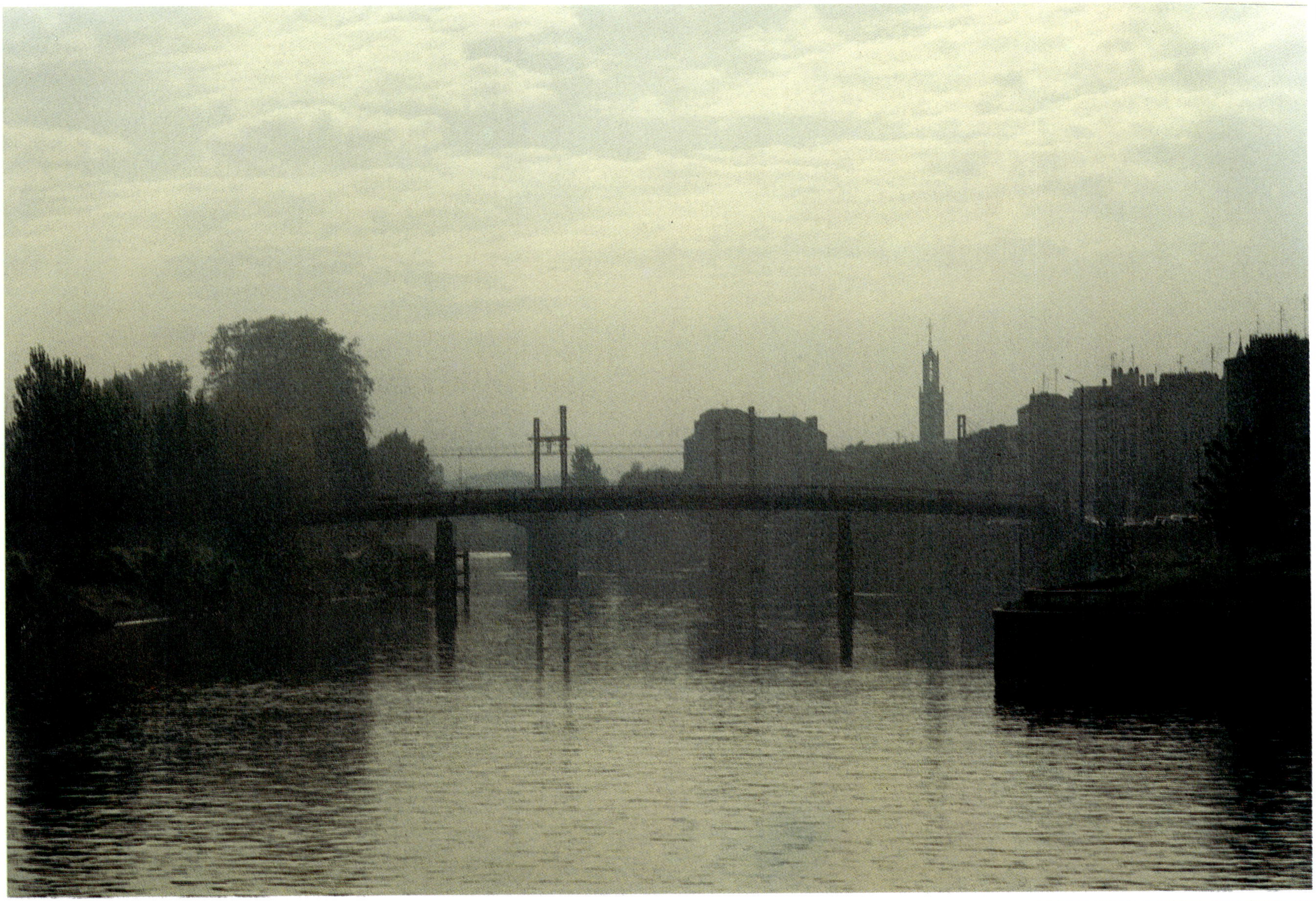

MEETING OF SEINE AND MARNE, PARIS

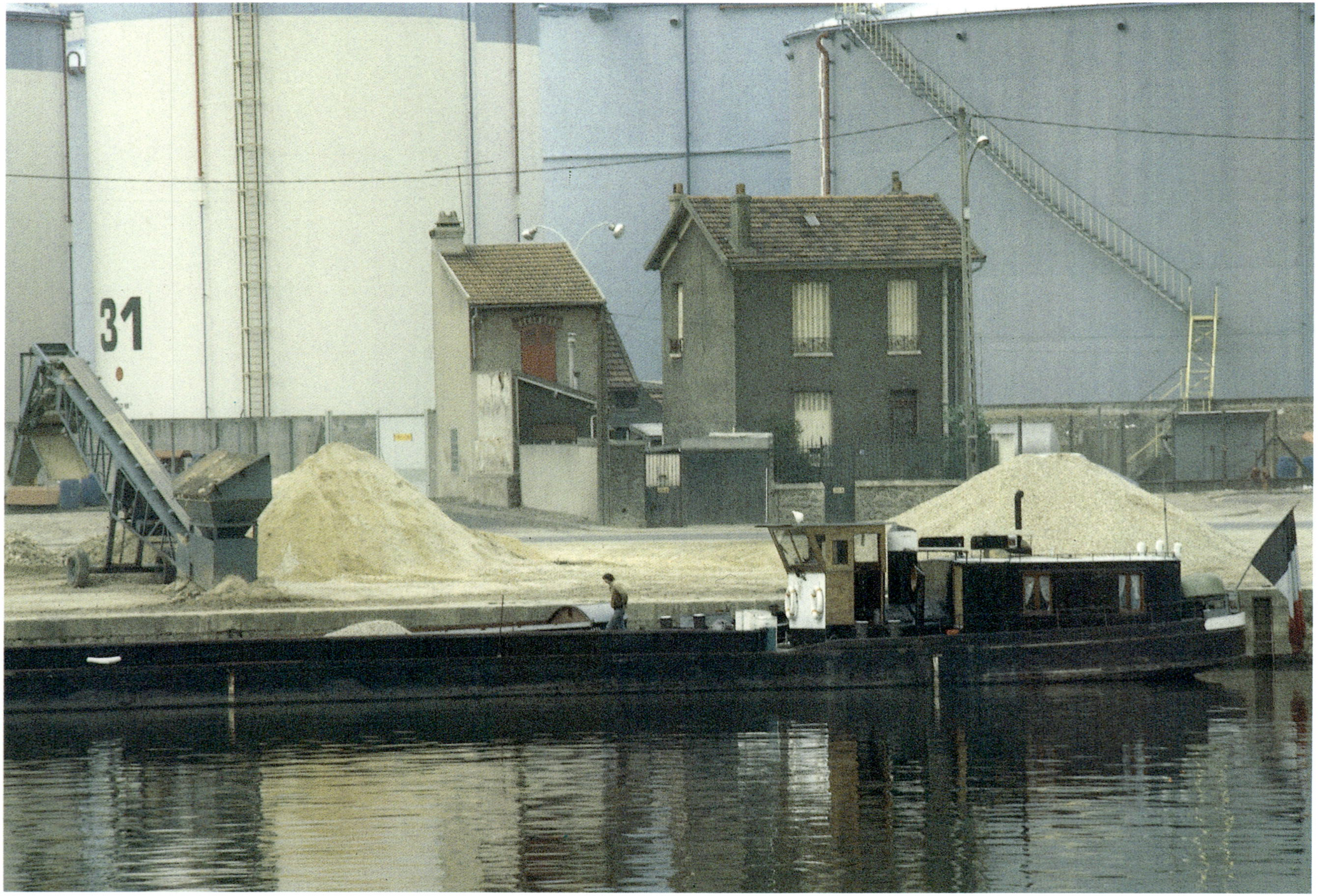

Choisy-le-Roi

PART II

PARIS

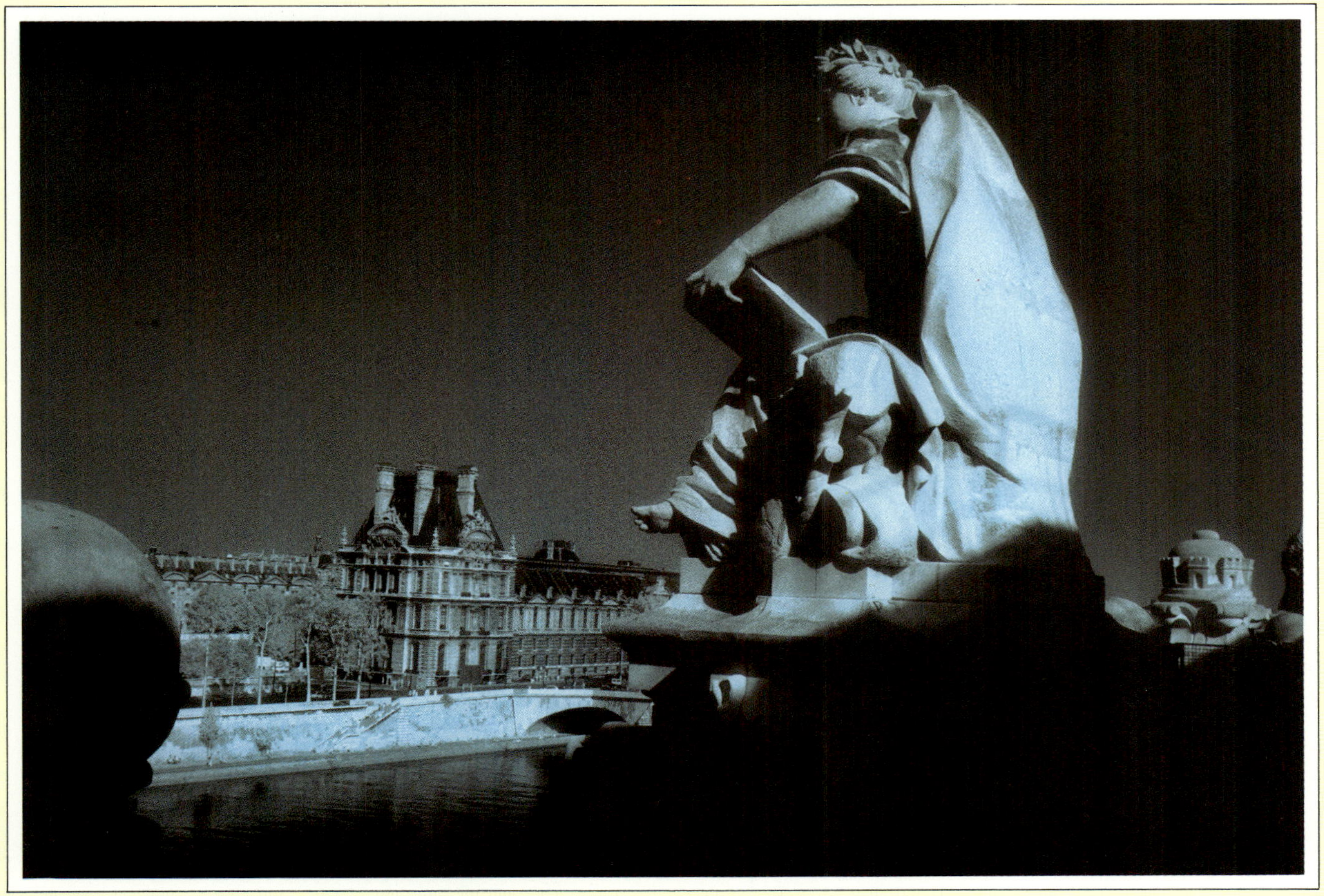

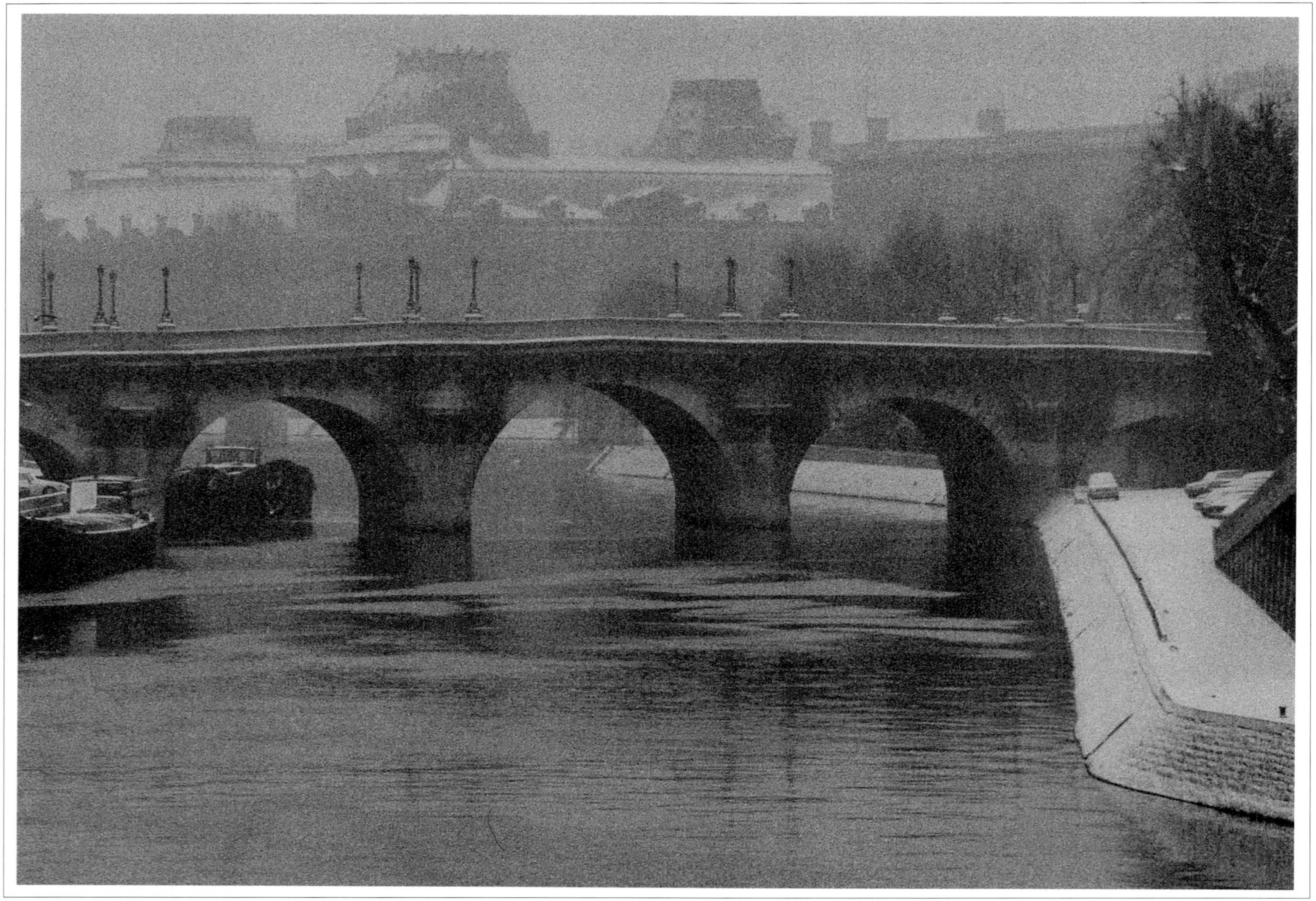

Pont Neuf, Winter

MISERY VALLEY

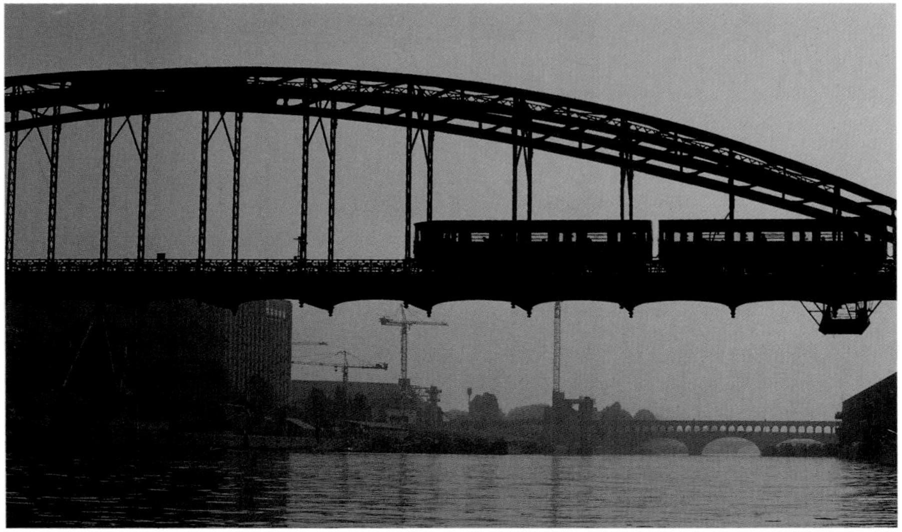

'Under the Bridges of Paris' was not only a song, it was once an exceedingly tricky feat of navigation. And sailors of the river, while artists talked of The City of Light, were more concerned with staying alive in what they referred to as Misery Valley. Most of us wax as lyrical as a *chansonnier* about that short, romantic reach between the Ile St-Louis and the Eiffel Tower. It packs so many landmarks into its three miles that the *bateau-mouche* commentary sounds like historical name-dropping. And we forget the dramas surrounding the river herself.

Until the Revolution of 1789, there were virtually two Seines in Paris: Royal and Popular; downstream and upstream. And never the twain did meet. Propulsion was entirely by man, horse, sail, or the river's natural current. Upstream Paris had the main commercial traffic, because loaded boats arrived with the current. From downstream, they had to fight against it. Upstream were the ports, the popular quarters with their raunchy low life. Downstream, it was the *ancien régime's* river: the royal Right Bank of the Louvre Palace; the aristocratic Left Bank with its fine town houses in Rue de Varenne.

METRO CROSSING THE SEINE

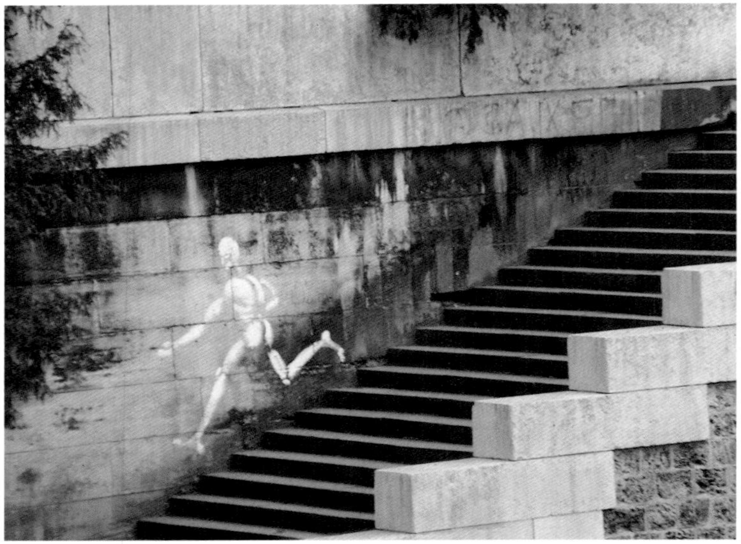

RIVERBANK GRAFFITI

The French Revolution got rid of the *ancien régime*, and the Industrial Revolution the transport problems – with the coming of steam. Eventually, the river below Paris became commercially viable and the two Seines joined up.

But first, the bad news. . . .

From the Romans to the Revolution, Paris treated the river of her origin like an ungrateful child her generous mother. The Seine had given her a perfect natural position: a slow-down of current causing sedimentation which formed three islands – the Ile de la Cité, the Ile St-Louis, and the Ile Louvier (no longer there); and a quiet reach of river upstream of these islands, easily forded at summer low water and crossable by ferry at winter high.

Formerly a fishing village of Gauls from the Parisii tribe, its strategic advantages were seized upon by the Romans with their usual astuteness. A road running north-south; a river running east-west. What could be better for logistics, and bringing in the bread and circuses? Absorbing the Gauls into the community, the Romans colonized Lutetia, as Paris was then called, and set up a port on La Tournelle quay. Came the end of the Roman Empire and the Dark Ages, the remaining citizens holed up in the fortified Cité, an island citadel built around its church, Notre-Dame. A protection against the Barbarians.

As the royal capital of France developed during the Middle Ages, the sheer take-off of trade involved a progressive spoilation of that natural quiet reach of river.

You can't go on narrowing and raising a river's bed indefinitely without trouble. The walls and quays were built higher and higher against flooding. Bridges with thick arches, as well as mills, water pumps, shipwrecks and builders' rubble, all had a damming effect. And the water level upstream of the Ile de la Cité could be as much as five and a half feet higher than the downstream end. With a concomitant speed-up of water.

No wonder the motto of Paris, taken from the Waterman's Guild, was *Fluctuat nec mergitur* – 'she has a rough passage but stays afloat'.

By the seventeenth century, the most dangerous part was the urban gorge bounded by the Ile de la Cité and the Quai de Gesvres, between today's Pont Notre-Dame and Pont au Change. The arches of one bridge were not in line with the other's, so the mariner had to change course in mid-rapids. Many would crash into the Devil's Arch of the Pont au Change, and at that speed death was certain.

Eventually, specialist pilots were trained to take the boats

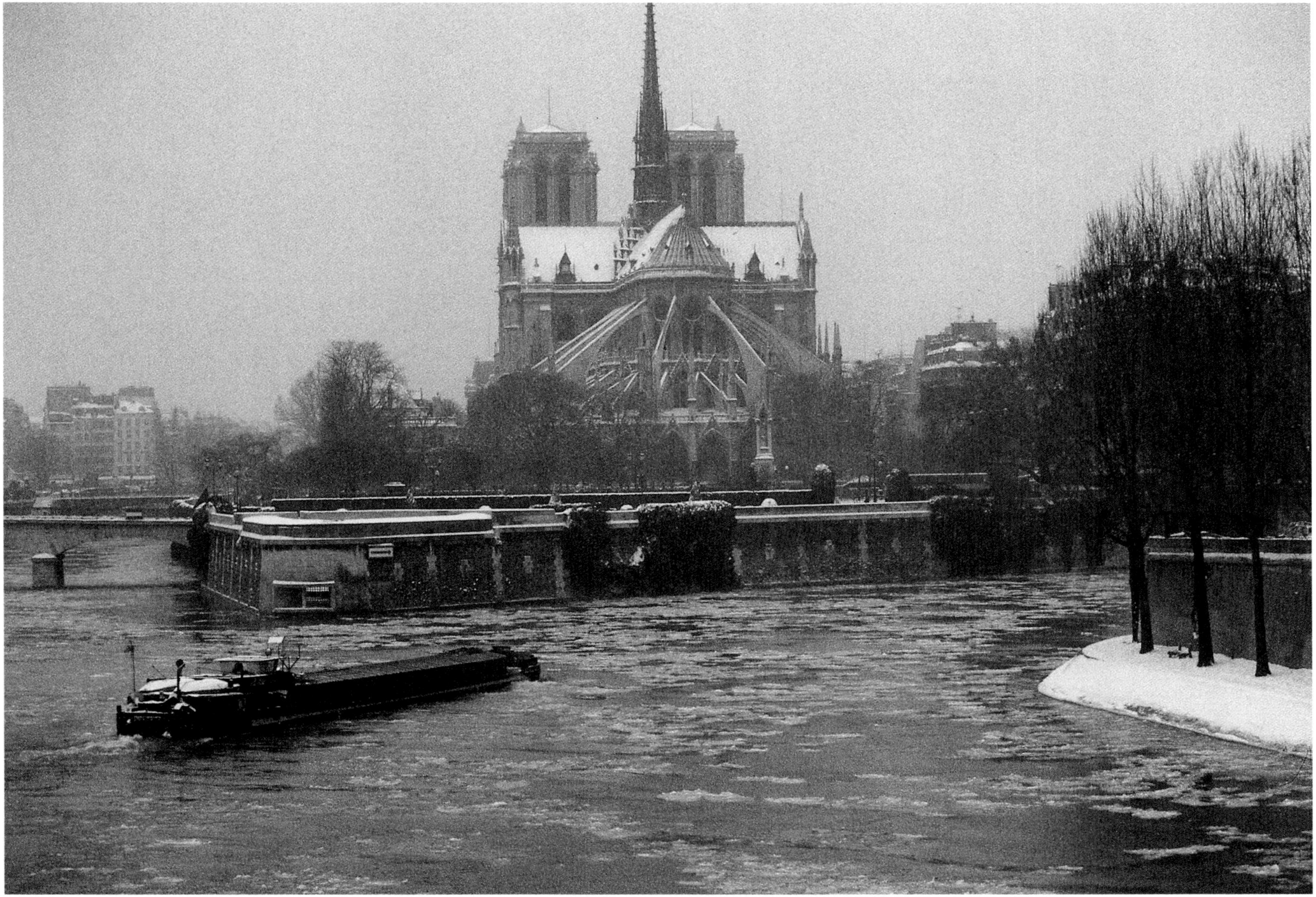

ILE ST-LOUIS, WINTER

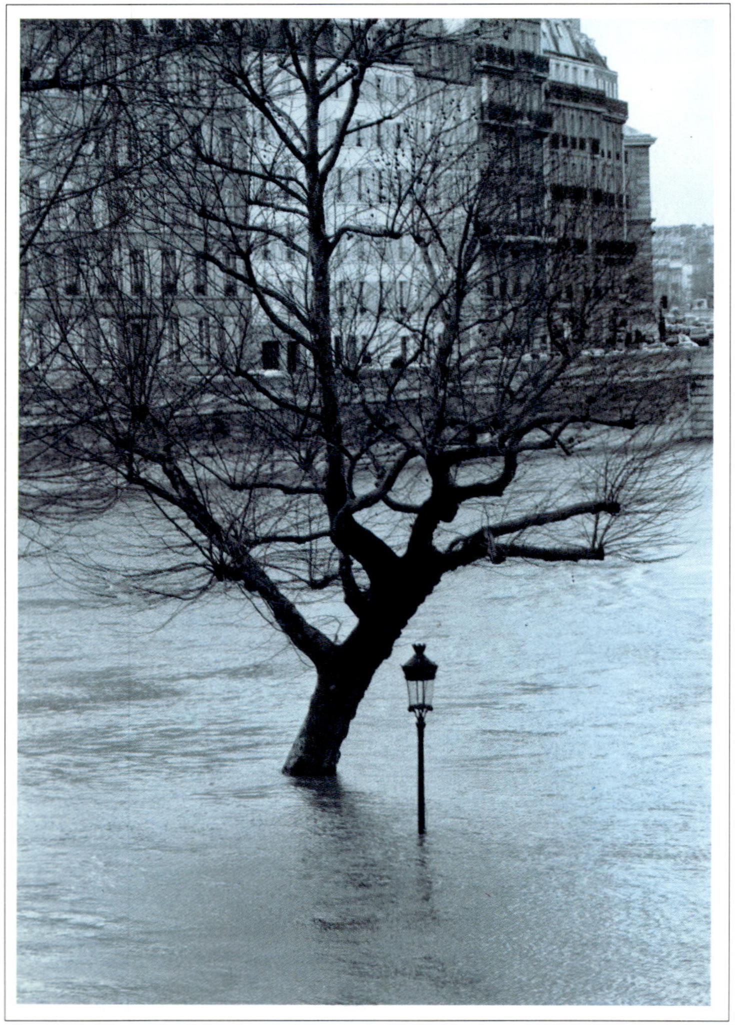

safely through Misery Valley; and to haul them back up again, the mechanical ingenuity of the French produced the *aquamoteur*. This was a stationary paddle boat, whose paddles, turned by the strong current, operated a winch-and-cable system pulling the boats upstream of the Ile St-Louis. Previously, they had been hauled by men with ropes round their necks.

It was, however, all right for some. The more fortunate could take an eighteenth-century water-coach from the Port St-Paul. Fifteen daily services carried passengers in different classes, from luxury cabins to deck. Hauled upstream by horse, the Seine water-coaches connected with others down the Burgundy Canal to the Saône river, and the Orléans Canal to the Loire.

Water-coach and *aquamoteur* were ancestors of the craft that, for me, epitomizes the zenith of Seine river transport, the paddle steamer. In the early nineteenth century, the two Seines – upstream and downstream of Paris – were showing signs of meeting up. And, with the arrival of the paddle steamer, Misery Valley became a memory.

Nobody evokes the spirit of the steamboat leaving Paris better than Gustave Flaubert in *L'Education Sentimentale*, as his hero, Frédéric, sets out for Nogent.

'On the 15th September 1840, about six o'clock in the morning, the *Ville-de-Montereau* let out great whirlwinds of smoke by the Quai St-Bernard.

People arrived out of breath; wine-barrels, cables and linen-baskets made it hard to circulate; sailors answered no one; people banged into each other; packages piled up between the capstans, and the hubbub was absorbed by the hissing of steam, which, escaping through plates of sheet-metal, enveloped everything in a whitish cloud, while the ship's bell, fore'ard, clanged incessantly.

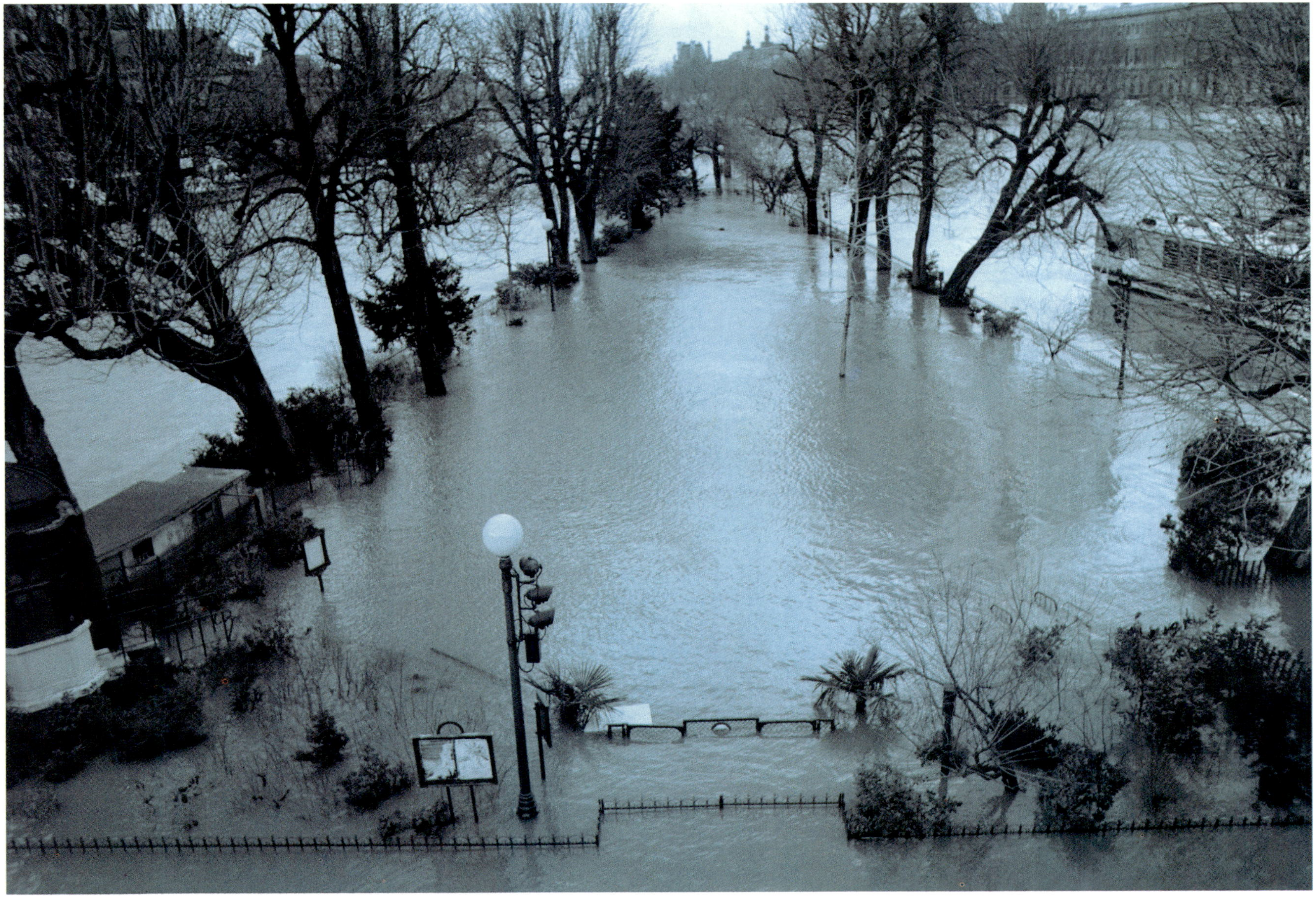

FLOODS: ILE ST-LOUIS (LEFT) AND SQUARE DU VERT-GALANT (ABOVE)

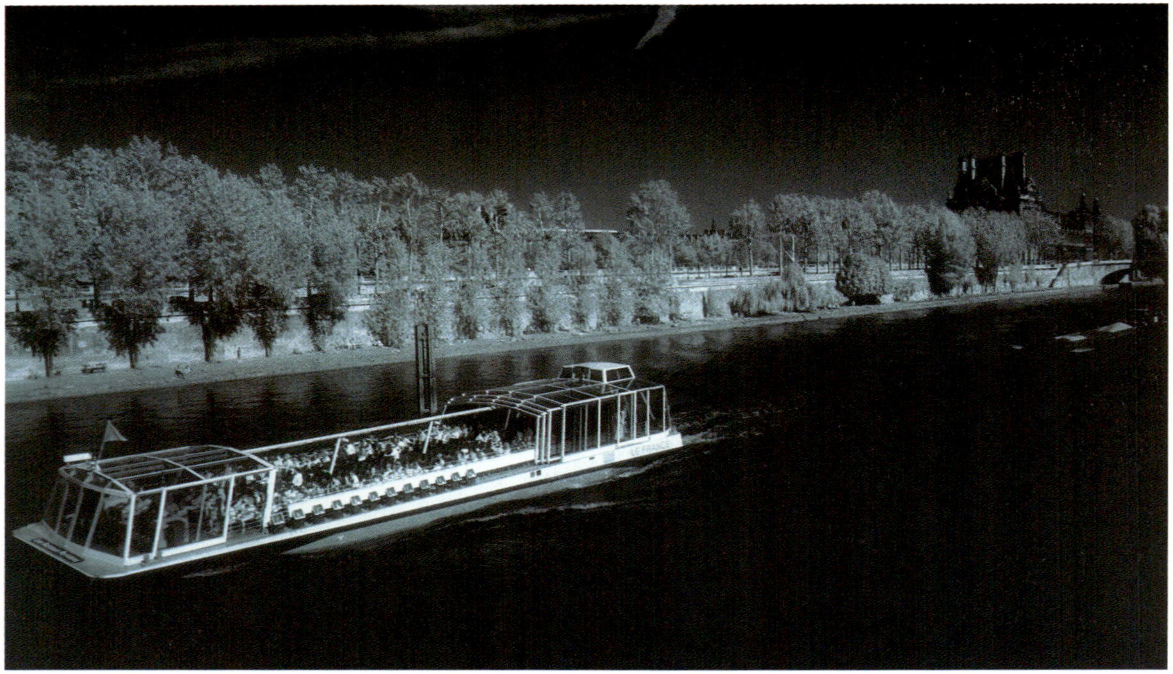

TUILERIES GARDENS

Finally the boat left; and the two banks, lined with shops, boatyards and factories, passed by like two wide ribbons unrolling. . . .

The tumult died down; everyone had taken their places; some, standing, warmed themselves round the engine, and the funnel belched its plume of black smoke with a slow, rhythmic rattling; little drops of dew rolled down the brass fittings; the deck shook with a slight vibration from inside, and the two wheels, rapidly turning, beat the water.'

Nowadays, most people first travel the Seine in a *bateau-mouche* – a great transparent alligator by day, a twinkling spaceship by night. These vast tourist boats have their own, spectacular floodlighting which casts a subtle light-show upon the passing Paris quaysides and embarrassed lovers. The origins of the *mouche* are arcane. I myself had always taken it to mean a boat like a giant water 'fly', flitting the tourists from the Pont d'Alma round the islands and back. In fact, it was named after the part of Lyons called Mouche, where the first propeller water-buses were made for the Paris Exhibition of 1867.

The more adventurous, in search of a Flaubertian 'current of fresh air' in the midst of the Paris fumes, live in houseboats on the Seine's banks.

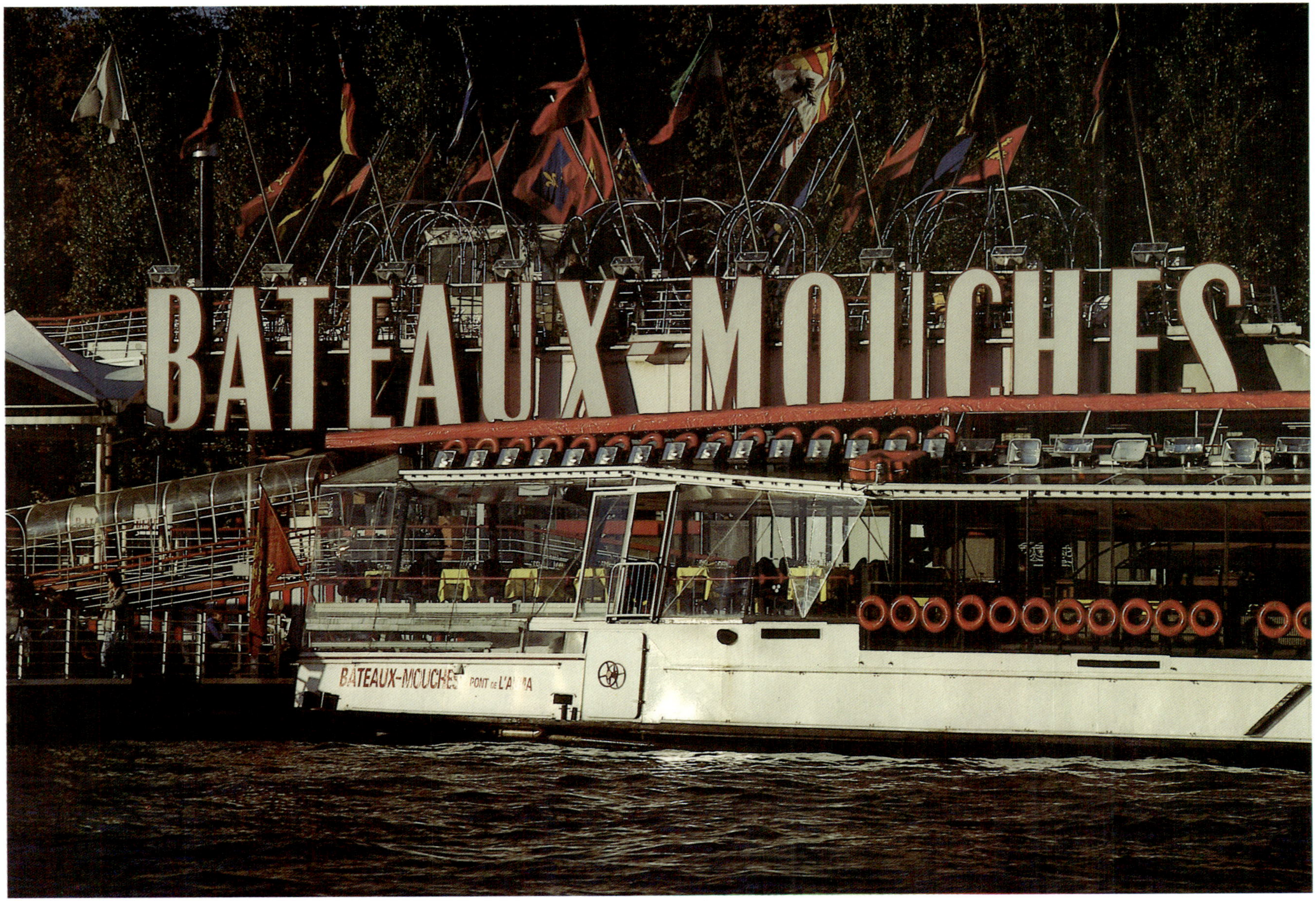

PONT DE L'ALMA

BARGE PEOPLE

Actor Pierre Richard looked as if his next movie role was piratical. Bearded, barefooted and Barbary-tanned, he greeted me on the deck of the *Eendracht*, a Dutch barge built in 1912, now his permanent Paris home. It couldn't be more central: the Place de la Concorde was hard by; a really bad flood would have the *Eendracht* in the Tuileries gardens, visiting the Orangerie and Monet's *Water-lilies* by water.

'I'm three minutes from the office at Alma,' Pierre told me, 'my press agent lives two houseboats away, and at the same time it's like a village here. In my previous Paris apartment, I never even knew the neighbours opposite. Here, I certainly know my neighbour: if my barge is moored on the outside, and he wants to take a trip, it's a twenty-minute manoeuvre for us to change places. So we have to get along – and I can always borrow bread or fuel for the cooker.'

Not at all the dude barge life-style a film star might be thought to lead. The living-room was simple – open plan with wooden ceiling in the central section where once coal had travelled. A piano was no trouble to the neighbours: 'The walls are double thickness – the interior wood and the hull. So my son plays sax at all hours, and no one complains.'

The river was specially romantic at night, Pierre said, the water mirror-flat and black, with the illuminated monuments and bridges reflected in it.

'One night, I and a neighbour went in my motor dinghy to the Ile St-Louis for a nice, quiet dinner *à la vénitienne*. First thing that happens: while we're in the restaurant, the boat goes missing. Luckily, we find it – moored round the other side of the island. How it got there, God knows! Then, on the way home, we hear this yelling under a bridge. We can't pretend we haven't heard. So we come in close to the bank. See a *clochard* beating up his woman. "Stop that, or we'll call the police!" I shout. And guess what? He doesn't stop. Instead, the woman we're trying to rescue tells us: "Fuck off!" So we do. And continue on our way, under the stars. But we've hardly been going a minute when we pass a barge-restaurant where a waiter's tipping garbage into the Seine. "That's illegal!" I yell. "Illegal?!!" the waiter yells back. "Who are you to talk, *salauds*, with no red lights on your boat?" Okay, okay – enough good citizenry for one night. We chug on. Until . . . there's this poor tourist, snoring away in a sleeping-bag on the river-bank and a *voyou* going through his backpack! I put on my best Molière voice, and yell "*Au voleur*!" For once, we win. In a flash, the thief is beating it up the steps to the quay. And we head full-throttle for our barges. Surprisingly, they're still there.'

The neighbour on this quiet dinner outing was marine architect Jacques Rougerie, who designs undersea buildings and exotic craft. His barge is his workshop – a superb water-side space lit by the skylight, with models of boats, designs for projects and its own aquarium. Jacques also has his offices just across the paving-stones of the river bank – up an iron ladder and through a door into premises once occupied by the

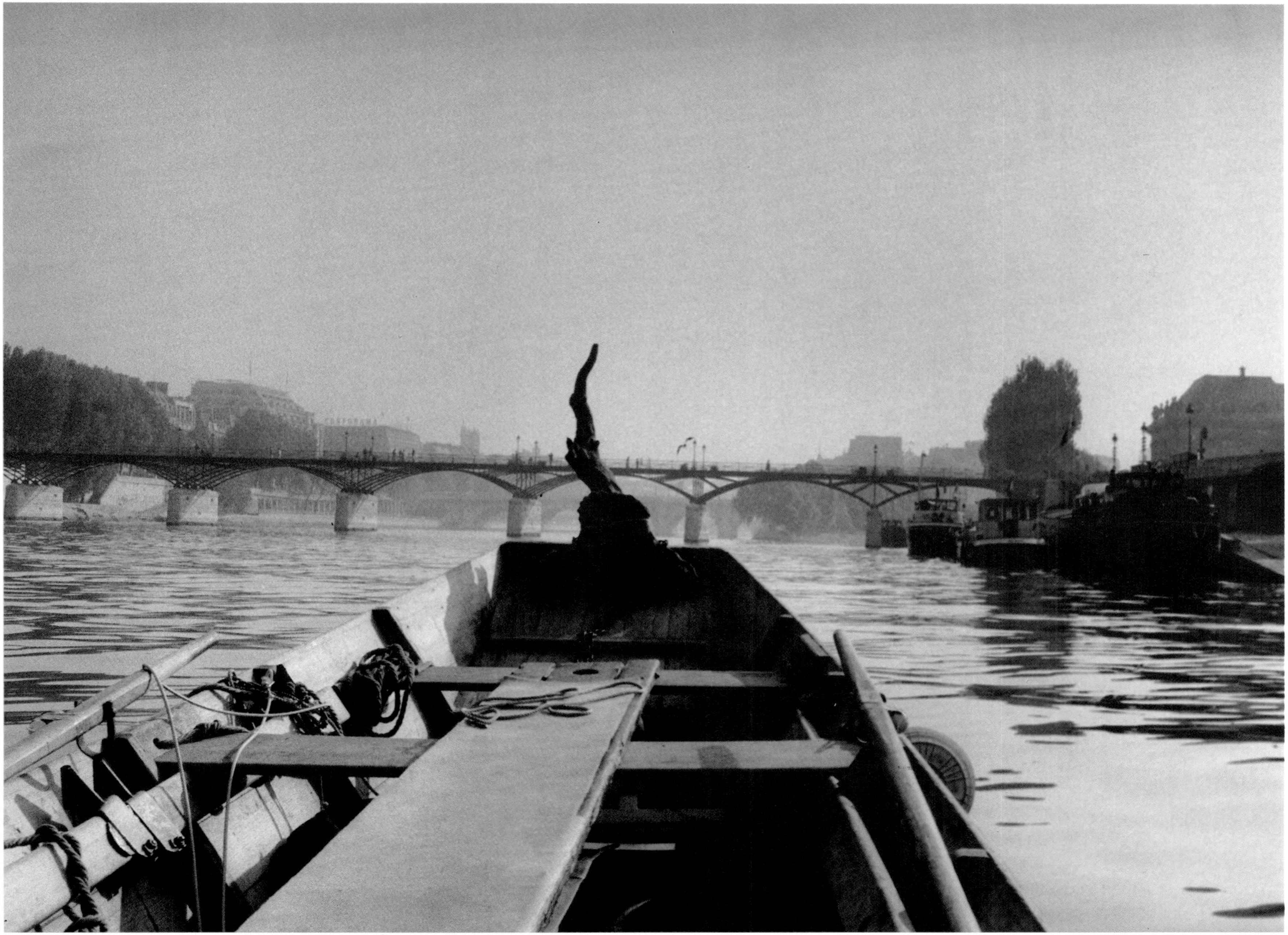

Pont des Arts

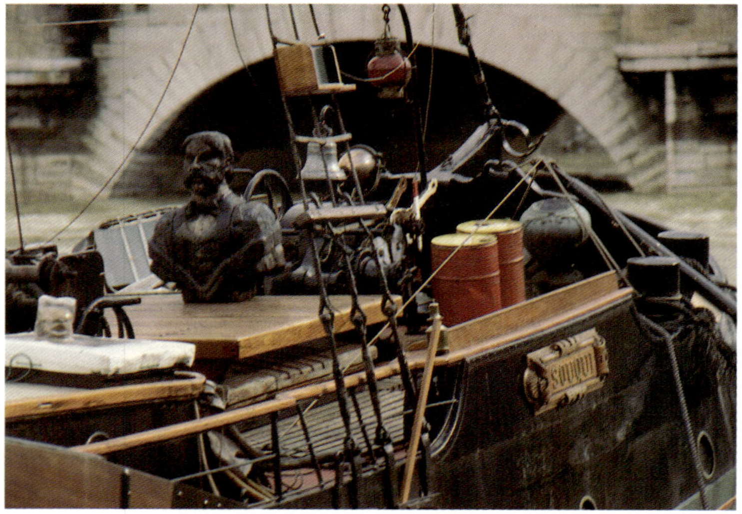

HOUSEBOAT

sewage-men of Paris, now a hive of clicking computers, buzzing telephones and staff of twelve.

'I have taken this barge on trips,' Jacques said. 'Nice to take off in your home – up the Marne or down to Rouen. Rouen only takes twenty-four hours. My companion, Violaine, and I have lived here ten years now. Paris is a world centre of marine architecture, and this is the perfect. . . .'

'I complain all the time,' Violaine interrupted, laughing. 'I'm short-sighted, and that's terrible on a barge! I bang my head. And look –' She had a plaster on her shin. 'I still bump into bits of barge, coming aboard. And remember the *clochard*, Jacques?'

One night the Rougeries came back late from dinner. Jacques, as usual, took a last look at his day's work, while Violaine went into their bedroom. She quickly returned. 'Jacques, you are terrible! Who's this *copain* of yours sleeping in our bed? He stinks.' Jacques went to investigate. It was no *copain* but a young giant of a *clochard*. 'What are you doing here?' 'Sleeping.' 'You'll have to go.' 'No, you go. I'm sleeping.' 'Then I'll have to call the police.' 'So call them.' The *clochard* went back to sleep. The police arrived. And the *clochard* wisely decided he would continue the night's sleep under the bridge, as usual.

Other incidents had more irony, contrasting the urban success of the barge-dwellers with the marginal characters around them. One summer's night the Rougeries were dining on deck by candlelight, so were their neighbours on the next barge. A morbid cabaret was provided by an exhibitionist who climbed over the parapet of the Pont Neuf and yelled: 'You shits, I'm leaving your stinking world – right now!' Jacques called the fire brigade. And just as they had succeeded in talking the lunatic down, the Rougeries' neighbour shouted: 'Idiot, you can't even kill yourself decently!' With that, the mortified exhibitionist jumped. Splash! into the water, right by the elegant diners' barge. When the firemen had hauled him out, the neighbour felt obliged to invite him for a drink.

Suicide attempts and accidents, however, were all too often fatal on that treacherous reach of the Seine. A barge-dwelling American artist, Duncan Caldwell, told me: 'There were two *clochards*, Michel and Napoléon. Both liked their wine. Michel also liked cooking *coq au vin* in a lean-to on the quayside. He went to get more water from the river, leant forward, and just toppled in. It was winter. In seconds he developed hypothermia and was pulled down by the undertow.'

Napoléon had more luck. One day, leaving a friend's barge blind drunk, he fell off the gangplank. They hauled him out,

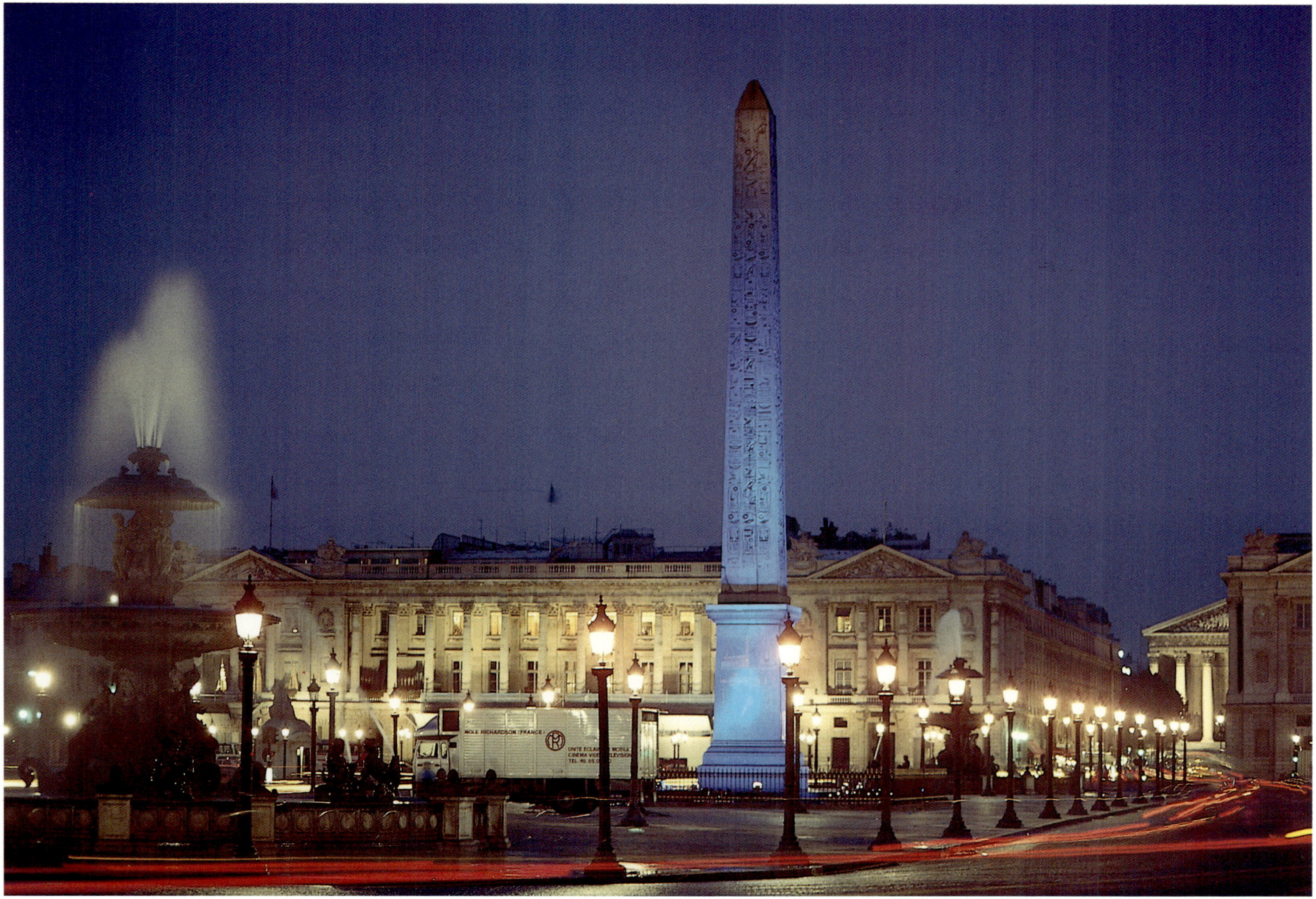

PLACE DE LA CONCORDE, NIGHT

apparently dead. But when the firemen arrived, he sprang from the blanket they'd wrapped him in and saluted. The fire chief saluted back, announcing in a military voice: 'Napoléon, your *avant-garde* has arrived!'

Another American Seine-dweller was the tormented cowboy actor, Sterling Hayden. A genuine sailor, he wrote two books on his barge: one called *Voyage*, about sailing round Cape Horn, the other, *Wanderer*, about kidnapping his own children to Polynesia after his Californian divorce. He felt, in some way, he had betrayed his working-class origins – and filled his houseboat with twenty tons of gravel to make it more working-class.

But most of the barge people nowadays are doctors, architects, lawyers and other urban professionals looking for a more relaxed life-style. Observing that the Assemblée Nationale was just across the river, I asked: 'And politicians?' 'No, I wouldn't go as far as that!' was Pierre Richard's wry comment.

Duncan, as an American, was justly proud of his part in defending the Seine against a truly mad waterfront renewal project of President Pompidou's: the demolition of the existing Seine banks and eviction of houseboat owners. The Port Autonome de Paris were furious. The port had authority over the houseboats, and the Government was outside the law in threatening to evict them. After a strong petition, the scheme was dropped, and houseboats remained. And shrubs and geraniums still adorn their decks. Every flood continues to be a barge-child's dream – when Papa has to row them to school.

I stroll down the Left Bank and, at every marvel, sigh with relief at prevailing sanity. Starting with Open Air Sculpture on the Quai St-Bernard, where the turning metal discs of Yoshikuni's vast metal mobile 'Shining Wings' catch the sunlight.

Modern architecture, too, at its oxydized aluminium best faces the Pont Sully. The Arab Institute – the work of nineteen countries, including France – combines Western and Eastern, inside and outside, present and past, science and art. The revolutionary windows, with their symmetrical Arabic design, open and close like a camera lens according to the strength of sunlight outside. From a spatial mezzanine, I look down on fifteenth-century astrolobes, their gold discs brightly lit against a backdrop of wintry barges obfuscated in a grey twilight.

Outside the Tour d'Argent, an Olympic team of Japanese gastronomes (they are in matching red blazers!) limber up before the exquisite meal for a mere 700 francs a head. Occasionally, real-live Parisians can be seen eating a truffle stew or turbot with Sauternes at that privileged round table which overlooks the Seine and its islands.

Foreigners again – at the famous bookshop, Shakespeare and Company. For 35 years the riverside browserie of George Whitman, former New Orleans seaman, has been a convivial meeting-place for expatriates and the ghosts of Ernest, Henry, Ezra, Scott, Zelda, Gertrude and Alice B.

At a bookstall near the Boul' Mich', the *bouquiniste* is rather less literary, a specialist in back numbers of girlie magazines. 'Pretty girls, M'sieur, are what I do best,' he tells me, his corduroy suit and pipe and flowing grey hair more suitable for fondling first editions of Sainte-Beuve. Proudly he shows me every *Playboy* since 1958, and a complete set of *Penthouse*. 'Very useful for research,' he said earnestly. 'For period costumes.'

Past the Mint and the Académie Française, I turn up Rue Mazarine to pay homage to François du Perrier, a seventeenth-century member of the Comédie-Française. This Perrier's water

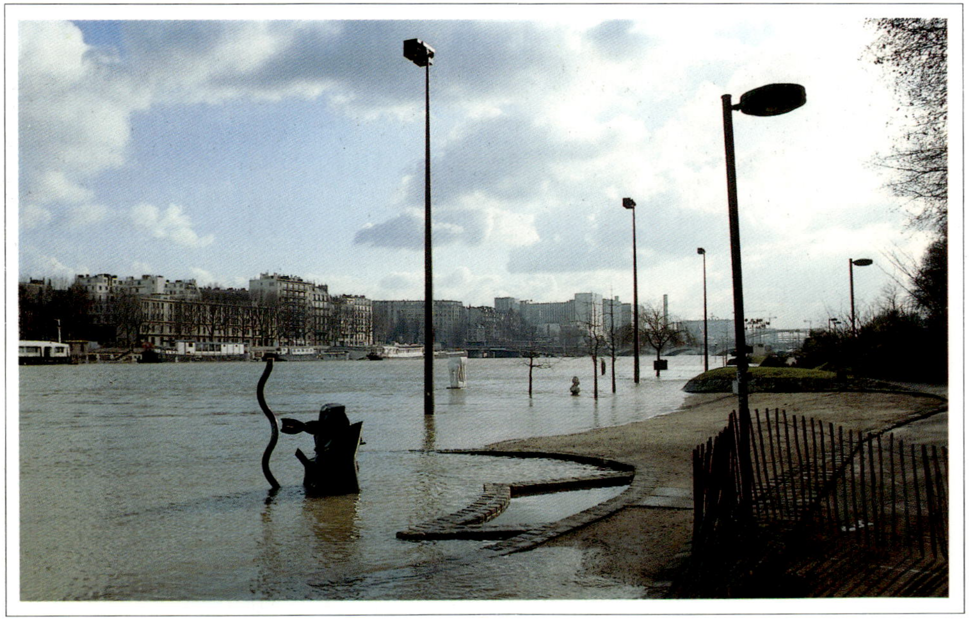

FLOODS, OPEN AIR SCULPTURE

was strictly the Seine's, for the versatile actor (he also had 32 children) was founder of the Paris fire brigade, from a house conveniently close to the river.

A nineteenth-century railway station, turned into a museum of nineteenth-century art – by the Seine. What could be more appropriate? Never was the river and its life more painted than during the Age of Steam. Witness Monet's railway-bridge, Renoir's riverside ball, Boudin's sailboats, Jongkind's Notre-Dame, Seurat's La Grande-Jatte, Sisley's floods – and so many other images of a Seine just across the road from the Musée d'Orsay.

Another crowd draw is the Plage de Paris, that admirable lido near the Palais-Bourbon, home of the Assemblée Nationale. Could be a reason its debates often play to a tiny house; hot, bored Deputies are off sunning themselves at the Piscine Deligny.

Or, perhaps, to reassure themselves of their capital's eternal allure, they stand for a moment on the Left Bank side of the Pont de la Concorde. On a clear day, in one slow movement of the head, one can see Montmartre, Sacré Coeur, Place de la Concorde, Eiffel Tower, Louvre, and Palais-Bourbon. Not to mention the Seine. The Seine of Lovers.

'. . . and it was a delightful refuge, a shelter in mid-crowd, with Paris rumbling around them on its quays and bridges, while by the water's edge they tasted the joy of being alone, ignored by the world. From then on, that bank was their corner of countryside, a land of fresh air where they enjoyed hours of sunshine. . . .' (Emile Zola: *L'Oeuvre*)

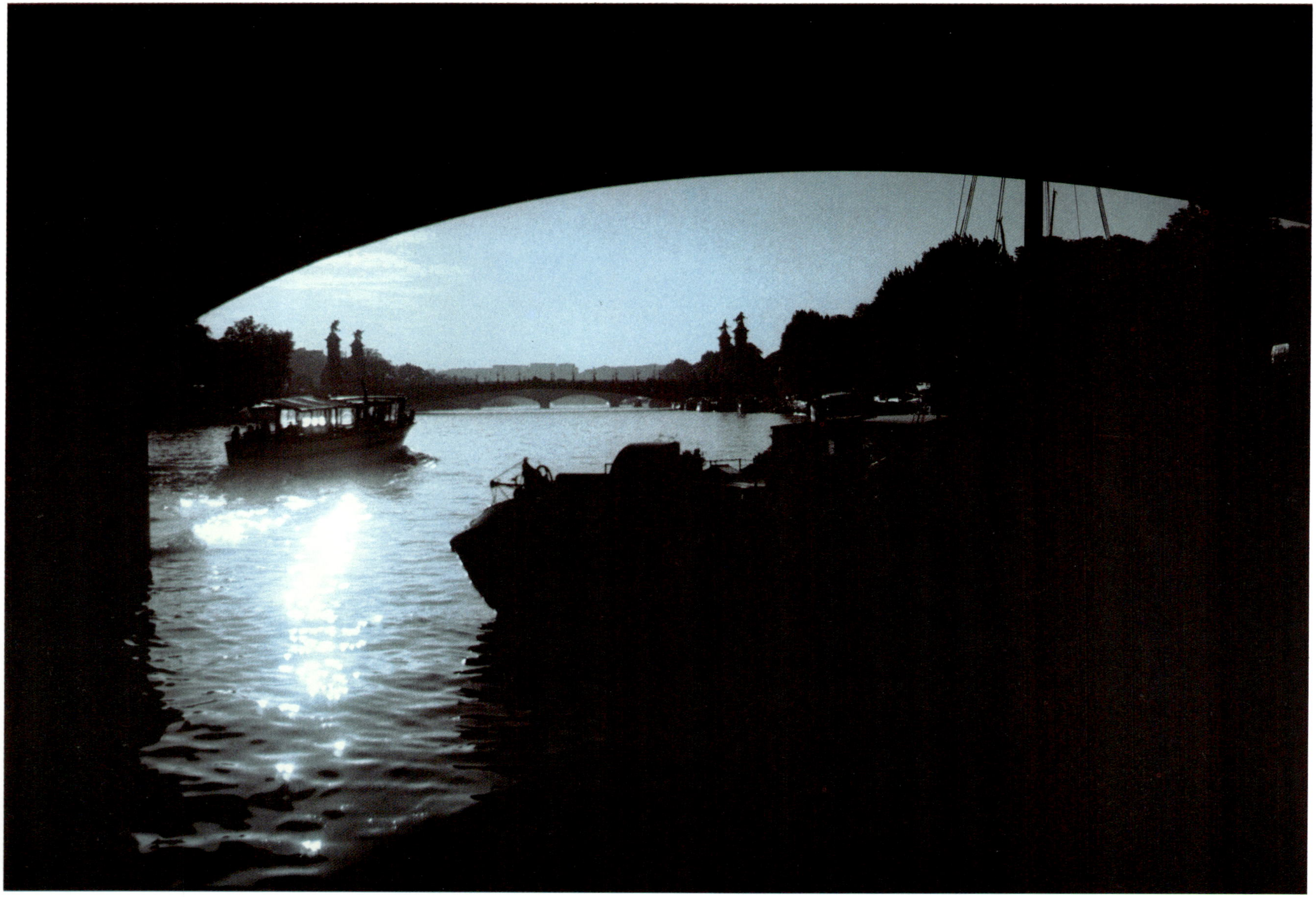

PONT DE LA CONCORDE

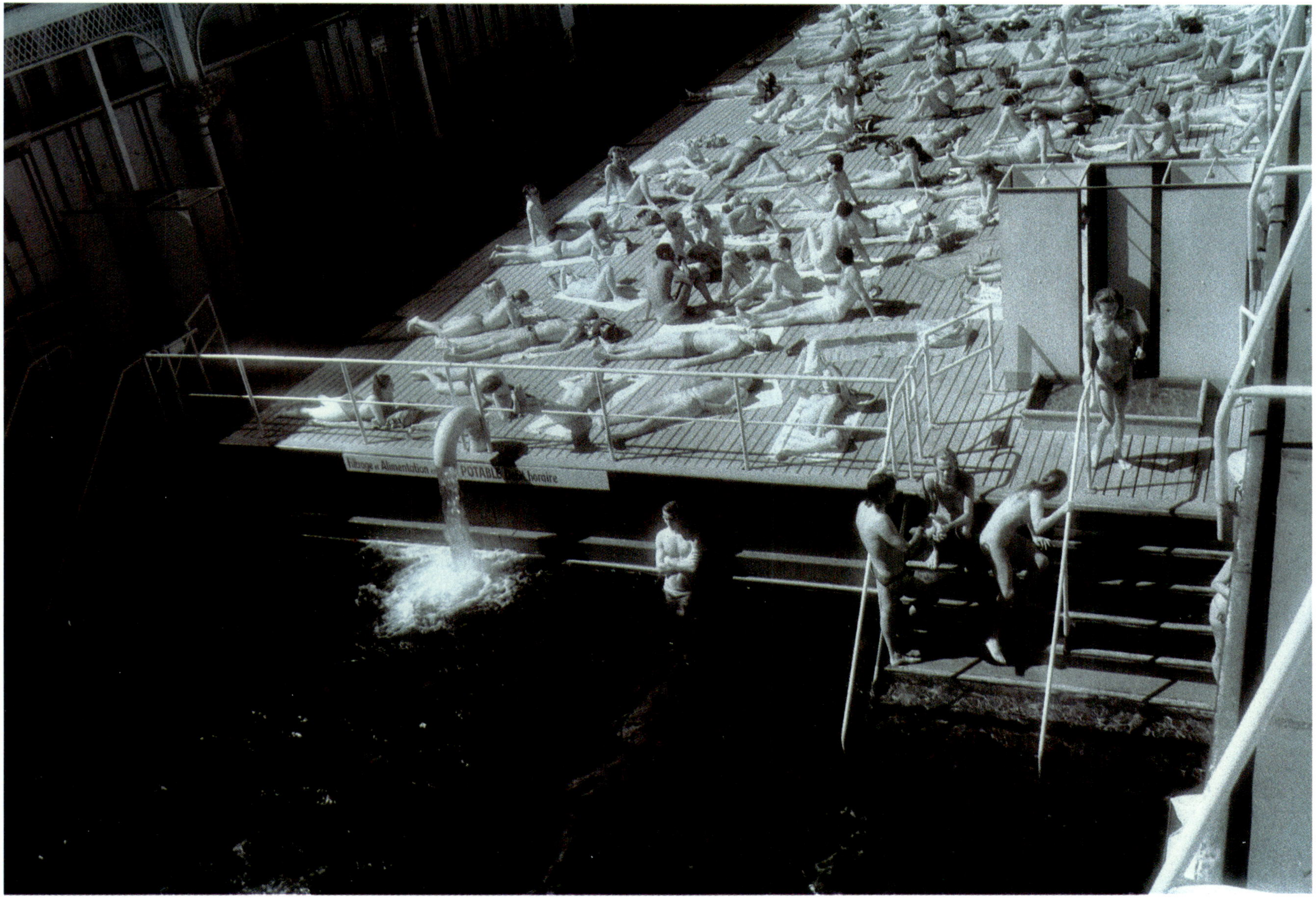

PISCINE DELIGNY

ISLAND LIFE

'Around the island,' said the shopkeeper, 'they fish eel, pike, barbel, carp and tench. For lunch, we've just eaten a delicious perch caught this morning.'

The island was not Bora-Bora or Saint-Barthélémy; it was the Ile St-Louis, in mid-Seine, in mid-Paris. And the fish-eater who lived to tell the tale was now serving customers in the family shop, La Maison de la Mouche, an angler's paradise on the Pont Henri IV. 'Ah, *dis-donc*, M'sieur, I don't feel too sick. Believe it or not, the Seine is perfectly healthy.'

I was skeptical. So he recommended I talk to a fisherman. I found my fisherman being photographed by a journalist, as he reeled in a handsome carp over the parapet. The journalist had been working a year on the article; piscatory pace in Europe's speediest city slowed down even a busy newshound. Nice work, this leisurely shooting and fishing.

'I give the fish I catch to friends,' admitted the fisherman. 'Except if it's a salmon, which is very rare.' His basket, already well filled with bream and roach, was proudly held up for the camera. But, looking down at the murky green water whence came the catch, I wondered if his friends were all that lucky. There were some very sick-looking weeds floating about just below us. My fisherman, although he did not eat his own catch, was not fazed by pollution. 'Special rubbish boats collect two thousand tons of shit thrown overboard by people every year.' 'But what about the industrial effluent and pesticides and toxic gum from paper mills,' I asked. The fisherman made a dismissive gesture, speaking passionately of purification plants capable of treating more than two million cubic metres of effluent a day.

'In ten years' time, it'll be Paris-Plage,' he assured me. 'People will be bathing in the Seine like they used to twenty years ago. And fishermen will have their own private pontoons again. You'll see.' It was nice to meet an ecological optimist, for once. 'Look – not an oil slick in sight.'

I showed him a newspaper cutting from *Le Journal de Dimanche*, in which Mayor Chirac answered an interviewer who suggested a 'blue' Seine might be an electoral caprice: 'I'll give you a rendezvous in three years' time, and we'll swim across the Seine together.'

'*Bouf*!' the fisherman exclaimed. 'Three years' time?! If you fell in right now, I'd jump in and rescue you without a qualm.'

I did not put him to the test.

Uninviting as the Seine water may sometimes look, the island it surrounds is a perfection of seventeenth-century houses on quiet quays – a city village that beats even Hampstead or Georgetown for peace and elegance. Neither of those has the river.

The Ile St-Louis was always a source of artistic inspiration. Wagner composed there, Baudelaire poetized, and Daumier drew. Great *portes cochères*, studded with huge nails, and interior courtyards guarded their privacy. As I passed Number 9, Quai d'Anjou, I imagined Daumier's carriage clattering out

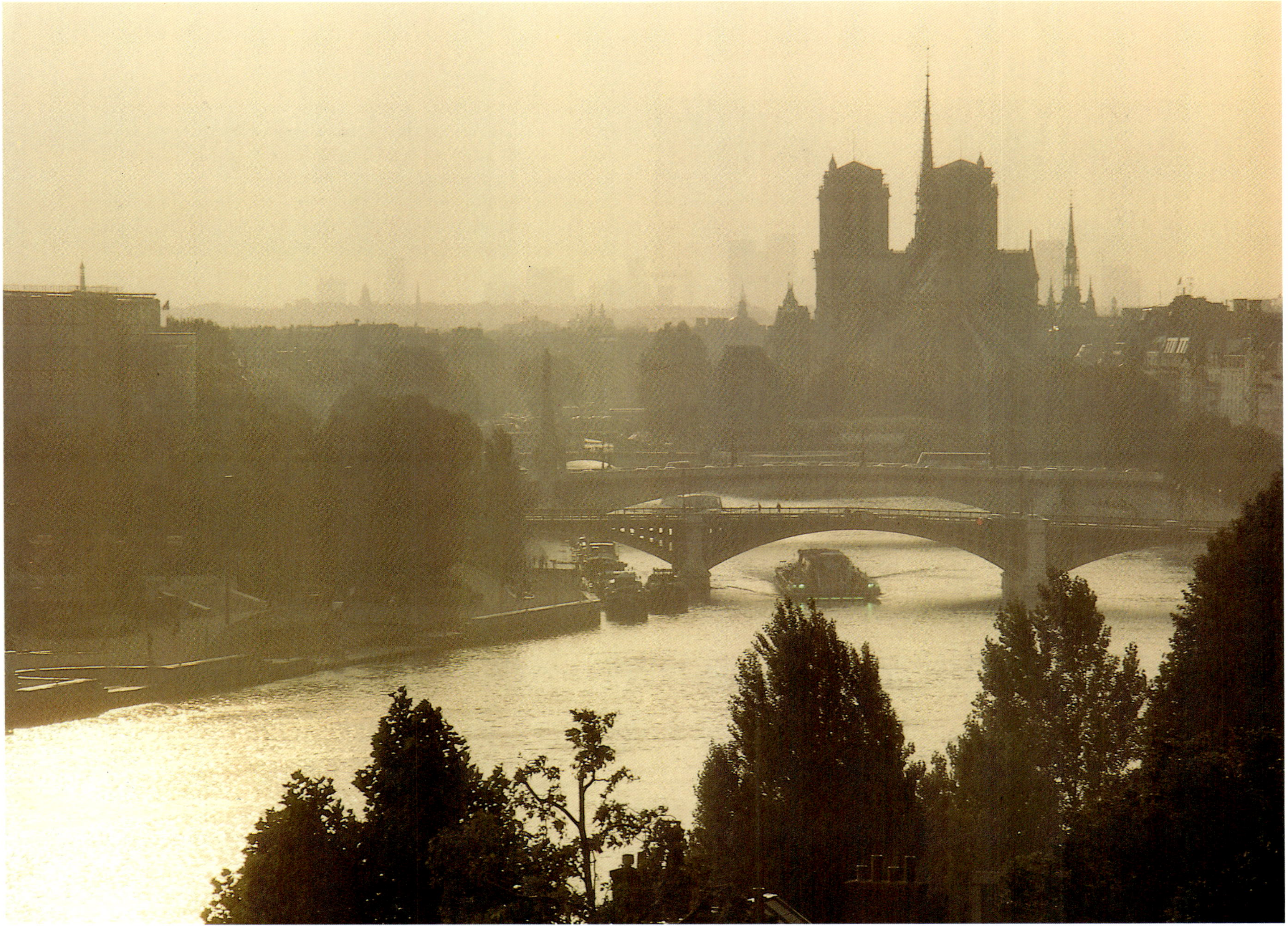

Notre Dame, sunset

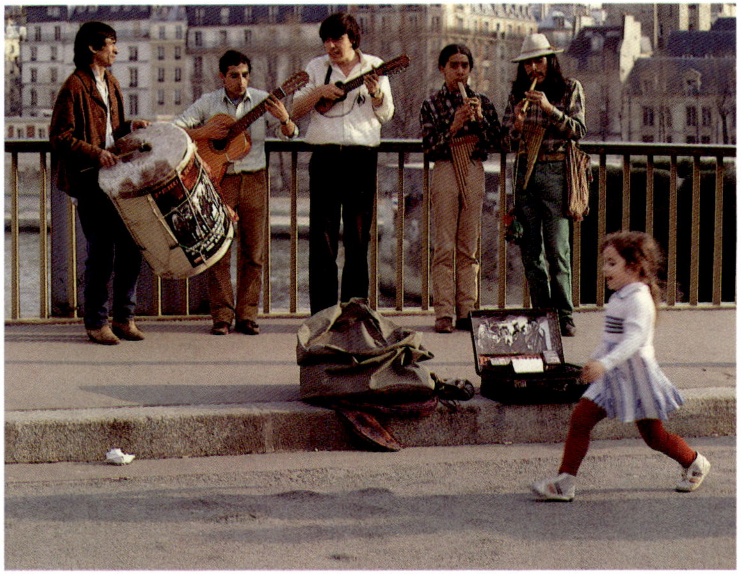

PERUVIAN STREET MUSICIANS, ILE ST-LOUIS

across the cobblestones, as he delivered yet another savage cartoon to his lithographer. Like Flaubert, he flayed the philistinism of the mid-nineteenth-century bourgeoisie. 'Typical art-lovers more and more convinced that art in France is over', was the caption for a cartoon of prim, disapproving viewers at the Salon des Beaux-Arts. An unattractive man comments to his equally unattractive friends: 'This Monsieur Courbet makes faces much too ugly. There's no one like that in real life!' And not long after, similar Salon-haunters would be scandalized by Manet and Monet, throwing new light upon the River Seine.

A funeral service with a counter-tenor singing Monteverdi greeted me at the baroque church of St-Louis-de-l'Ile. But, in spite of the elaborate singing within and the ornate hearse without, casual Arab workers, loading old church pews into a truck, brought a village ambience to the easy-going main street that seemed far removed from Parisian stress.

And Berthillon ice-creams! I remembered a time when Carey was lucky enough to inhabit 51, Quai Bourbon; of the village shops, Berthillon was her favourite, though by no means totally stress-free with its long queues and sometimes irritable staff. We avoided it by eating our Berthillon sorbets at the café Flore de l'Ile, overlooking the river and the back of Notre-Dame.

Below the café, on the river bank, a man was prone, basking in the November sun, stripped to the waist. On the Pont St-Louis, as I crossed the narrow channel between the two islands, a young violinist played an autumnal lament.

Such quiet residential charm is rare on the larger Ile de la Cité. In spite of its many wonders, it is tourist land – lines of coaches surrounded Notre-Dame as though a Cup Final were being played inside. La Sainte-Chapelle, the Law Courts, the Flower Market and the Conciergerie are tourist musts. But there is none of that intimate, island atmosphere until you reach its western tip.

Here I sensed the Parisian joy of Zola's lovers: the seventeenth-century triangular Place Dauphine, named by Henri IV after his son, the future Louis XIII. The Conciergerie was still a royal palace in those days; Monarchy, Law and Church were conveniently concentrated on this one island. With the pressure on land for mightier purposes, it was far-sighted of Henri IV to make over Place Dauphine for private residences, and a modest but charming little hotel is named after him, lest we forget. Elsewhere, lawyers can browse at the legal book-shops, and lunch at the Caveau du Palais.

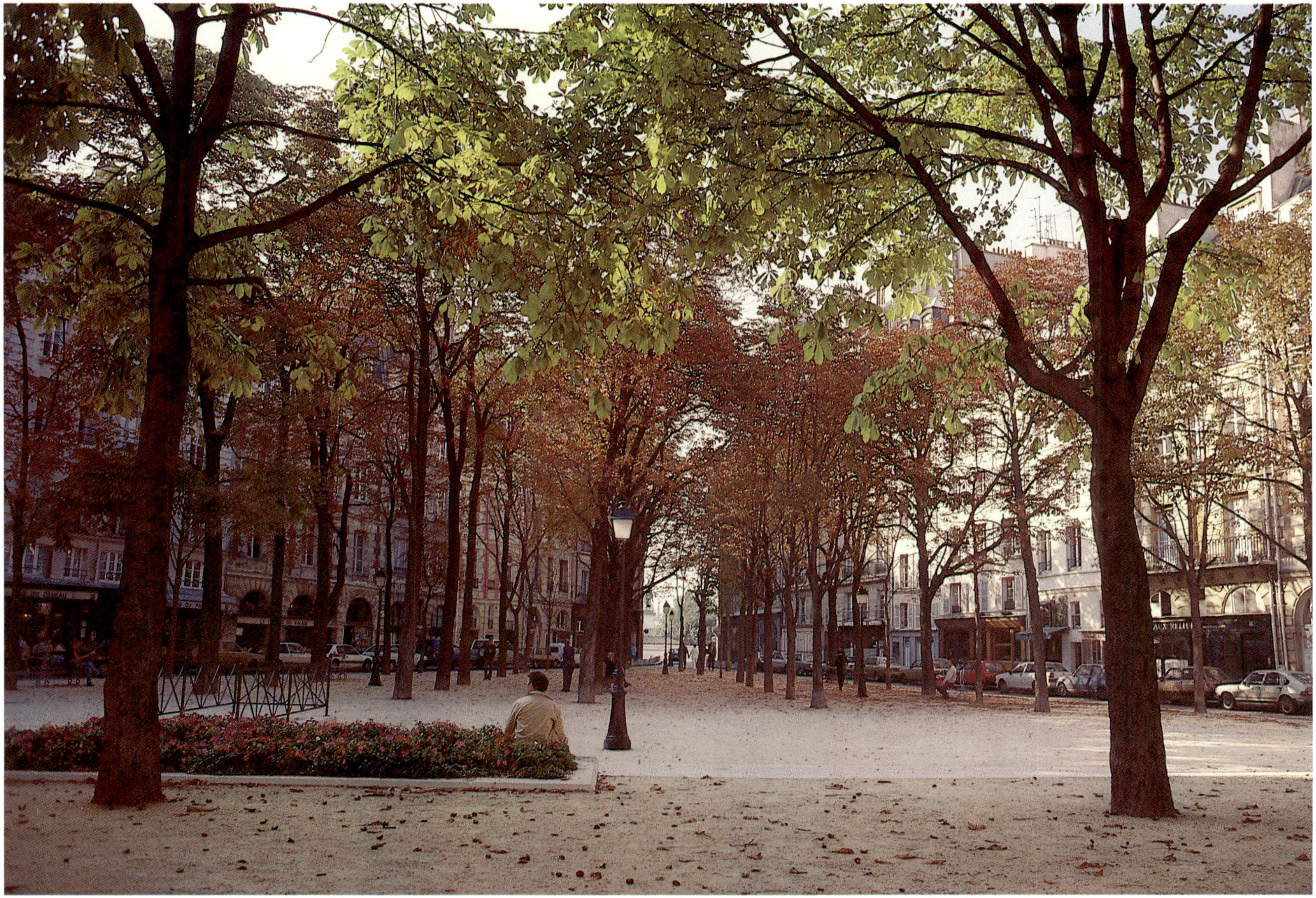

PLACE DAUPHINE, ILE DE LA CITÉ

At the apex of the triangle, a narrow alley led me on to the Pont Neuf, Paris's oldest bridge, built in 1578. Across and down steps to the Square du Vert-Galant (nickname for Henry IV – 'bright old thing'), I found myself in crisp, wintry sunshine among the chrysanthemums and trees of a little garden. With the Seine on either side, the garden narrowed to a point, mirroring the triangular Place Dauphine, and it was like being on the prow of a ship. Beneath a voluminous weeping willow, a heavy girl was sitting in her lover's lap. Schoolchildren, being snapped at by their bearded young teacher, took no notice of the lovers who kissed and kissed, oblivious of all but each other.

'Ah, what beautiful sunsets they had on their weekly strolls! . . . And the dusk deepened, and they parted with that last dazzling effect still in their eyes, aware of Paris as triumphant accomplice in their inexhaustible joy, for ever restarting that walk together along the old stone parapets.' (Emile Zola: *L'Oeuvre*)

Even alone, the Right Bank is eminently strollable.

In November, the smell of chestnuts roasting on street corners cuts through the carbon monoxide.

Next best thing to being on the Ile St-Louis is the view of it from the Pont Louis-Philippe – upstream, downstream, and a tantalizing glimpse, beyond bridge, narrow street and river's Left Bank branch, of the distant dome of the Panthéon.

At a bookshop on the Quai de L'Hôtel de Ville, I ask for a book on La Seine. Salesgirl: '*La Scène? Oui, M'sieur – du théâtre ou du cinéma?*' Perhaps, being so close to it, she takes the river for granted.

A chilly autumnal mist rises off it. From the grey, gloomy quayside, I look through vast windows into the mayoral opulence of the nineteenth-century Hôtel de Ville's reception rooms, chandeliers a-glitter, curtains draped, caryatids and statues staring impassively at Mayor Chirac's guests and keeping their thoughts very much to themselves.

How do the booksellers at their quayside stalls stand the constant roar and fumes of the traffic? Sweeter sounds come from young American pianists playing Scarlatti or Egyptian folk-singers at the Théâtre de la Ville. Equally international, just behind it, is the sixteenth-century Tour St-Jacques, once a meeting-place of pilgrims on their way to Santiago de Compostela.

'One finds everything at La Samaritaine' goes the slogan of the Seine-side store; I treasure its cinema commercial in which the present Queen of England, on a State Visit to France, has left her crown behind, careless thing, and picks up a spare at La Samaritaine.

The Louvre has even less of a riverside feeling; all its action is in the interior courtyards and galleries. But it does now have the festive new glass pyramid by Chinese architect, I.M. Pei, with its attendant waterworks which remind us of the Seine's vicinity.

A long stretch of greenery – chestnut and plane trees – is the Seine's hinterland from the Tuileries gardens to the Pont Alexandre III, a gift of Tsar Nicholas II for the World Paris Exhibition of 1900. When the one hundred Venetian lamps come on, its two bronze Pegasi look as though they are about to fly off into the Paris twilight, as does Apollo's Chariot on the nearby Grand Palais.

This is Exhibitionist Paris at its best – and beyond Place d'Alma, the river curves south–west to another open space, this time Place du Trocadéro, dominated by the Palais de Chaillot on its hill above. Thirties dictatorial in architecture, it provides, nonetheless, the best view of my favourite Paris monument.

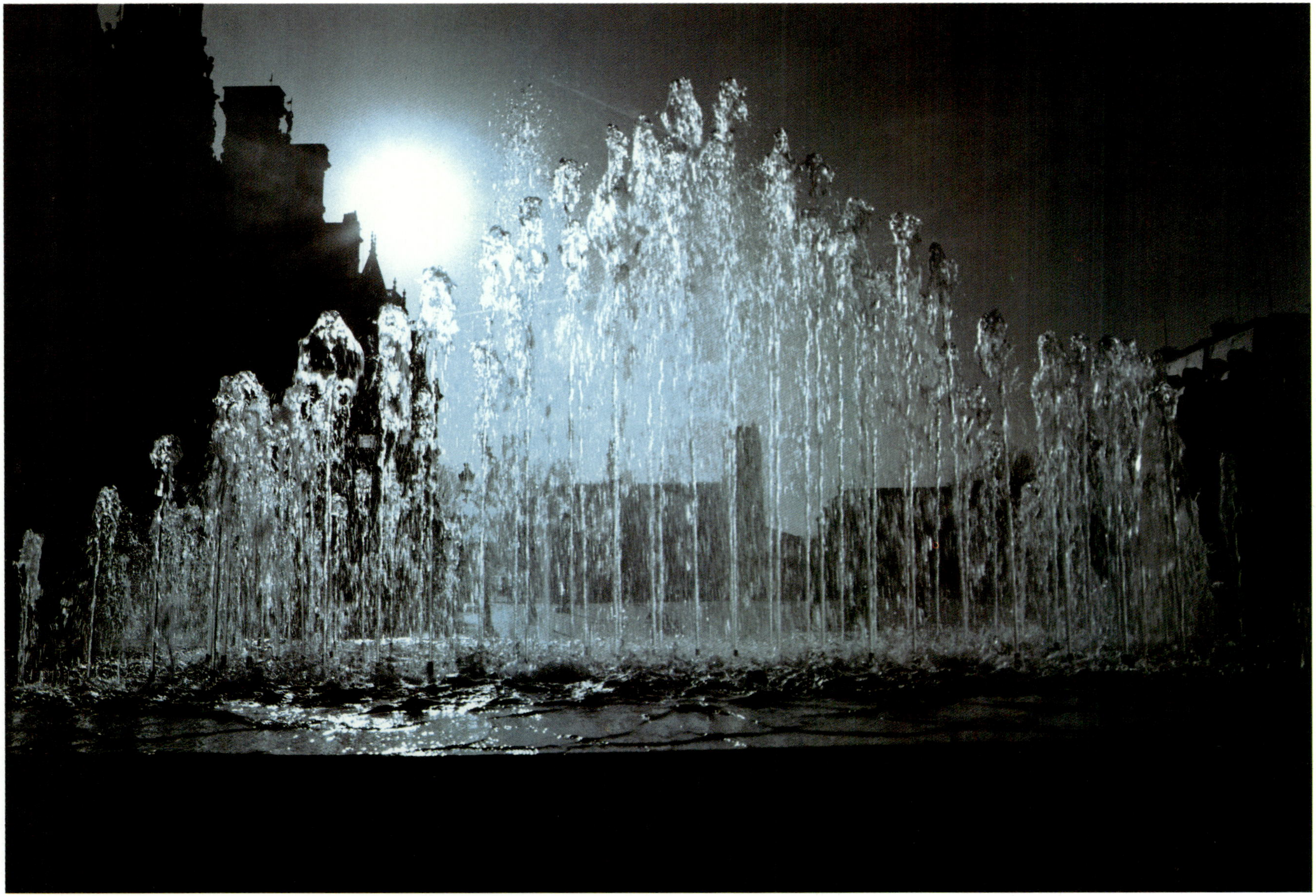

HÔTEL DE VILLE

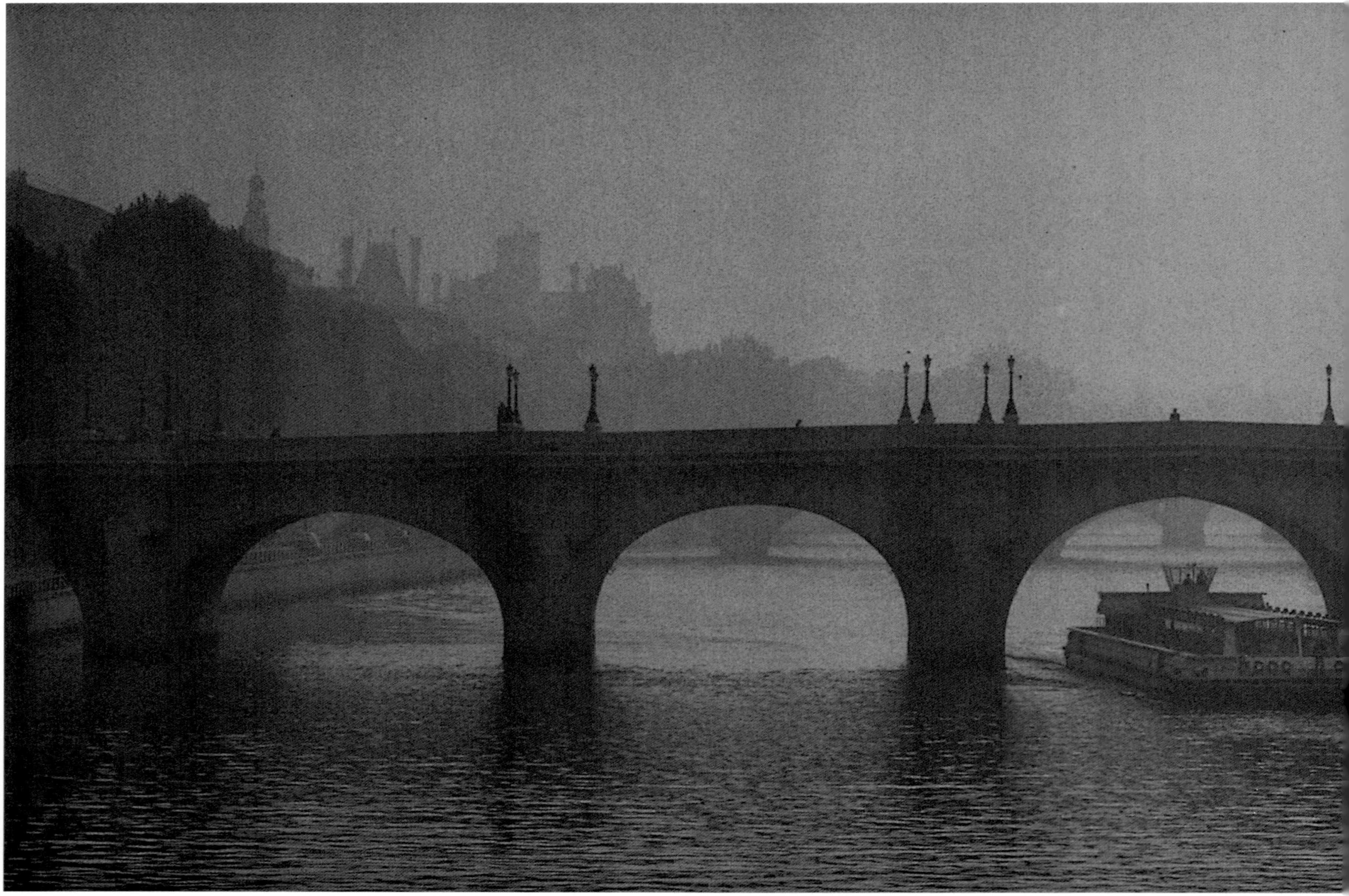

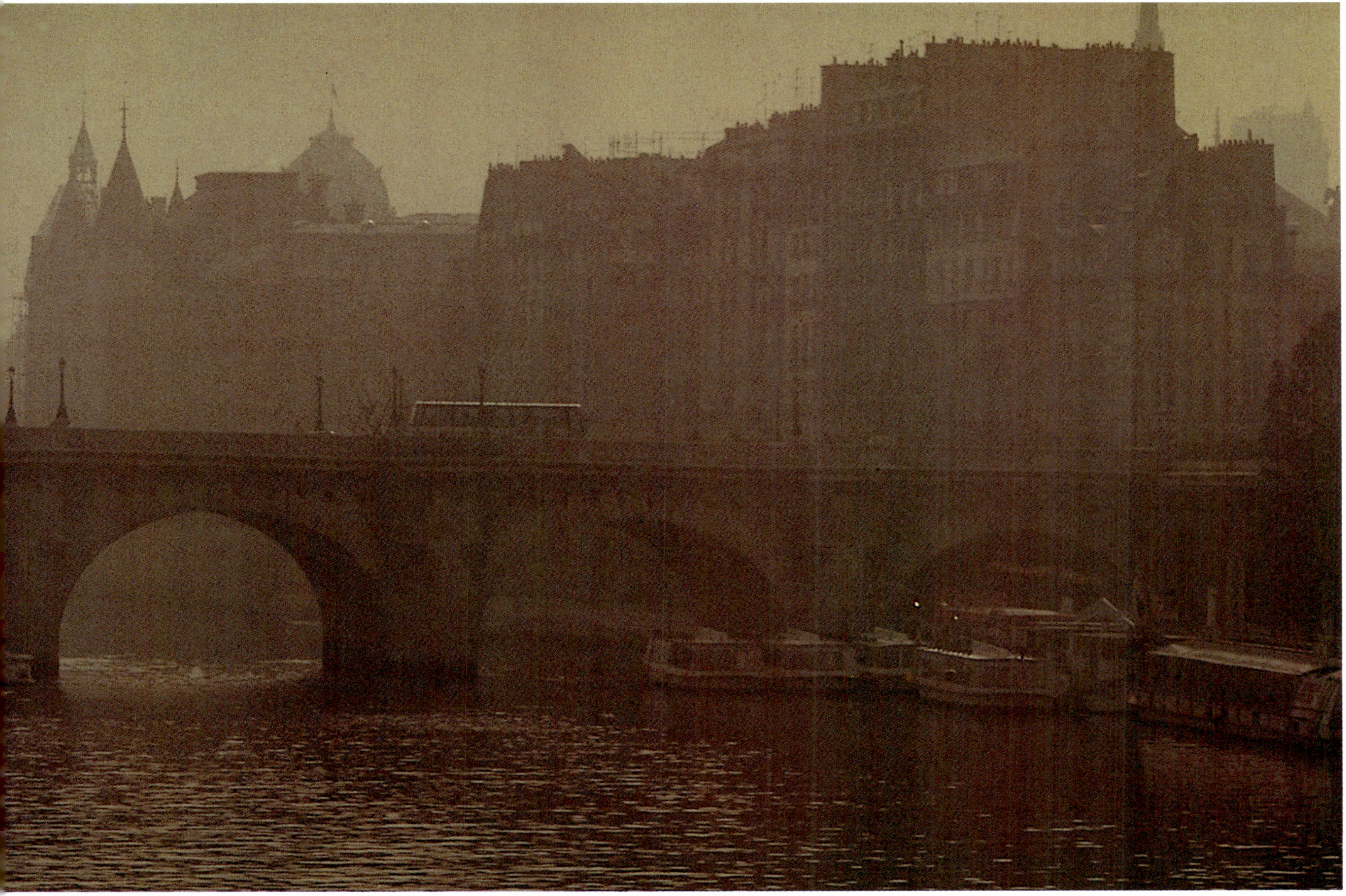

PONT NEUF

NEW VIEW FROM OLD IRON

The Eiffel Tower was one hundred years old in 1989.

At sunset, looking across the river to the perennial Hollywood 'establishing shot' of Paris, I watched streaks of orange reflected on the flamboyant Beaux-Arts latticework. It made me think of a Jules Verne period space rocket. And indeed, at the birthday celebrations, a show-biz bonanza finale began with a laser effect turning the iron lady into a shimmering rocket to rival her contemporary sister, Ariane.

For a moment, the Eiffel Tower seemed to disappear spacewards, then to return to earth, as the crowd let out a great sigh of relief. The massed stars of stage, screen and radio, backed by Can-Can girls and fashion-house models, burst into a specially written Hymn to the Rights of Man, and their last noble note set off The Greatest Firework Display on Earth. Not content with that, across the river, between the wings of the Palais de Chaillot appeared a gigantic birthday cake 82 feet high and 65 feet across, made by a hundred pastry-cooks who cut it and distributed it to the crowd. Let them eat cake. Paris had done the iron lady proud.

The Eiffel Tower was not always so popular. Architect Gustave Eiffel excitedly claimed that Paris would be the only city with a 984-foot flagpole. His 'flagpole' weighed seven thousand tons, its height can vary by six inches according to the weather, and you are advised to take sandwiches if you attempt the 1,652-step climb to the top.

To many, it seemed like a vulgar indulgence. Among the three hundred signers of the protest were the composer Gounod (*Ave Maria*), the writer Guy de Maupassant (a passionate lover of the Seine), and Charles Garnier, architect of the Opéra (frankly, who was he to talk?). To no avail: by the turn of the century, artists and poets were beginning to applaud its vigour and tensility – among them, Dufy, Pissarro, Seurat, Cocteau and Apollinaire. And this beacon of so-called bad taste, an oasis of modernity among Gothic masterpieces, was a reminder of popular Paris – the Paris of the music hall, *bal musette*, street market and fair. The Eiffel Tower is androgynous; both iron lady and phallus, a symbol of Parisian freedoms as representative, in their way, as Parisian culture.

The tower can now be reached by *vaporetto*, Mayor Chirac's nostalgic new river-bus system. It took me less than a couple of minutes to get from the pier to my place in the eternal queue for the ascent.

With much Industrial Revolution clatter and clank, we lifted off beyond the yellow pistons, and soon the Seine was sparkling below us, the Palais de Chaillot monolithic and Mussolinian beyond. Slowly, as we slid up the curve of the west pillar, the distant skyscrapers of La Défense appeared on the horizon.

All change at the second platform. Toy barges below left a neat mini-wake behind them. A couple of tourists clutched each other as we took another six-minute ride to the top. I felt naked as a fledgeling. But the gentle upward propulsion between skimpy ironwork was only pleasantly scary. Just a twinge of

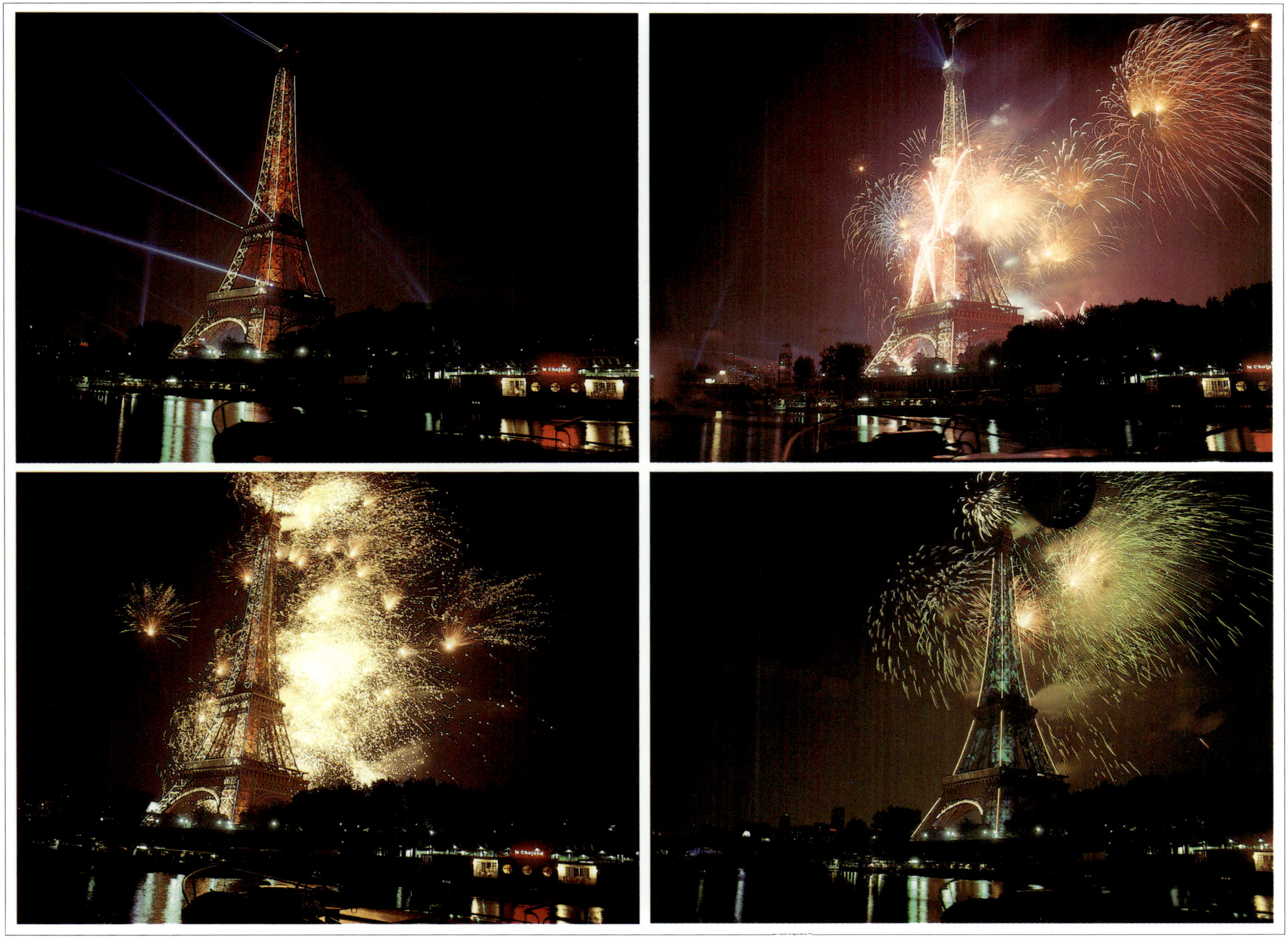

EIFFEL TOWER CENTENARY, 1989

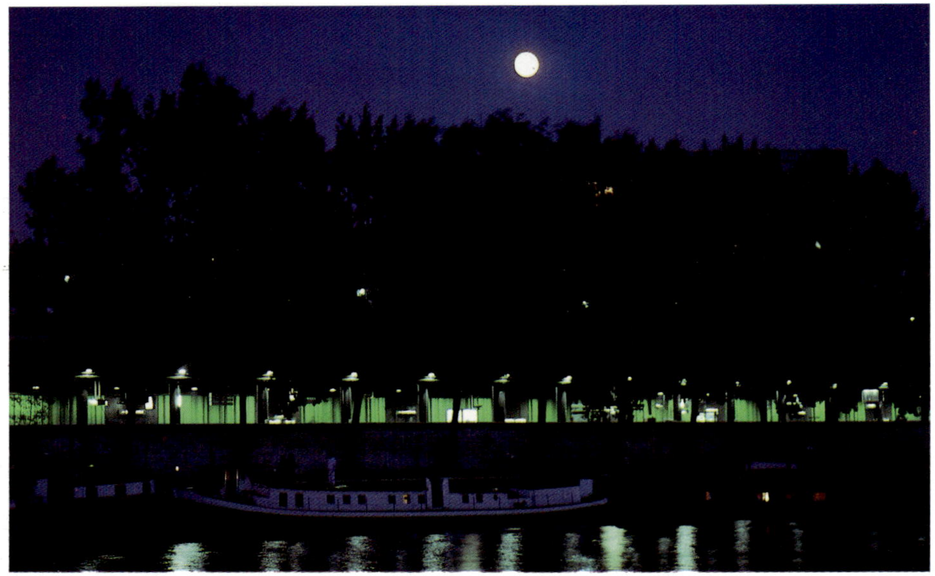

HOUSEBOAT, QUAI BRANLY

vertigo, a touch of claustrophobia as the crush of bodies grew tenser the higher we went.

On the top platform, it was like being in a plane suddenly brought to a standstill in mid-flight. Weird. No sway in the wind, the observatory was amazingly steady, the terrace caged against potential birdmen's flights of fancy.

For a Seine-lover, nothing gives a better impression of the river's curve through Paris and its importance to Baron Haussmann when he replanned the city: the spoking-out of wide tree-lined avenues, his use of the bridges and open spaces. At Place d'Alma, the miniature traffic converged from two riverside avenues and a bridge; also from the Champs-Elysées, via three avenues, and from Trocadéro by a fourth. Somehow the traffic sorted itself out and got from the hub on to the spoke it required, until it came to another hub and set out on yet another spoke. The Paris of Haussmann, seen from my eyrie, was a city of hubs and spokes. Bicycle City in the land of the Tour de France.

The onset of winter had cleared the smog, I had never had such a view. Paris small within its gates; Paris sprawling in its high-rise outskirts; the Seine curving and snaking, as it turned north past a fiery sunset; Paris of hills – Mont Valérien, Montparnasse, La Butte-Chaumont and Montmartre.

As we descended, familiar landmarks came into sharper perspective. The Arc de Triomphe, covered in green and red sacking for restoration, reminded me of the Pont Neuf 'packaged' by the artist, Christo. Over the Pont de Bir-Hakeim trundled a little blue Métro train, disappearing between the slightly sinister twin domes of riverside houses before plunging

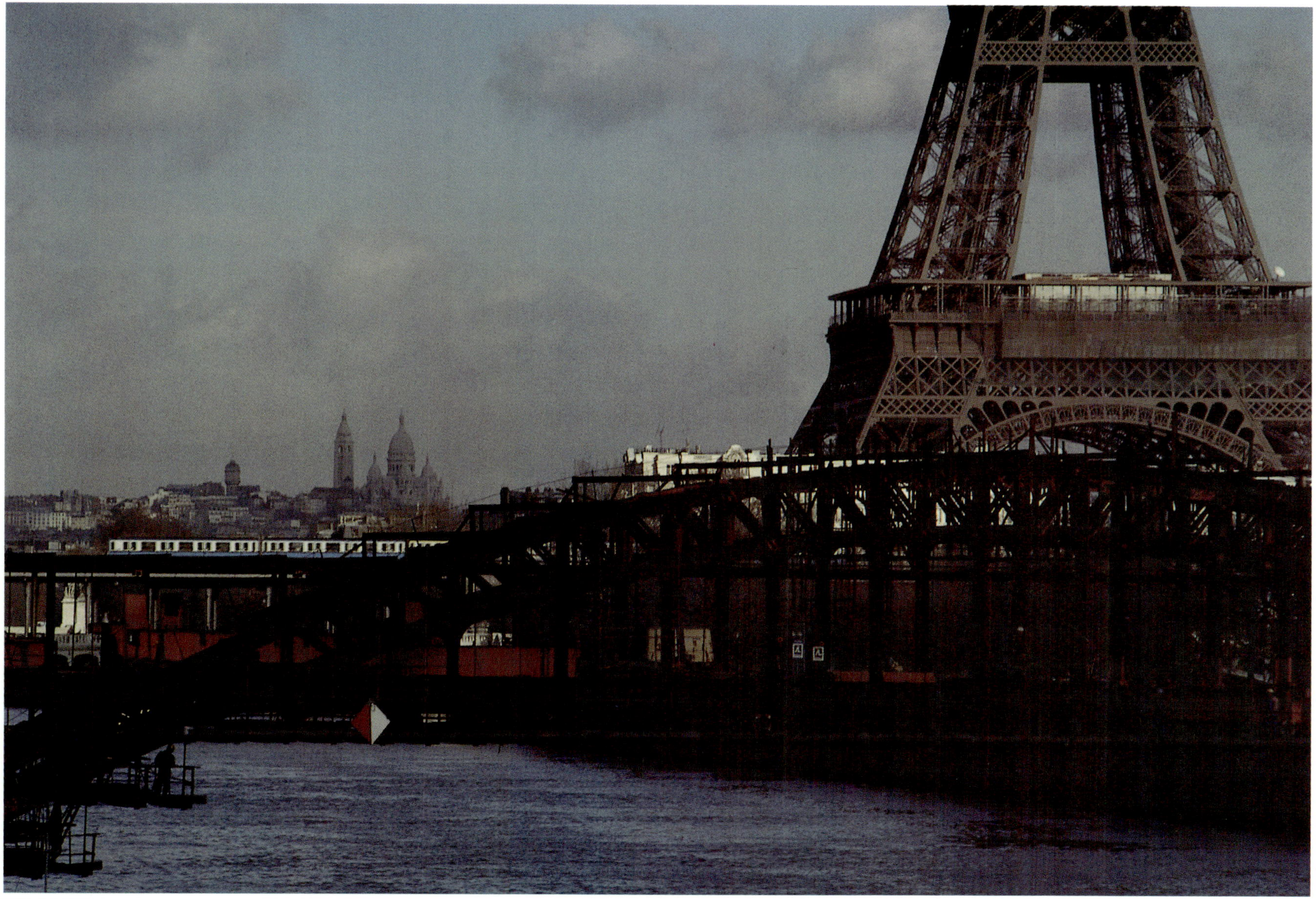

PONT DE BIR-HAKEIM

into the Passy tunnel; I imagined some mad old countess looking out from an *oeil de boeuf* window and murmuring, as she watched our descent: 'Pull it down! Pull it down!'

Well, they didn't. And they won't. A conman once nearly succeeded in selling the Eiffel Tower for scrap metal; the scam failed. The tower is blessed with survival.

Downstream, reminders of the 'royal' river, pre-Eiffel Tower, remain. Among the steeply wooded slopes and suburban houses of Sèvres is the famous porcelain factory. In 1756 it belonged to the king, and the royal monogram of intertwined L's (for Louis) was the china's trade-mark, and royal blue one of its colours.

For the sport of kings, no racetrack could be more delightfully placed than Longchamp. Where the Bois de Boulogne meets the river, it is country racing in a city. Degas and Manet worked there, perfecting their unforgettable images of horses and jockeys. And what could be pleasanter than to arrive by boat for the 'Arc de Triomphe', have one's race picnic on board, and wander over to the grandstand, relaxed and replete for the first race?

Saint-Cloud, on the opposite bank, was once Napoleon's favourite home. The eighteenth-century house was burned down by the Prussians in the siege of 1870, leaving a thousand-acre park overlooking the Seine and the Bois de Boulogne.

'I reached the Seine to take *L'Hirondelle* which would put me down at Saint-Cloud.

How I loved waiting for this boat on the landing-stage! It seemed as though I were leaving for the other end of the earth, for new and wonderful lands. I watched for the boat's appearance, there, there, beneath the arch of the second bridge, so small, with its wisp of smoke, then bigger, bigger, continuing to grow; and, for me, it had all the excitement of a liner.

It moored and I boarded.

Sunday trippers were already on board, with showy costumes, dazzling fripperies, and big, scarlet faces. I placed myself aft, standing, watching the quays go by, and the trees, houses, bridges. And suddenly I saw the huge viaduct of Point-du-Jour spanning the river. This was the end of Paris, the beginning of the country, and the Seine, beyond the double line of arches, grew abruptly wider, as though given space and freedom to become all of a sudden a fine peaceful river about to flow across plains, at the foot of woody hills, in the middle of fields, on the edge of forests.' (Guy de Maupassant: *Souvenir*)

Napoleon had made just such a journey, but in the opposite direction. To the Pont de Courbevoie, the paddle steamer *La Dorade* brought the former Emperor's body on its triumphant 1840 return from St Helena. Having made imperial progress up the Seine, the coffin was transferred to a hearse and taken, in a snowstorm, across Paris to Les Invalides.

Below the bridge, on the long, beautiful island, those nostalgic for the suburban riverside pleasures of the Belle Epoque dine on the balcony of La Guingette de Neuilly. Near here, Seurat painted his vast *Sunday Afternoon on the Ile de la Grande-Jatte*, an idyllic combining of some forty elements on a riverside lawn – weekenders, their children, animals, boats. Many Impressionists had a favourite stretch of river, and this was Seurat's: bathers at Asnières, the bridge of Courbevoie with fishermen on their floats and the inevitable pencil-thin chimneys – factories still distant but already an insidious presence creeping into the sunlit landscape.

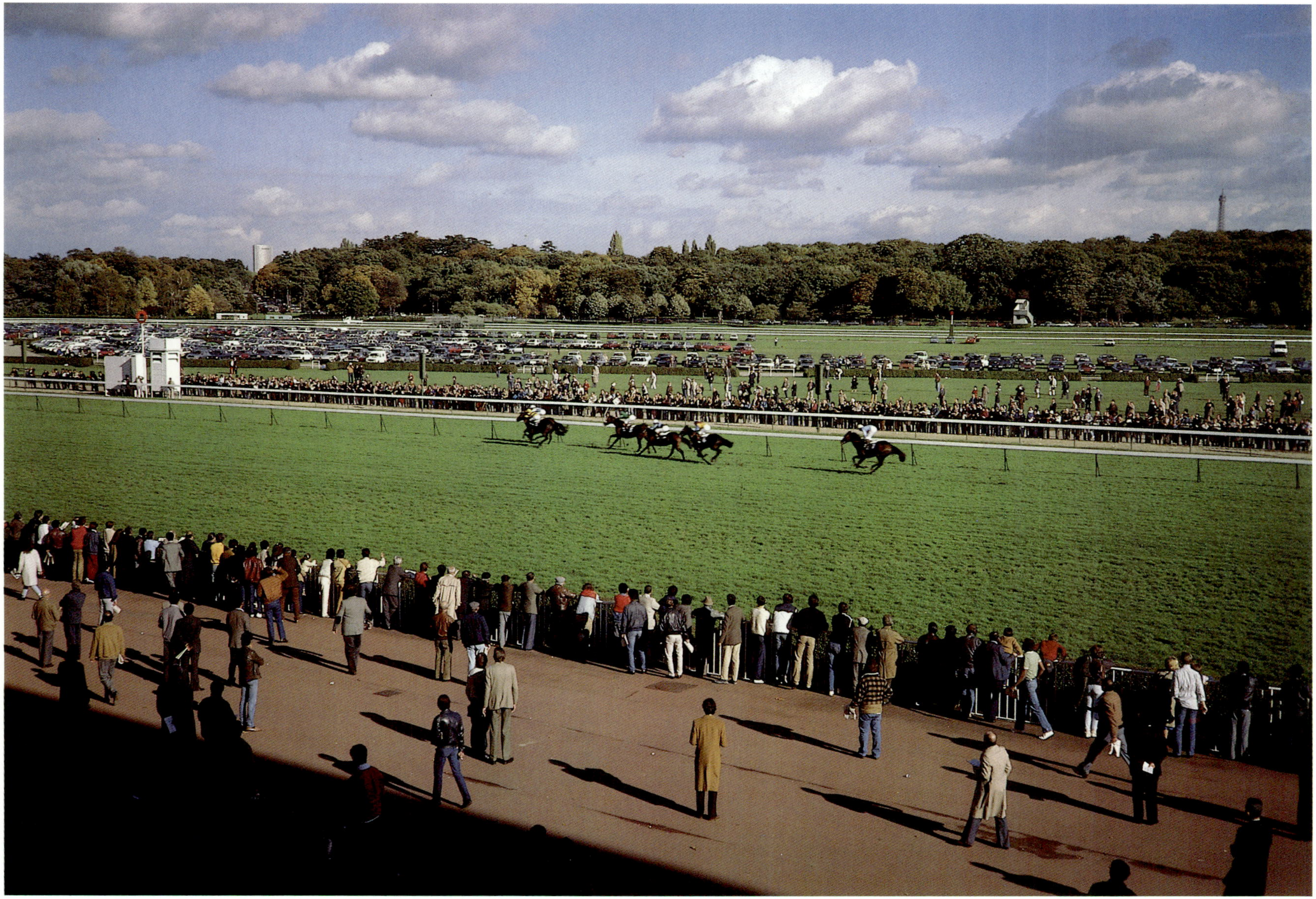

LONGCHAMP RACETRACK

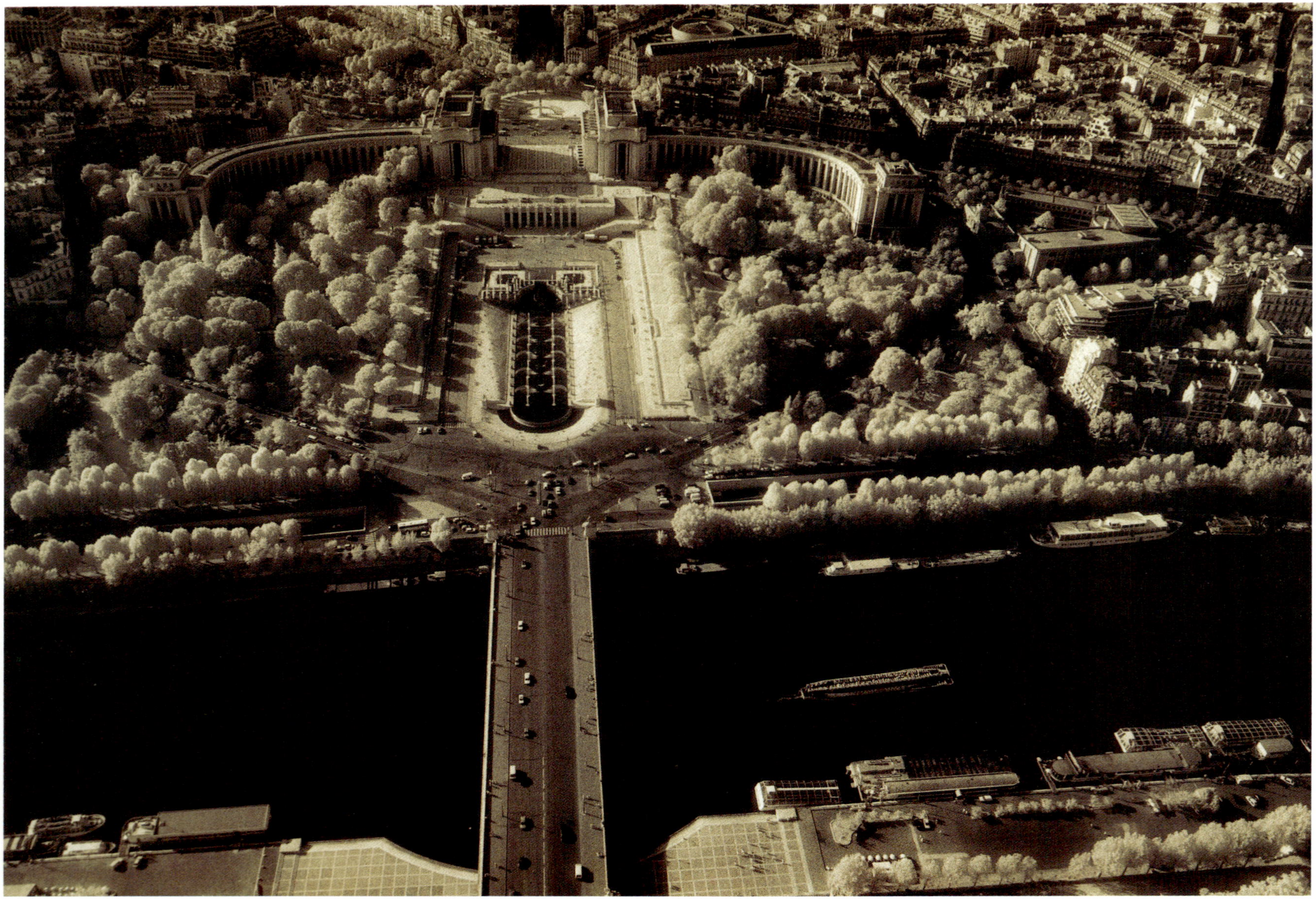

PALAIS DE CHAILLOT FROM THE EIFFEL TOWER

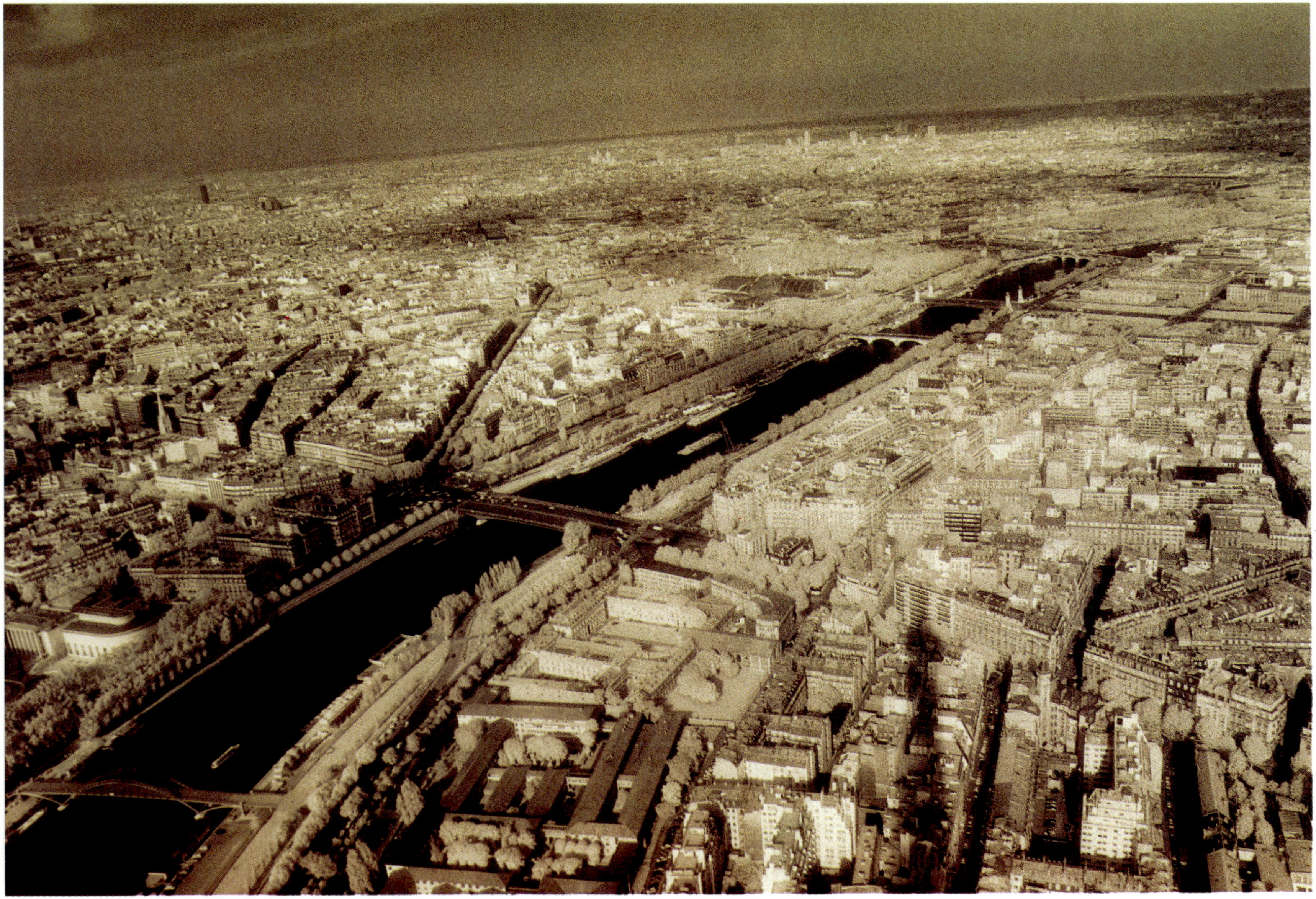

The Seine east of the Eiffel Tower

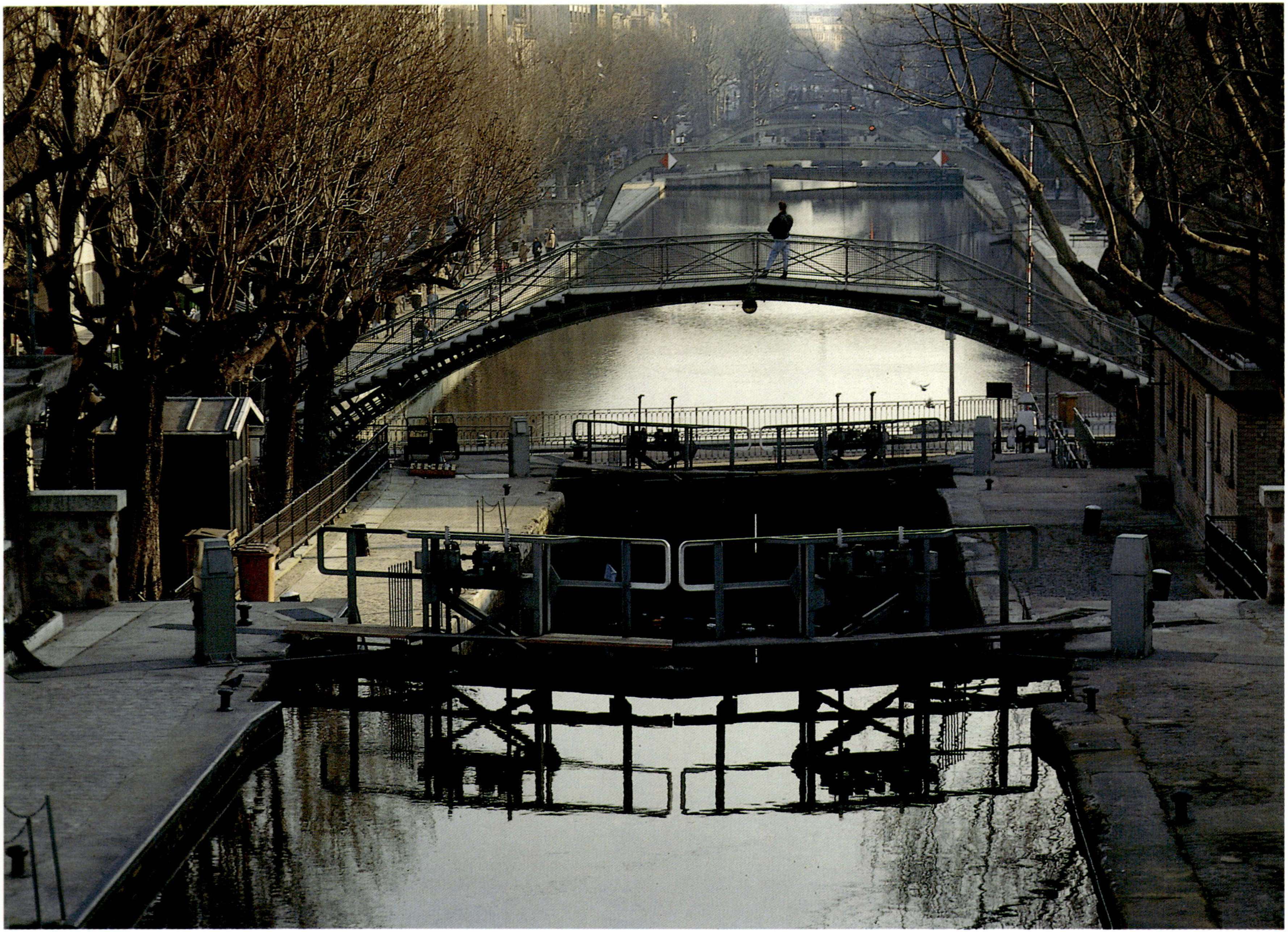

Canal St-Martin

CANAL CRUISE

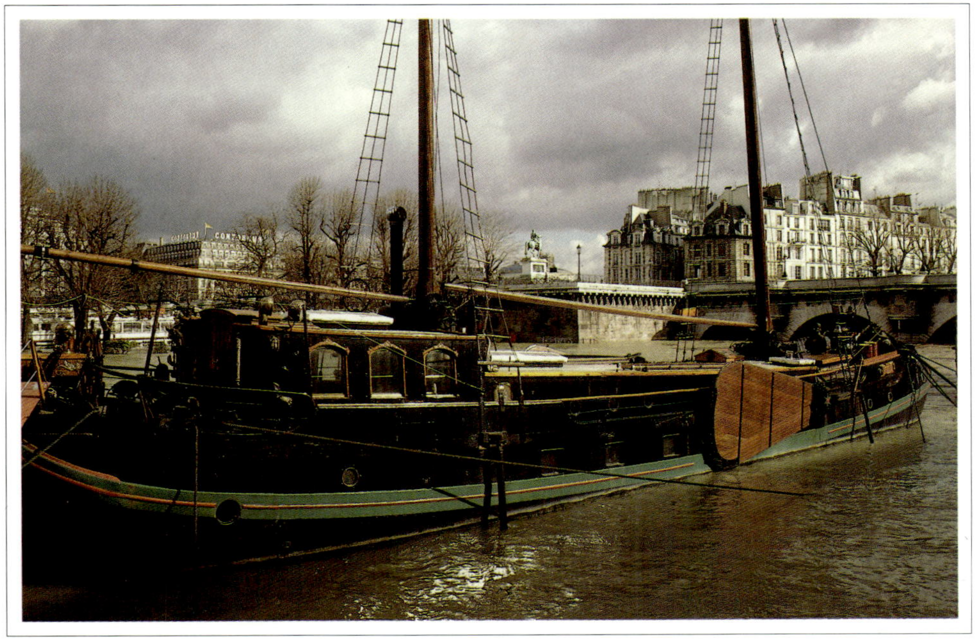

HOUSEBOAT, PONT NEUF

'Industrial Paris? Where?' asks the casual visitor, accustomed only to the sanitized tourist beat. Answer: much of it on the western meanders of the Seine, where the 'royal' river downstream ceased its hoity-toity isolation and overcame difficulties of navigation with the coming of steam.

Just as you think you must be getting into the country, comes the heavy stuff. A reminder that a quarter of French industry is concentrated in the Paris region – from pharmaceuticals to machine tools, motor cars to telecommunications.

It began some fifty years before those chimneys in Impressionist paintings.

The Parisian Seine, whose narrow shallowness could not cope with the commercial shipping and public river transport of the Industrial Revolution, earned herself a most convenient bypass.

A system of canals joined upstream Paris to downstream Paris, cutting off a long loop of the river from just east of the Ile St-Louis to the Ile St-Denis in the northern industrial suburbs. In these days of depleted river transport, it is hard to envisage its importance. A friend gave me a yardstick: 'Just imagine how much stone was needed for the first Métro line from Port Maillot to Vincennes. It came from the quarries to Paris by boat.'

And these canals are still navigable.

One Sunday, nearly a century later, our boat turned to starboard into the Canal St-Denis. A signpost announced: 6½ kilometres (4 miles) to the Canal de L'Ourcq. Our detour from the Seine took us along an inland waterway system begun in 1821 and completed in 1825, once as important an artery in the life of Paris as the river herself.

A rise of 91 feet must be negotiated during those four miles, involving passage through seven double-locks. One lock is now used for pleasure boats, the other for commercial traffic.

A notice told us it was forbidden to park in the locks. Hardly surprising: the surroundings were very pleasing; small, nineteenth-century houses with neat gardens, and often trees lining the bank like a country canal.

Suddenly, between warehouses, we glimpsed the St-Denis basilica, burial place of the Kings of France. The legend of the saint whose name it took is a French schoolchild's favourite. In the third century the first bishop of Lutetia, appropriately (for a wine-growing area) named Dionysius (Denis, in French), converted the locals from paganism to Christianity. For his pains, he was beheaded on the hill which is now Montmartre. Whereupon he picked up his head and walked away with it under his arm. He kept walking until he fell, and on that sacred spot was founded the church of St-Denis, early Christian martyr.

Simenon country again. A man very like Inspector Maigret was puffing his pipe on the canal bank. Our captain told us the canal was drained once every seven years, revealing not only dumped cars but the corpses of missing people. In the Second World War, the Resistance used it as an arms cache.

We achieved our seven locks and arrived at the junction of three canals in northern Paris. Coming up from the bottom of the last 33-foot deep lock was like rising from the dead. The dank and slimy walls of a tomb seemed to bear in on us, cavernous and menacing, and it was a relief to see the wide open waters of the Bassin de la Villette, the canal junction. The Canal de L'Ourcq passes through 67 miles of delightful woods and fields to the north-east, formerly used for delivering firewood. But we were to turn into the Canal St-Martin.

Here, we began our 2¾-mile, 9-lock descent through the city of Paris back to the Seine.

At Port de la Villette, once a thriving inland harbour, the feeling of past greatness was still present: an occasional eighteenth-century house with fanlight windows among the recent apartment blocks; a fine Customs House, where food was taxed on its arrival in the capital; disused warehouses on wharves to be developed into shopping malls and discothèques. Gentrification had already come to the Canal St-Martin.

Streets seemed to cross the canal every minute or so, and each time our boat approached one of the electronically-controlled bridges, a bell and light warned people that, in sixty seconds precisely, the bridge would rise on its gantry to let us through. Cameras on either side of the canal set off the alarm. Very different from the old-time locks, operated manually by a lock-keeper – and in the very heart of computerized Paris!

And then we reached the famous little hotel, location of

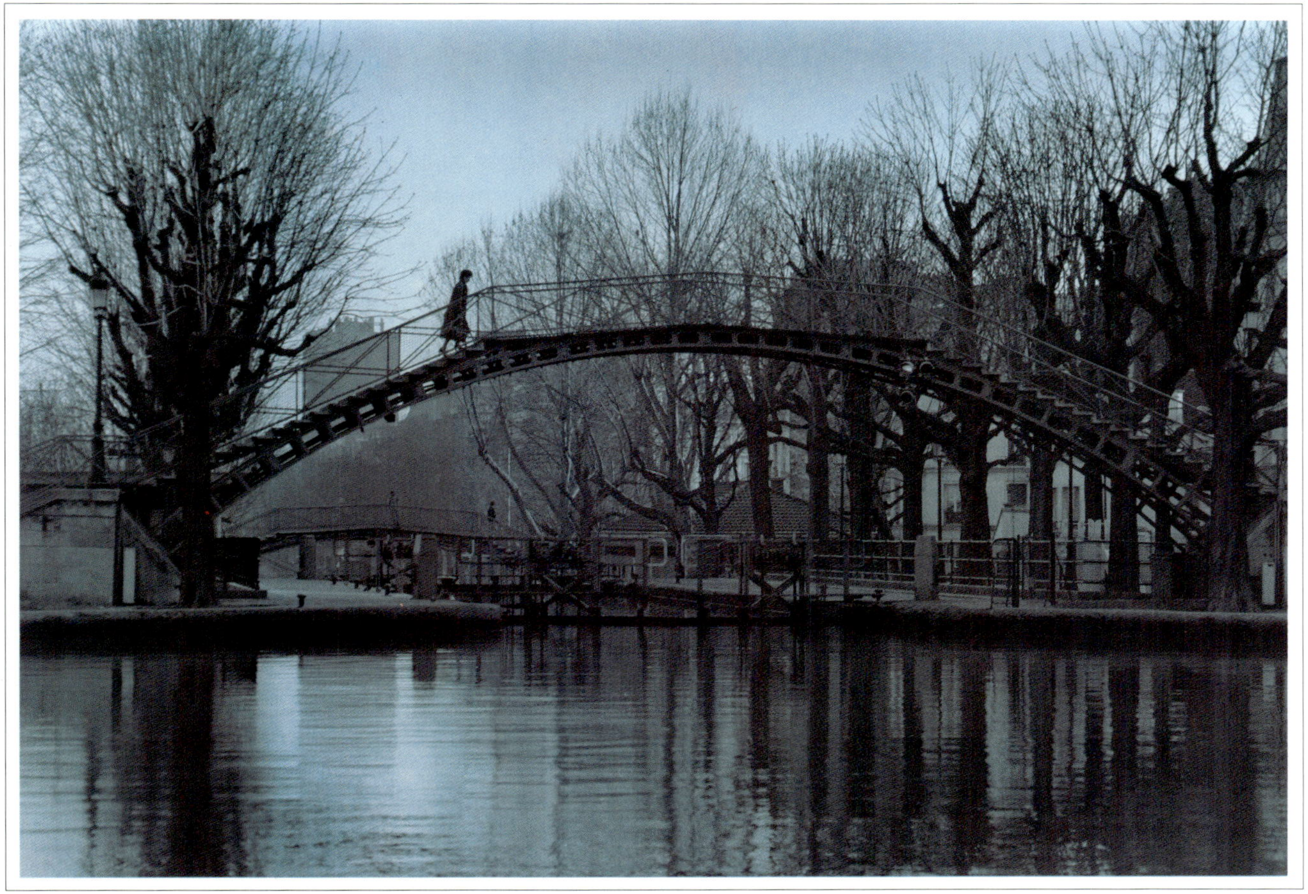

CANAL ST-MARTIN

the film *Hôtel du Nord*, starring Louis Jouvet and Arletty. The hotel had been classed as a *monument historique* and was scheduled to be a cinema museum. Remember the quayside ball for the 14th of July? The hotel with its runaway lovers? The scene with Jouvet and Arletty on the bridge? Jouvet tells her he needs a change of atmosphere. Arletty retorts: 'Atmosphere? Atmosphere? Is my mug made of atmosphere?'

Tree-lined canal streets bordered our stately progress, down, down, through lock after lock, bridge after bridge. Footbridges, bridges that turned, bridges that went up and down. Until, eventually, we slid into the tunnel that took us 1¼ miles underground from the Quai Valmy to Place de la Bastille.

The lights of the boat cast a subterranean shimmer on the stone walls and vaulted arches. Then, jumping more than a

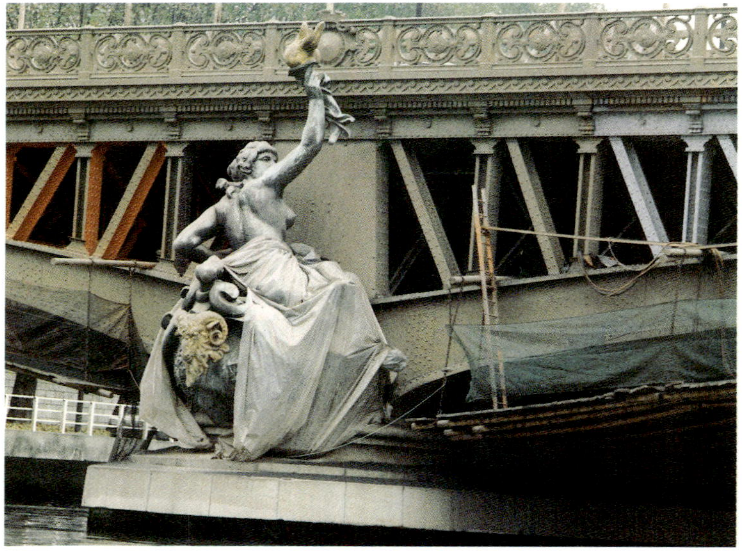

PONT MIRABEAU

century, we emerged into dazzling sunshine and new development. The old Bassin de l'Arsenal, once crammed with seven hundred cargo craft from Burgundy and the North, had recently been converted into a modern yacht marina.

Above the banks, we could see the column of the Bastille and the new Pop Op, that controversial opera house which opened on 13 July 1989, to celebrate the Bicentenary of the Revolution, and very nearly caused another with its teething troubles.

American, British and Italian flags were flying at the moorings. The banks were a profusion of roses, lawns and young trees. And the harbourmaster, over his public-address system, directed the coming and going of craft in several languages.

And through the final lock at Quai de la Rapée, we turned to starboard again, back into the Seine.

That day, I learned from our captain about an important development which eventually made Paris through-traffic possible without the canals. In 1867, the Ecluse de Suresnes, was opened: a giant three-lock barrage at the western approaches, which brought bigger boats to and from the now sufficiently deep water of Paris itself. Thanks to this, the 'royal' downstream and 'popular' upstream became a democratic entity – one Seine once and for all.

The sheer length of river, snaking in a double S through the western Paris region, concentrates its industry amid the former royal palaces and present dormitory towns.

From the island Renault factory on the Ile Seguin, diesel pushers guide vast barge-trains of five hundred cars downstream to other factories on Renault's riverside production line.

Meanwhile, a battered but buoyant French movie industry is just managing to keep afloat at the film studios of Boulogne-Billancourt; international big business thrives in the skyscrapers of La Défense, Manhattan-sur-Seine; and at Asnières, an incineration plant burns the city's garbage, recycling it into gas vapour which heats the Paris Métro.

The northern bend of the river, as it curves away from St-Denis, is heavily industrial. And it is hard to associate Gennevilliers with the first performance in 1783 of *The Marriage of Figaro*, banned by the Royal Censor. Amid wooded hunting country, in a château's private theatre, to an audience of aristocrats whose manners he mocked, playwright Beaumarchais mounted his biting, scandalous comedy. Today Gennevilliers is the Port of Paris.

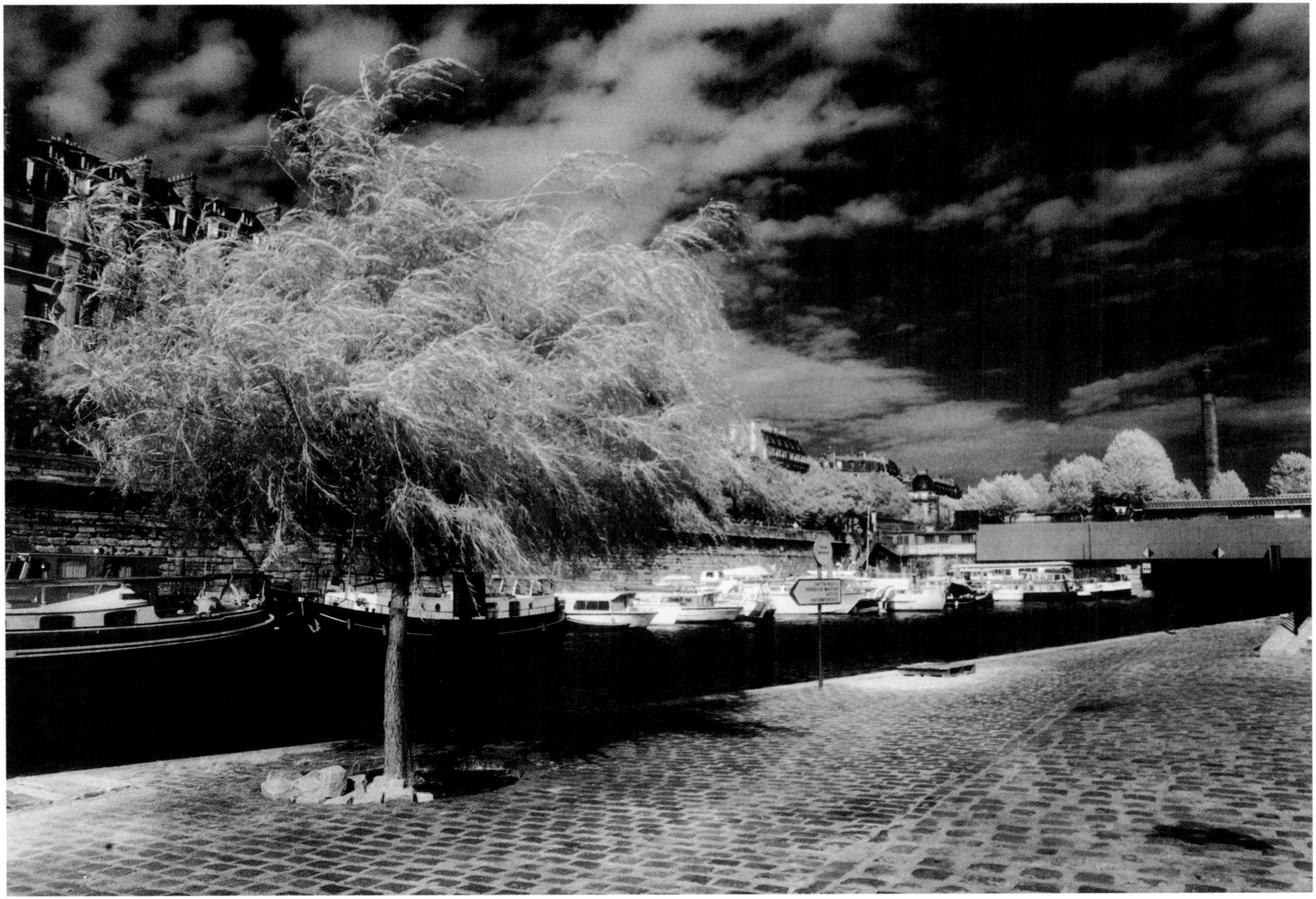

BASTILLE, PARIS YACHT MARINA

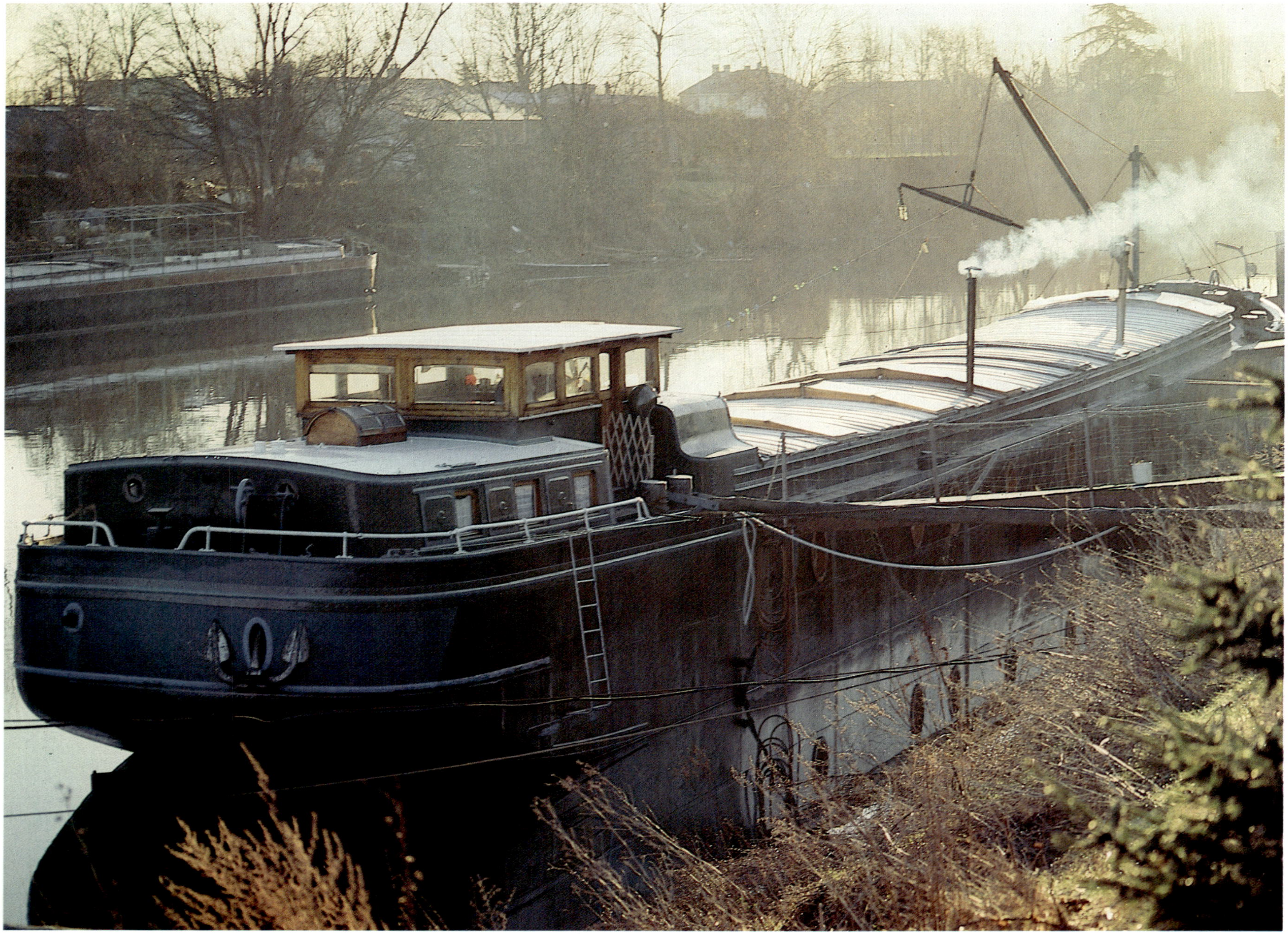

Barge, Port Marly

PORT OF PARIS

On a raw December day, when that particularly nasty French drizzle called *bruine* was falling upon a scrubby, junky stretch of Seine, I stood by a coal dump and thought of England.

Not with any disaffection. Nor because of the rain. It was partly because Gennevilliers was situated on a near-island, bounded by that northern bend, 2¾ miles across by land, 12½ miles meander by river. And partly because of France's developing nineteenth-century *entente* with Perfidious Albion, burying the hatchet with her after the Napoleonic Wars and transferring it to Germany after the Franco-Prussian War. England was now the goodie; even Napoleon liked the idea of a Channel tunnel and secretly traded with Britain while at war with her. Not far from that very coal dump, British anthracite had been brought up the Seine. And the north-west flatlands of this near-island more than a century later became the Port of Paris, a two-and-a-half day voyage from the Port of London.

The Paris Port Authority covers the waterfronts of the Seine from Melun upstream to Bonnières downstream. But it is at Gennevilliers that its installations are most impressive. Completed in 1950, but conceived in the seventeenth century when the biggest cereal silos were there, the Port of Paris covers nearly a thousand acres, including more than a hundred enterprises dependent on the river: petroleum; cereals; metallurgy; coal; container transport; and building materials which make up an astonishing 94% of all river transport! There are six docks with a 13-foot draught and 7½ miles of moorings. Pusher convoys carrying up to five thousand tons can be serviced.

But enough impressive facts and figures. Why did so little seem to be going on the day I visited?

I expected to see 'Freycinet' self-propelled barges, unloading cargo with their own cranes; tanker barges busy at Avia, Esso, Antar, Elf and Mobil; and pusher barges being coupled together like freight trains.

A lone container truck from Nordisk transport (Paris-Milan) was getting a wash at the *Lavage Poids Lourd*, conveniently placed on the river bank. Along the Route de la Seine, a police car with nothing better to do trailed me for a time. And the shiny aluminium structure of a new light industry factory seemed in no hurry to be finished.

Sunday, was it?

I looked at my watch. The day indicator had stuck between Wednesday and Thursday. And one-and-a-half-million tons of merchandise was supposed to pass through this port every year. I couldn't see even a measly ton.

The six-lane highway to the main port was empty. How come? We were, after all, at a port only twenty minutes from the gates of Paris. Where was everyone?

Then, at last, an encouraging line of cars greeted me at the Customs House, its owners no doubt clearing a few of their one-and-a-half million tons of merchandise.

At Bassin 1, the main dock, I took a walk. There were a few

seagulls about. And where there are seagulls, there are boats. I looked. There were a few boats, yes, but no crews. I walked on. I came to a bright blue crane which said 'Paris-Terminal'. A huge wall of containers faced me. The crane was not lifting any of them. A freight train stood empty nearby.

With this wintry drizzle, it was certainly not the 14th of July. Maybe there was a dock strike.

On my way back to the car, which I'd parked near the line of cars at the Customs House, I passed the Restaurant Inter-Enterprises. It was packed. An aroma of food whetted my appetite. And I suddenly realized: those other cars had been parking not for the Customs House but the restaurant!

The Port of Paris had stopped for lunch.

From the Port of Paris, it is a short sail to the water and sky which reflected each other for the Impressionists, and that stretch of river where Parisians once enjoyed the river's sensual pleasures.

Nobody sets the scene better than Guy de Maupassant, that astringent Norman short-story teller and chronicler of bourgeois morality.

In 'Paul's Girl', Maupassant excels in depicting a world of sweaty oarsmen and perfumed *poules* mingling with petit-bourgeois families and men-about-town in search of a girl. This, too, was the ambience Renoir captured in *The Oarsmen's Lunch*, *Couple Dancing* and *The Ball at Bougival*.

Paul, a politician's son, and his girl are on an outing to a regatta at Croissy; they seem happy enough, until the arrival of a group of lesbians, proud and immune to the jeers of the crowd; to Paul's horror, his girl greets one of the lesbians; their idyllic outing turns sour, and during a ball at La Grenouillère, notorious café-restaurant, Paul's girl goes missing; distraught, he searches for her, fearing the worst; indeed, he finds her in the arms of the lesbian; and, humiliated that her lover is not a man, he throws himself in the Seine and drowns.

The prism separates many colours, and Maupassant shows us not only the light greens and yellows and sky blues of abandoned pleasure, but the reds and indigos of sexual tension. His is a dazzling impression of the emergent power of independent-minded women, contrasted with the brute strength of the oarsmen. And the seedy dramas behind those seemingly idyllic riverside scenes of Renoir's.

Here are some random extracts that show the two layers of Maupassant's river story – surface sunshine and weeds below. La Grenouillère – The Froggery – took its name from the current slang word *grenouille* for good-time girl.

The immense raft, covered with a pitch roof supported by wood columns, was joined to the charming island of Croissy by two footbridges, one of which penetrated into this aquatic establishment, while the other linked it, at the end, to a tiny islet planted with one tree called 'The Flowerpot' and, from there, reached dry land near the bathing place.

The oarsmen exposed their brown skin and bulging biceps to the heat of the day; and, like strange swimming flowers, parasols of red, green, blue or yellow silk, belonging to the girls steering, blossomed at the back of the rowing-boats.

A July sun burned in the middle of the sky; the air seemed aflame with gaiety; not a flicker of a breeze stirred the leaves of the poplars and willows.

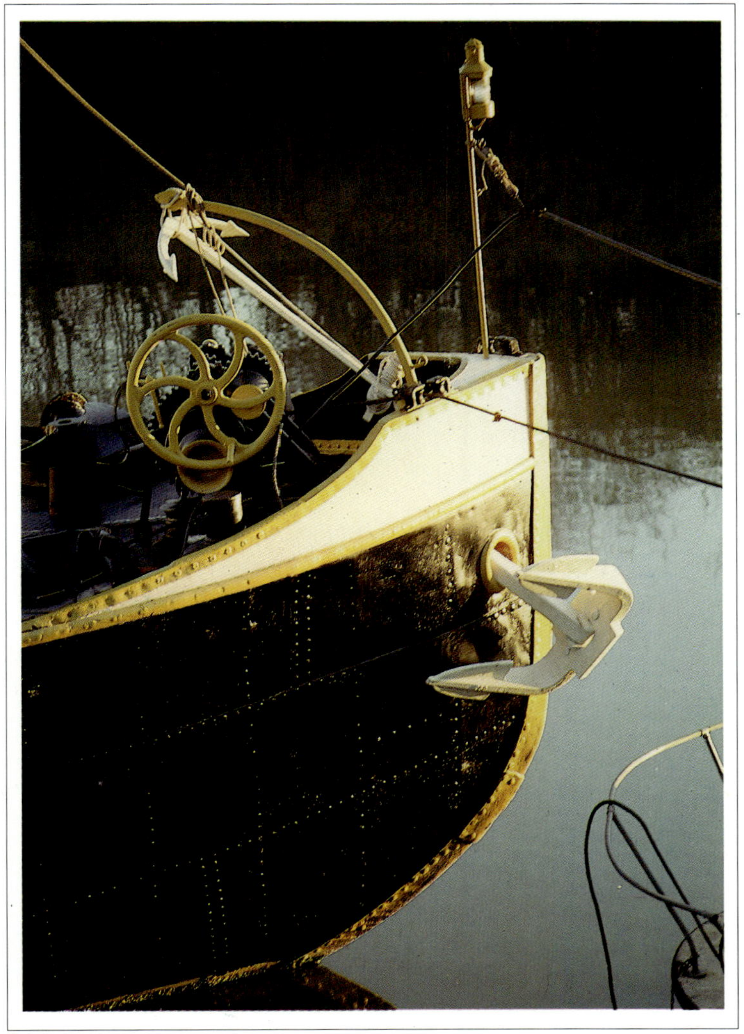

Not for nothing was it called 'The Froggery'. By the side of the raft where one drank, and very near the Flowerpot where one bathed, women of an ample roundness came to display their wares naked, and attract customers.

The show was the river, the incessant coming and going of craft held the eye. Boatwomen were stretched out in armchair comfort, facing their strong-wristed men, watching with disdain the dinner-seekers trawling the island.

The oarsmen returned with their eternal bawling, and then went off again to the ball at 'The Froggery'.

The organizer of the can-can, majestic in his tired evening suit, faced all and sundry with the ravaged countenance of an old purveyor of cheap pleasures at bargain prices. . . . They danced: couples facing each other capered about like mad things. . . . Women with disjointed thighs leaped up and down with skirts flying, showing their underwear. . . . Men crouched like toads, making obscene gestures. . . .

The intoxicating poetry of this summer's night took Paul over in spite of himself. . . .

. . . he found himself by the river, facing the rapids by moonlight . . . The river was there. Did he know what he was doing? Did he want to die? He was deranged. However, he turned back towards the island, towards Her; and, in the night's calm air filled with the faraway but persistent strains of cheap dance music, he let out a terrible cry, his voice desperate, sub-human, high-pitched: 'Madeleine!'

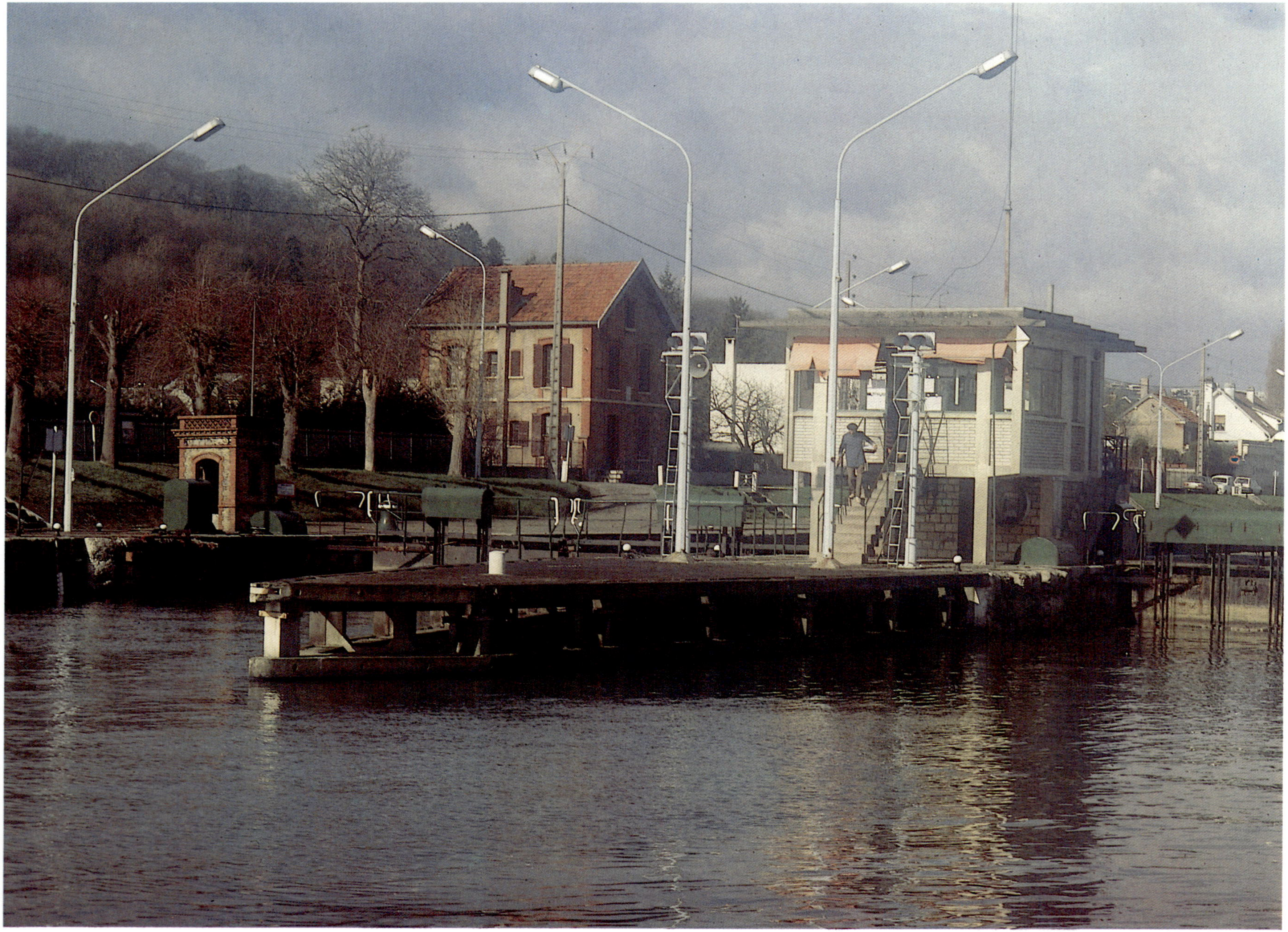

THE LOCK, BOUGIVAL

IMPRESSIONIST BEND

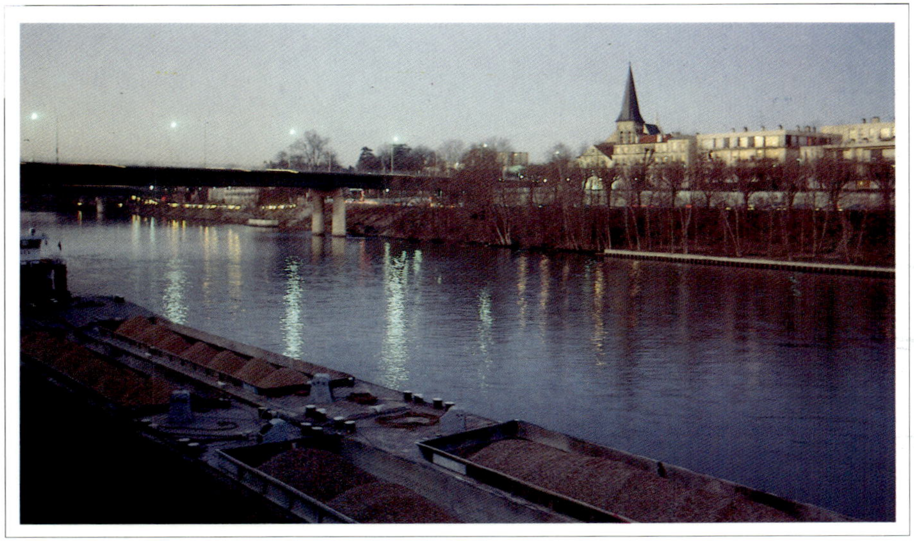

CHATOU, DAWN

Renoir, suffering the slings and arrows of outraged art critics, left the social comment to Maupassant and declared: 'For me a painting should be something likeable, joyful and pretty. Yes, pretty! There are enough aggravating things in life without us fabricating still more.'

Plagued by rejection and lack of money, Renoir took refuge at his parents' house at Louveciennes, a village on the wooded slopes above the Seine near Bougival. Monet, equally depressed, joined his friend there in 1867. And the therapy of riverside low-life lead to art historian Kenneth Clark's claim: 'It was at La Grenouillère, the café by the Seine, that Impressionism was born.'

In fact, the canvas was much wider, the 'sensationalists with rainbow palettes' going further and further in their experiments with light and shade. The river seemed inexhaustible: from Argenteuil, nearly opposite the present Port of Paris, where Monet later lived, down the long straight stretch to Bezons; from the tip of the island that snakes past Chatou and Croissy to its end just beyond the Pont de Bougival; from the curve at Bougival, as the river changes direction from south-west to north-east, past Port-Marly to the bridge at Le Pecq.

It was Impressionist Bend. In the space of some ten years, between 1867 and 1877, the landscape and figures of that comparatively short stretch of river were painted by Monet, Renoir, Manet, Sisley, Bazille, Caillebotte and Pissarro.

The countryside, a fifteen minute train ride from central Paris by the new St-Germain line, was a place to forget academic art. No more Roman warriors and biblical nudes, nor Winterhalter's Empress Eugénie and her ladies-in-waiting in a stagey woodland, nor the poetic landscapes of Corot.

What upset the Salon des Beaux-Arts about Manet's *Lunch on the Grass* in 1865 was not so much that the lady lunching was naked, but that her two gentlemen were wearing everyday clothes instead of togas or shepherds' tunics! But it was just the 'everyday' qualities of the river people and their natural surroundings that appealed to the Impressionists who wanted to capture a fleeting moment, a particular light, the fugitive expression on a face. They wanted to take art out of the studio and, with the new zinc tubes making paint easily transportable, set up an easel on a river bank or, in Monet's case, a boat converted into a studio. 'You can't work on anything outdoors for more than half an hour,' said Monet. 'It changes too much.'

Impression, Sunrise was the Monet title for a misty morning Seine, with a little boat approaching, and the orange sun reflected in the water at a moment never to be repeated. Art critic Louis Leroy, lampooning an imaginary old buffer of an artist viewing the painting with incomprehension, has him refer to 'these impressionists', and that was the origin of the label Renoir hated: 'schools' were for academics, 'Impressionists' for art historians.

One tends to associate Impressionist Bend with summery images. In fact, Monet's first Bougival painting looking towards La Grenouillère, which was closed for winter, shows ice-floes, with black poplars, grey sky, and five lonely figures dotted about the snow.

Winter also appealed to Pissarro in *Chestnut Trees at Louveciennes*, with its red-brick surburban house and muffled woman-and-child. And to Sisley, who had a particular penchant for Port-Marly, painting its lock under snow, a boatman punting between the ice-floes, with the quayside houses and wooded slope as backdrop. Floods also had their fascination for Sisley – boats gliding between the trees and approaching the door of a flooded Port-Marly inn.

Water from the Seine had been pumped by the ingenious *Machine de Marly* to feed Louis XIV's fountains at Versailles, rising 535 feet above the river via 13 water-wheels and 225 pumps, making a ladder of short canals. Only the Roman-style aqueduct at the top survived, its dark and slightly ominous presence in the background of Monet's *The Seine at Bougival*.

In 1870, work at Impressionist Bend was temporarily suspended by the Prussian siege of Paris.

Monet returned to find the road-bridge at Argenteuil destroyed by war, and his first picture, in 1872, shows it under repair. The camaraderie of the Impressionists was stronger than ever; Manet, whose family owned property in Gennevilliers, found Monet a house in Argenteuil. A wealthy yachtsman, Caillebotte, supported the profligate Monet by buying his pictures, and later distinguished himself as a painter with *Sailboats at Argenteuil*.

Argenteuil was a schizophrenic suburb, half-rural, half-industrial. Wine-makers and asparagus-growers mixed with steel-workers in its cafés. But Monet loved living close to its railway-bridge, his fascination with the Age of Steam evident in pictures like *Men Unloading Coal*. He was able to withstand malaria from the mosquitos when the Seine fell in summer, and the stench of floating garbage from Baron Haussmann's sewers, used to fertilize the fields of Gennevilliers.

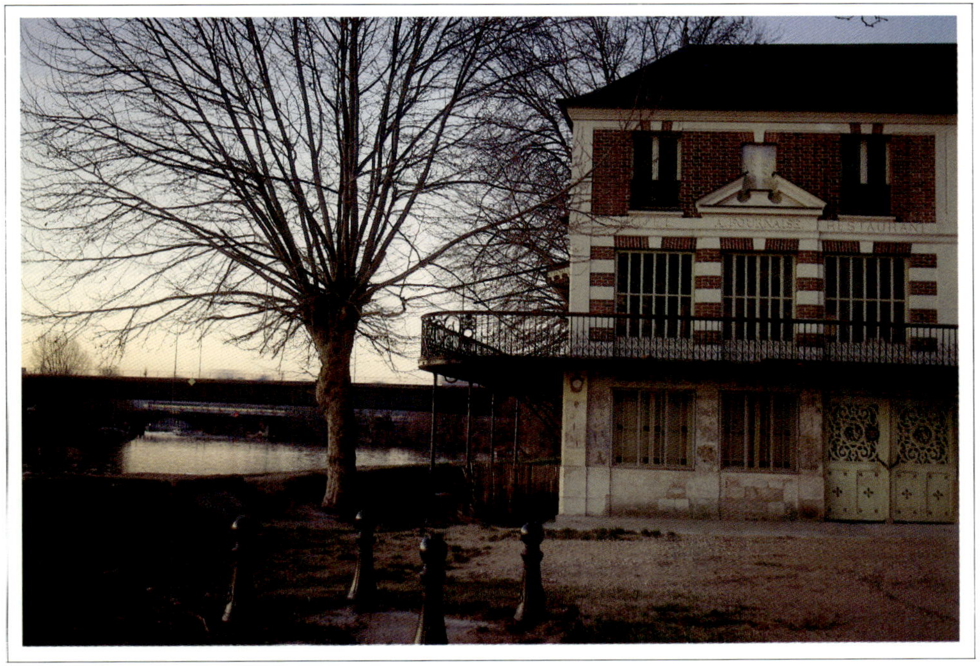

CHATOU, RENOIR'S FAVOURITE RESTAURANT

Monet and Renoir returned to their first love: the atmosphere of regattas and boating. These and the quiet reaches of the river at Argenteuil made the strongest impact during the 1870s and finally gained hard-won respect for the group which hated to be called a group but, on the whole, was proud of its co-operative spirit.

By the end of the 1870s, the Impressionists began to move on to other painting-grounds. And Impressionist Bend was left to the pleasure-seekers.

In 1900, it made art history again.

Derain met Vlaminck on the train to Chatou. The engine was derailed. And thanks to this happy accident, the two artists had time to continue their conversation. A friendship began which was to last a lifetime.

Chatou became known as 'The Argenteuil of *Les Fauves*', a riverside town where a new school blossomed, this time wilder and even more rule-breaking. They worked in purest primary colours, their paintings almost like children's in their directness and brightness, as in Derain's *Bridge at Le Pecq* and *Two Barges*, and Vlaminck's *Gardens at Chatou*.

Twenty-year-old Derain's parents were wealthy shopkeepers in Chatou. Vlaminck, four years older, of Dutch origin, had been bumming about the town as a delivery boy and strolling musician, when this chance encounter with Derain led them to set up in a studio together on the island.

Derain was the more restrained. Full of self-doubt, he needed to loosen up at the nearby riverside Restaurant Founaise. But Vlaminck was much less disciplined. 'I've never worked. I paint,' he said, squirting the paint on to the canvas, directly from his tubes, and boasting that he had never been inside the Louvre.

And although Derain found the Impressionists 'too realistic', he and Vlaminck were the natural, final inheritors of Impressionist Bend. 'Take me as I am,' said Vlaminck, like a character from Maupassant, 'warts and all.'

Bougival today. At the *crêperie* 'Sous Les Quais', the pancakes are named after famous movies: 'Alien' (chili and green salad), 'The Wages of Fear' (sausage, mushroom, egg and cheese). The in-crowd of Bougival, now an upmarket suburb of Paris, watch rock videos and Snoopy on a huge screen.

Outside, traffic spoils the quayside. Christmas decorations in the Impressionist house above the *crêperie*, lacy curtains draped at sunlit windows, white shutters, twin mansarded attics. A coal barge passes with dazzling white laundry on a line hung over the black coal. Above the town, steep wooded slopes, uncluttered and countrified; patches of mist hanging in the trees and rising off the river.

The island is bourgeois respectable. Signs forbid one to wash cars on the waterfront; the Portuguese help does that in the car-port. The Bougival lock (1838) is now very modern, but its site hardly changed since Sisley's painting.

The Ile de Chatou today. A barge festooned with electric light bulbs looks Christmassy (the French can work wonders of decoration with a simple white bulb). Green fields, parks, leisure complexes. A group of men are playing *boules* at 4 p.m. in the fading sunshine of the year's shortest day. Beyond a power-station, the road ends at a barrier, and a notice announces the imminent opening of a nine-hole golf-course.

All that remains of the *Machine de Marly* is one pillar in the Seine. But St-Germain-en-Laye is very much all there. The Pavillon Henri IV restaurant is doing a brisk trade in pre-Christmas business lunches; here, high above the Seine valley, chef Collinet invented 'Sauce Béarnaise' in 1847, which is commemorated by a plaque. A châteaubriand steak with the sauce costs 360 francs for two.

To walk it off, a visit to the Château, now an archaeological museum with important Gallo-Roman remains from the Seine Valley. And a stroll along the Grand Terrace, landscaped by André Le Nôtre in 1663. A noble perspective beyond the ornamental lakes and conical bushes gives on to the river. On the very edge of the forest of St-Germain, I stand at the belvedere and marvel at its view. Directly below, the bridge of Le Pecq, the lock at Bougival, the viaduct of the high-speed Métro; in the distance, Mont Valérien (5 miles), the retro power station at Gennevilliers (7½ miles), the Eiffel Tower (9¼ miles), and Sacré Coeur (10½ miles).

On, downstream to Maison-Lafitte, where commuter country peaks in a plethora of beautiful homes on opulent avenues, shooting off like rockets from myriad star-shaped *rondpoints*, whizzing you deeper and deeper into the forest. Easy to get lost. Few strangers have ever been known to arrive at a dinner engagement on time, generally ending up at the riverside racetrack or the maze of stabling around the Square de Kain. After directions from stable-lads at the Centre Hippique, you will surely find yourself among the pleasure boats moored along the Route de la Digue or on some sandy forest track known only to horse and rider. At dawn, when you finally give up on your dinner date, a reassuring sight is the stable-lads exercising racehorses in the morning mists rising from the Seine.

And city pleasures and pressures are well upstream.

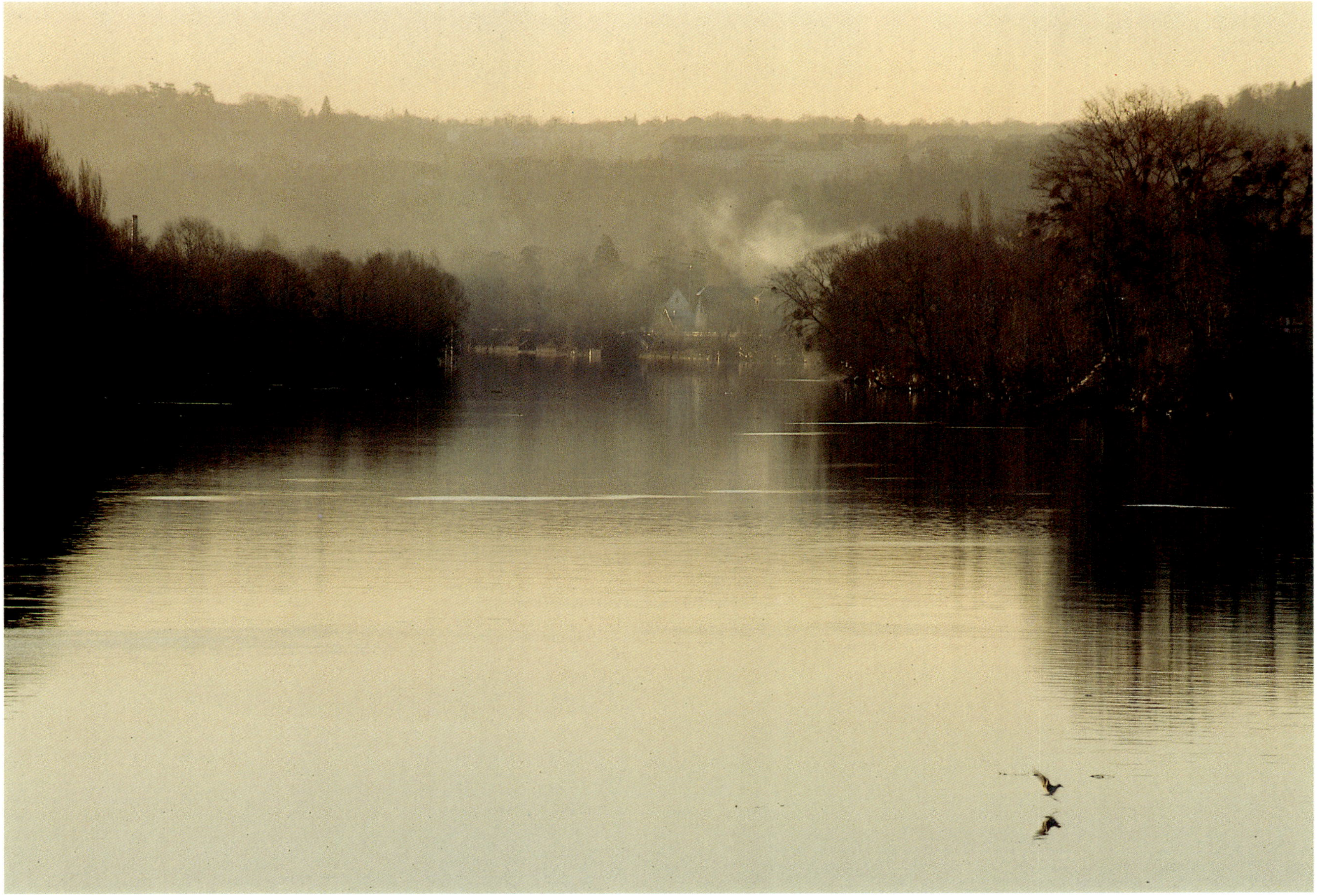

Port Marly, sunrise

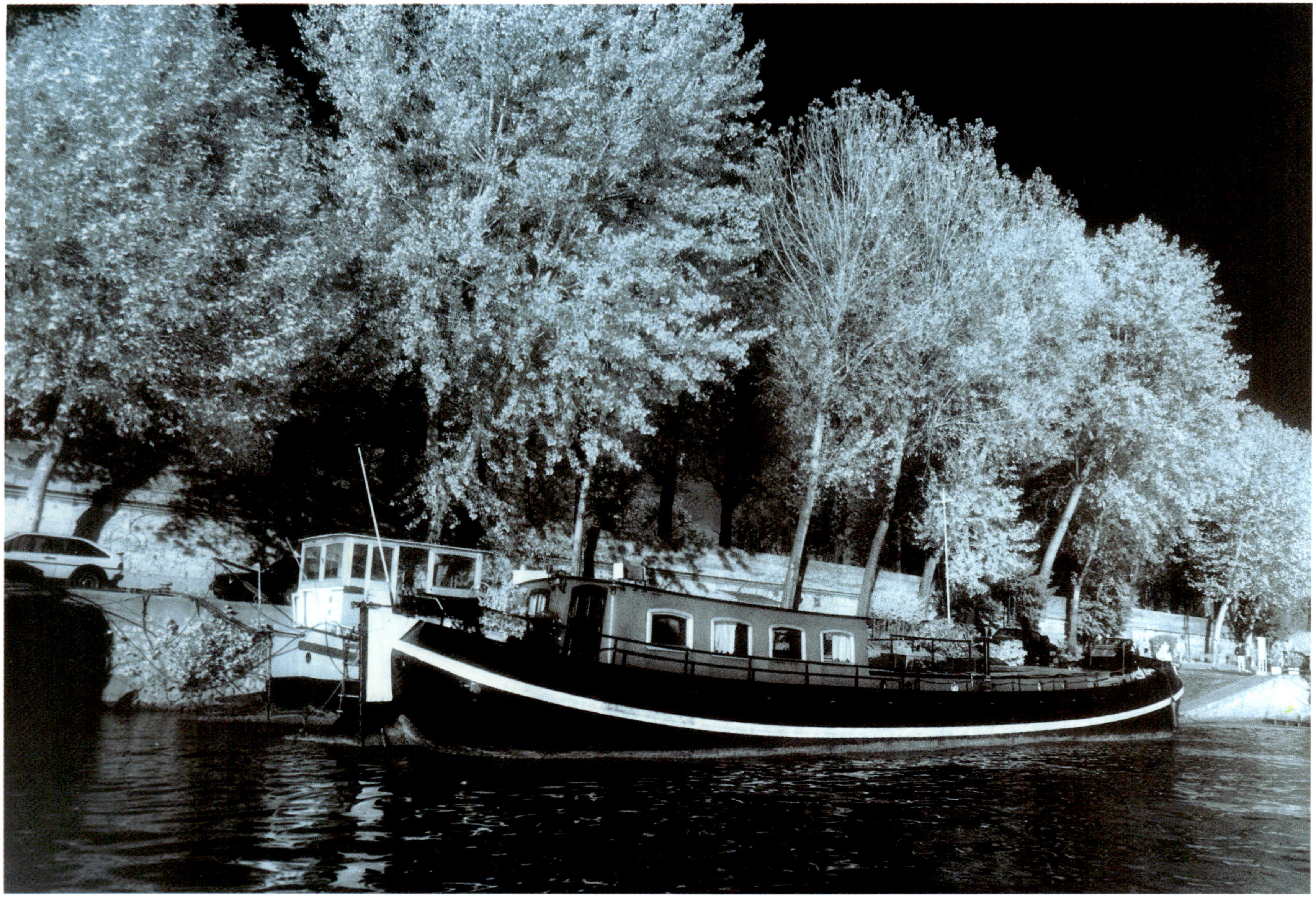

HOUSEBOAT, PARIS

PART III

PARIS TO THE SEA

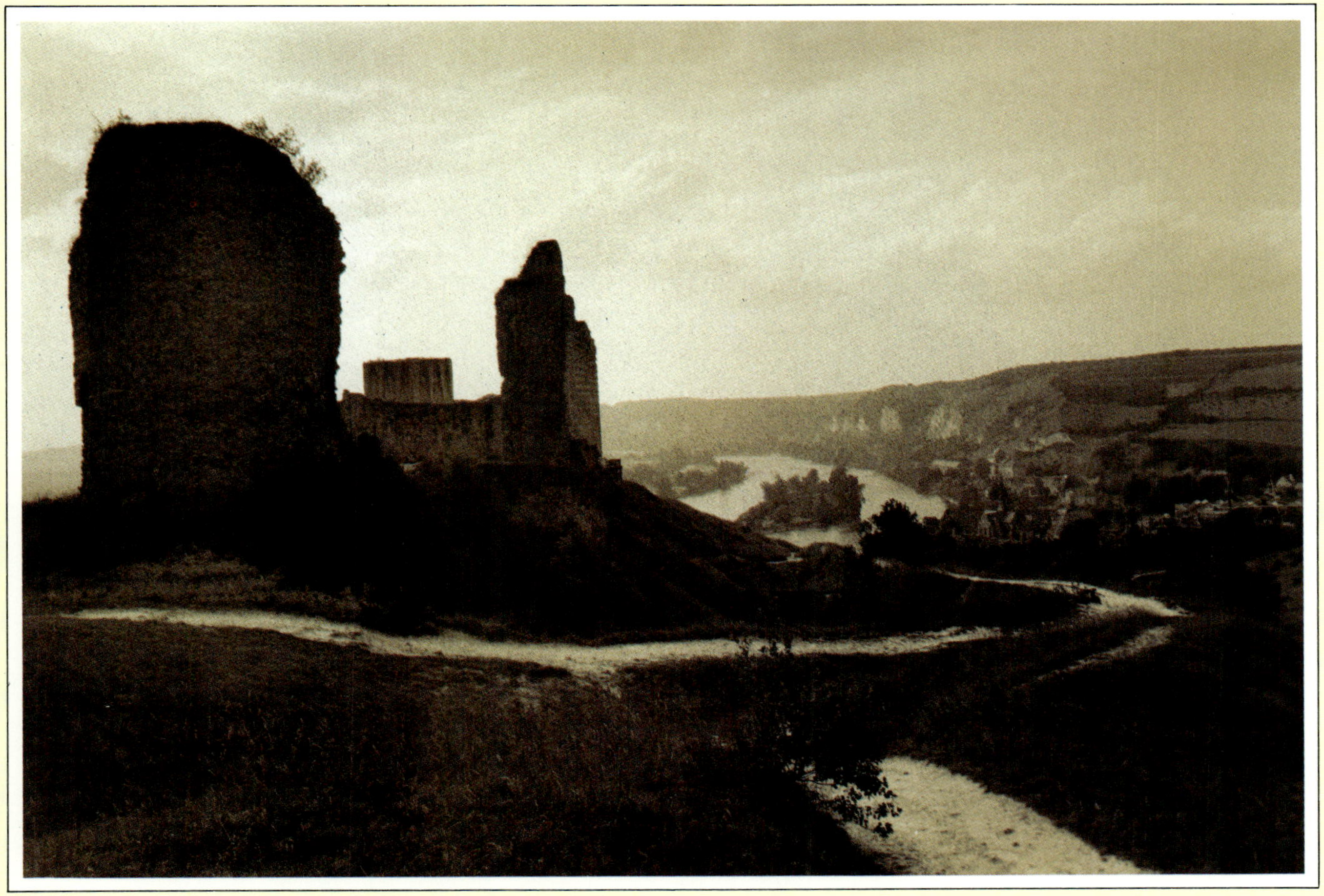

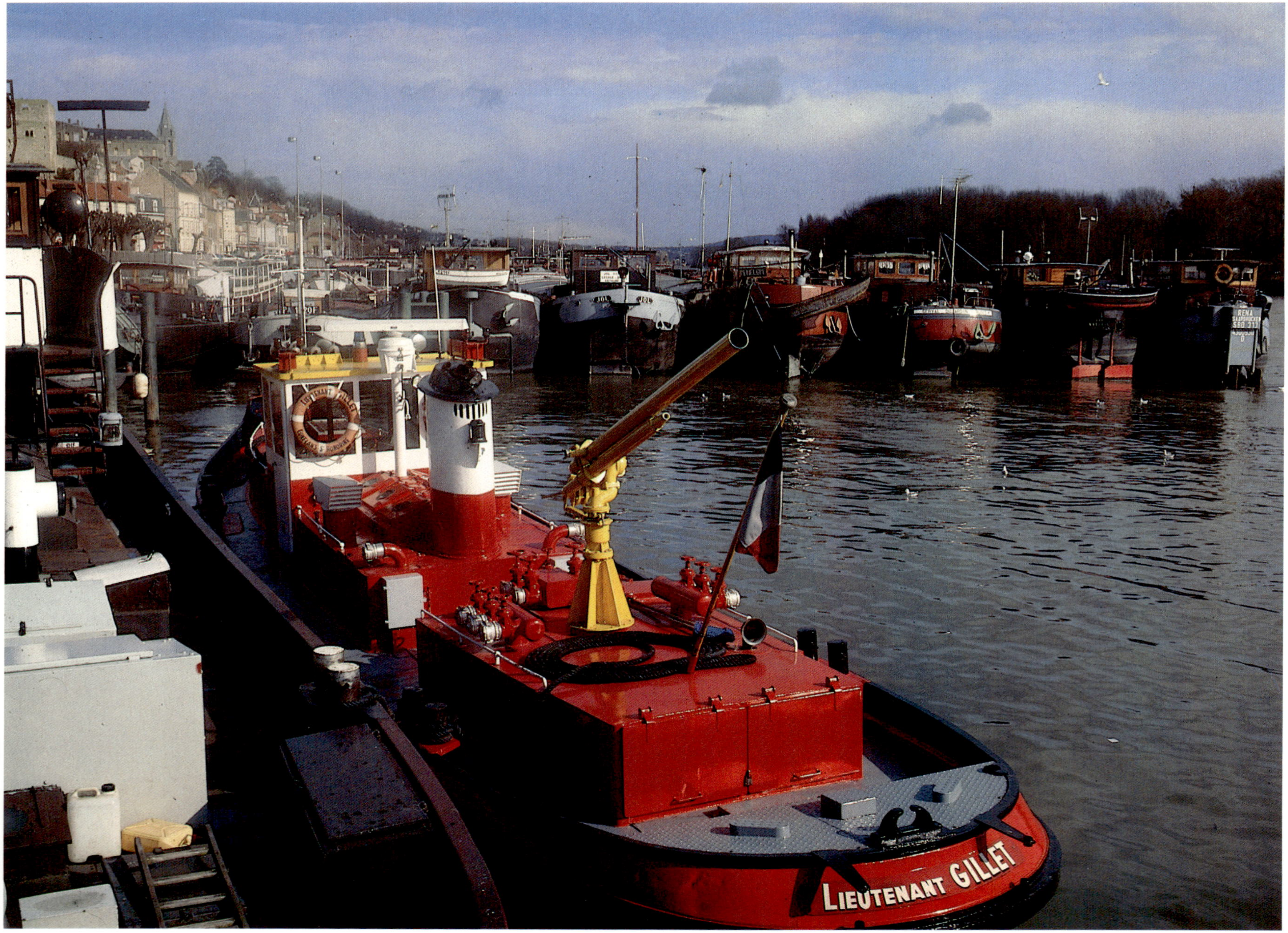

FIREFIGHTING BOAT, CONFLANS-STE-HONORINE

BARGEE'S CAPITAL

I stood on a grassy promontory. To the north was the Oise, to the west and east ran the Seine. And here, at this spectacular river T-junction, a barge swooshed down beneath the railway bridge, and, as it turned into the Seine towards Paris, I noticed that the bargee's car, travelling on deck, had Belgian plates. From Belgium, through the canals, they come; and from Germany and Holland, too. Down the Oise to Conflans-Ste-Honorine, the French bargee's capital.

This tip of headland, where the rivers meet, was a public garden with masts and flagpoles and a war memorial to the dead of the Inland Waterways. Many wars had passed this way, and much destruction. Including, sadly, as road and rail overtook river transport, a wrecking yard for old barges. Wood-panelling was burned; anchor chains were thrown into a backwater where, like a horrific serpent, they coiled and writhed beneath the clear, still surface.

Conflans-Ste-Honorine was not only a meeting-point of rivers, but of landlubber market gardeners and fluvial artisans. Farmer and river-dweller were sometimes indistinguishable, and it was once quite normal to find a chicken-coop on a coal-barge.

We were 37 miles from Paris by *la rivière*, as the bargees called it, and a mere twenty minutes by train from the Gare St-Lazare. The river, below Paris, doubles the crow-flying distance to the sea by its meanders, and the difficulties of navigation made Conflans an important staging-post for towing.

Till the end of the eighteenth-century, towing was by human teams. Currents were sometimes so strong that it took forty men and women to pull a boat upstream. Eventually, the tow-paths were paved, and horses could be used. But, owing to the channel's frequent change of side for each meander, the horses had to cross the river up to forty times between Rouen and Paris. Ferries were insufficient. And the journey could take up to a month, even in the most favourable conditions.

With the coming of steam, increased foreign trade, and the greater importance of the lower Seine, Conflans came into its own. Two road bridges were constructed in 1840; two rail bridges by 1900. Coal-barges from the mines of northern France arrived via the Oise, and stopped over, to be made into convoys for the chain-tow to Paris.

Brought down the Oise by horses, the coal-barge would moor along the waterfront, opposite 'Le Week-End' café, until a sufficient number made up a 'train' of fifteen barges. The tow-boat itself was about the length of a barge, using a chain laid along the river bed; the chain came up over the boat and a system of steam-driven winches pulled the tow-boat forwards on the chain. If the chain broke, disaster; also, if the tow-boat's captain forgot to lower the funnel for bridges. Tow-boat watching was a sadistic sport of schoolboys in the 1860s.

Propeller-driven tugs did away with the laborious chain-tow; by 1914, hundreds of tugs were operating on the Seine. And Conflans was the centre of tug companies nicknamed 'The Wasps', 'The Blues', 'The Tritons' and 'The Barnums'. Origin of

'The Barnums' was the sailor's joke that the company's horses had once worked the circus, so agile were they still!

It was an artisanal trade. A bargee's family travelled with him. Aft were the captain's quarters: parents' bunk, children's cot by a cosy coal-fired stove, wash-hand basin, oil-lamps and a ship's bell with a crucifix, bargees being traditionally religious. In the middle of the boat was the cargo. And fore'ard lived the crew.

All had a special affection for Conflans. It was a stopover for many purposes. For the boat: repairs, sale, purchase, conversion to diesel or petrol propulsion. For the crew: loading new cargo and wild nights at one of the many waterfront cafés, which held mail for them and gave advice of all kinds – from which brothel was the best to which dentist the least painful. For the captain: contracts for insurance or freight. For his wife: stocking up at the market on Place Fouillère. For his children: either leaving or going back to the special State boarding-school for children of the Inland Waterways. And for the whole family: Sunday Mass at *Je Sers* ('I Serve'), the chapel-on-a-boat still to be seen on the waterfront.

CHAPEL, CONFLANS

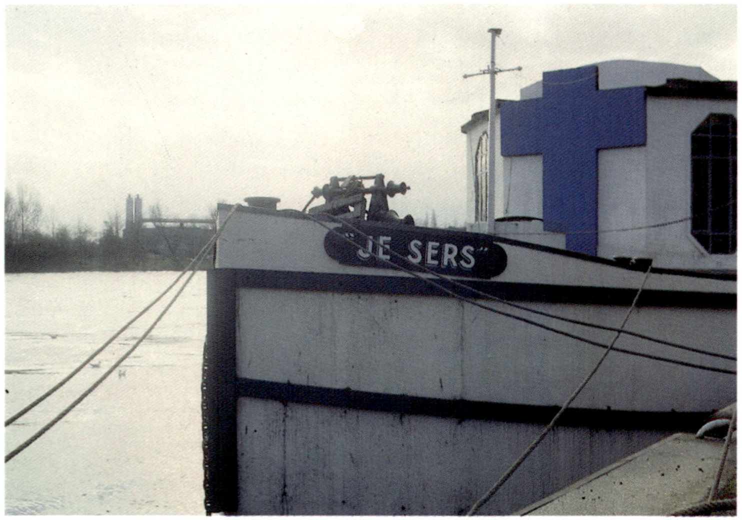

It's hardly surprising that the townspeople of Conflans had a special affection for the artisans of the Inland Waterways, too. But after the First World War the business became less artisanal. It cost a lot for a captain-owner to adapt his boat to self-propulsion, let alone buy a new one. And by 1960 the tugs he relied on for a tow had disappeared. Companies with powerful diesel pushers handled the heavy stuff – using convoys of car transporters or construction material barges. For the captain-owner, it was a case of adapt or sink. The self-propelled *automoteur* soon became the most commercially viable single-unit barge.

A certain melancholy pervaded the charm of Conflans-Ste-Honorine. Too many barges, up to seven abreast along a 1¼-mile stretch of river, seemed idle. Not many sailors were enjoying the excellent 60-franc menu of sardine salad and blade of pork with lentils at the 'Auberge du P'tit Bonheur'. Along the traffic-free Old Tow-Path, retired couples ambled in the afternoon sun, past a boatyard called 'Ambiance Yachting' for the wealthy commuters of nearby Maison-Lafitte.

I walked up a narrow, cobbled street, which led to the church of St-Maclou and a belvedere overlooking the river. But even better than the view of barges, bridges and the distant forest of St-Germain was the Château Gévelot. Its delightful nineteenth-century conservatory disguised a children's favourite – The

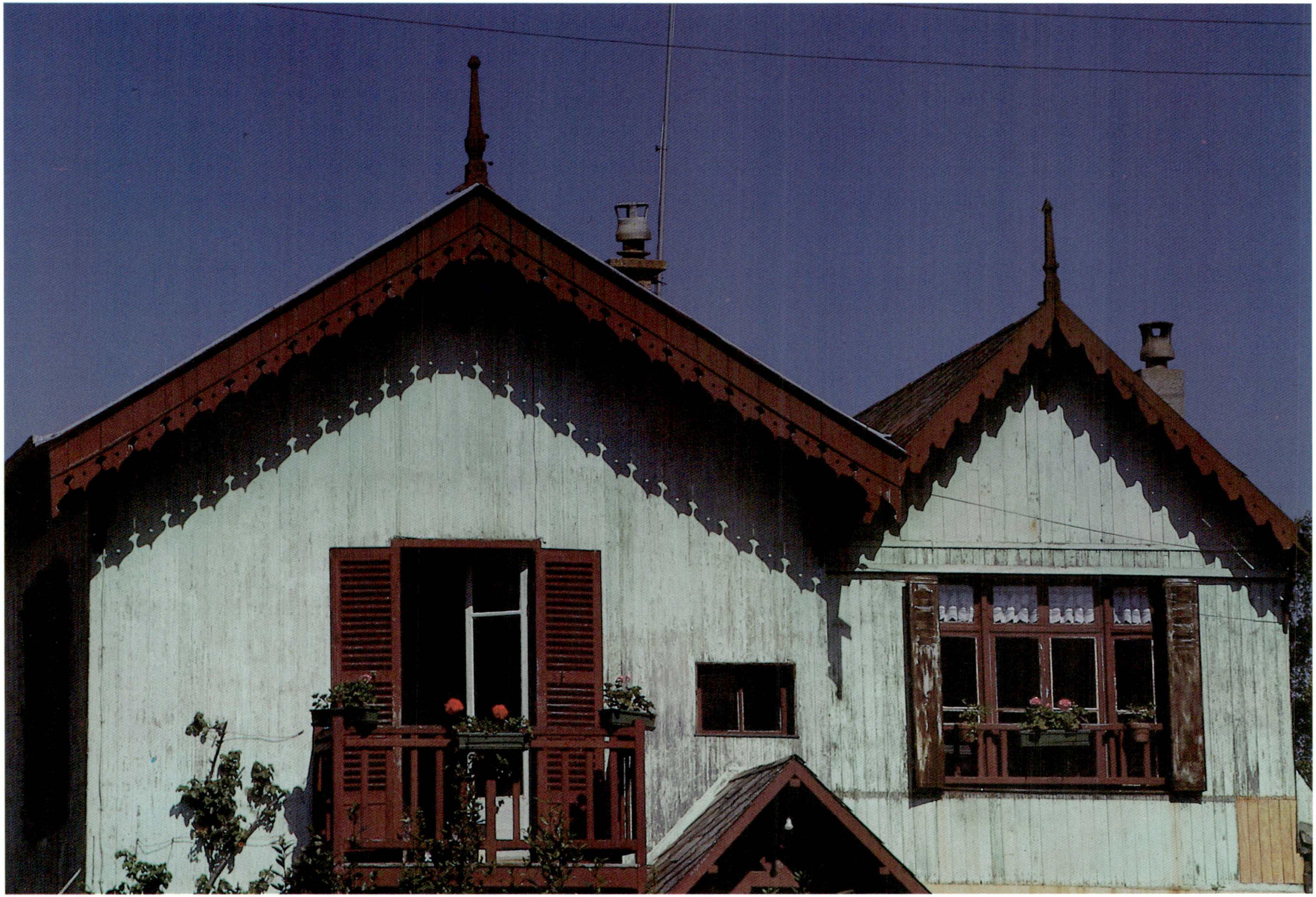

RIVERSIDE VILLA

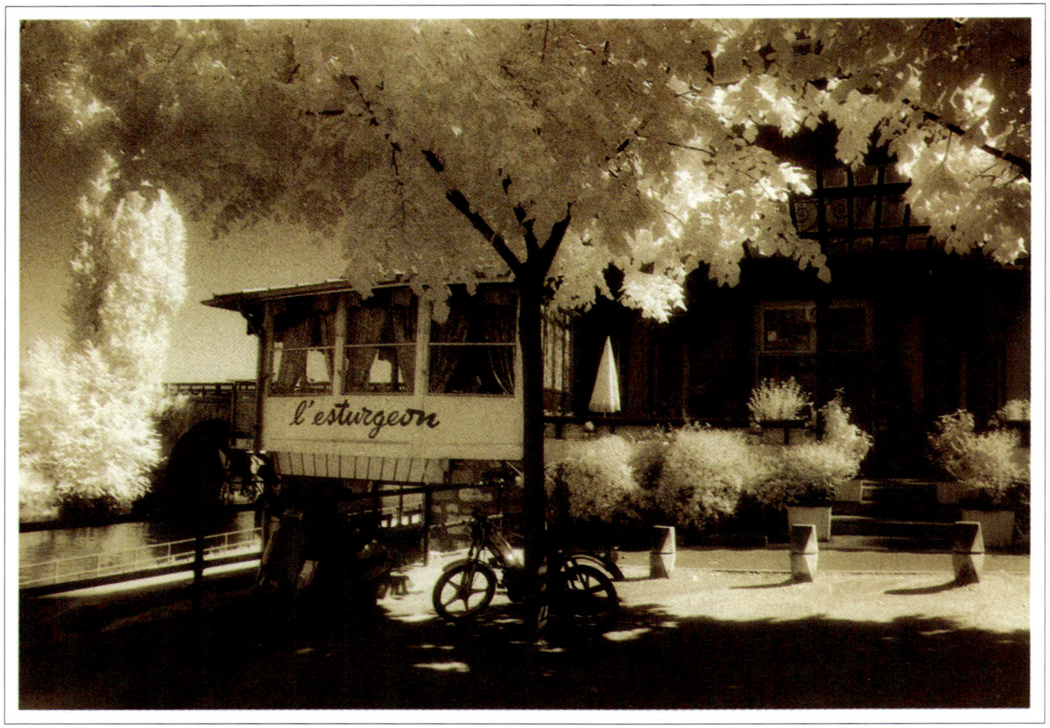

L'ESTURGEON RESTAURANT, POISSY

Museum of the Inland Waterways. Model boats abound, from the early *galiote de basse-Seine*, with its sail and huge rudder for control in tricky, tidal currents, to the super-powered pusher *Esso-Lutèce*. But it was still a museum. And museums mostly speak for the past.

In 1987, it is ironic to note, French barges were hired by 250,000 tourists. More than six million took a cruise or a river trip. In 1989, MS *Normandie*, the luxury six-day shuttle from Paris to Honfleur, carried 106 wealthy Americans in $1,000 staterooms.

Was the Seine itself, I wondered, in danger of becoming a museum?

Old people, old memories.

Along Cours de 14 Juillet, Poissy, a shady avenue makes pleasant walking for a lone *pépé* in a beret. Everything is period. A red vintage Bentley with Paris plates glides elegantly past L'Esturgeon Restaurant, a perfectly preserved nineteenth-century *guingette de luxe*. An Impressionist terrace overlooks the ruins of the Pont St-Louis; wrought-iron and fluted glass,

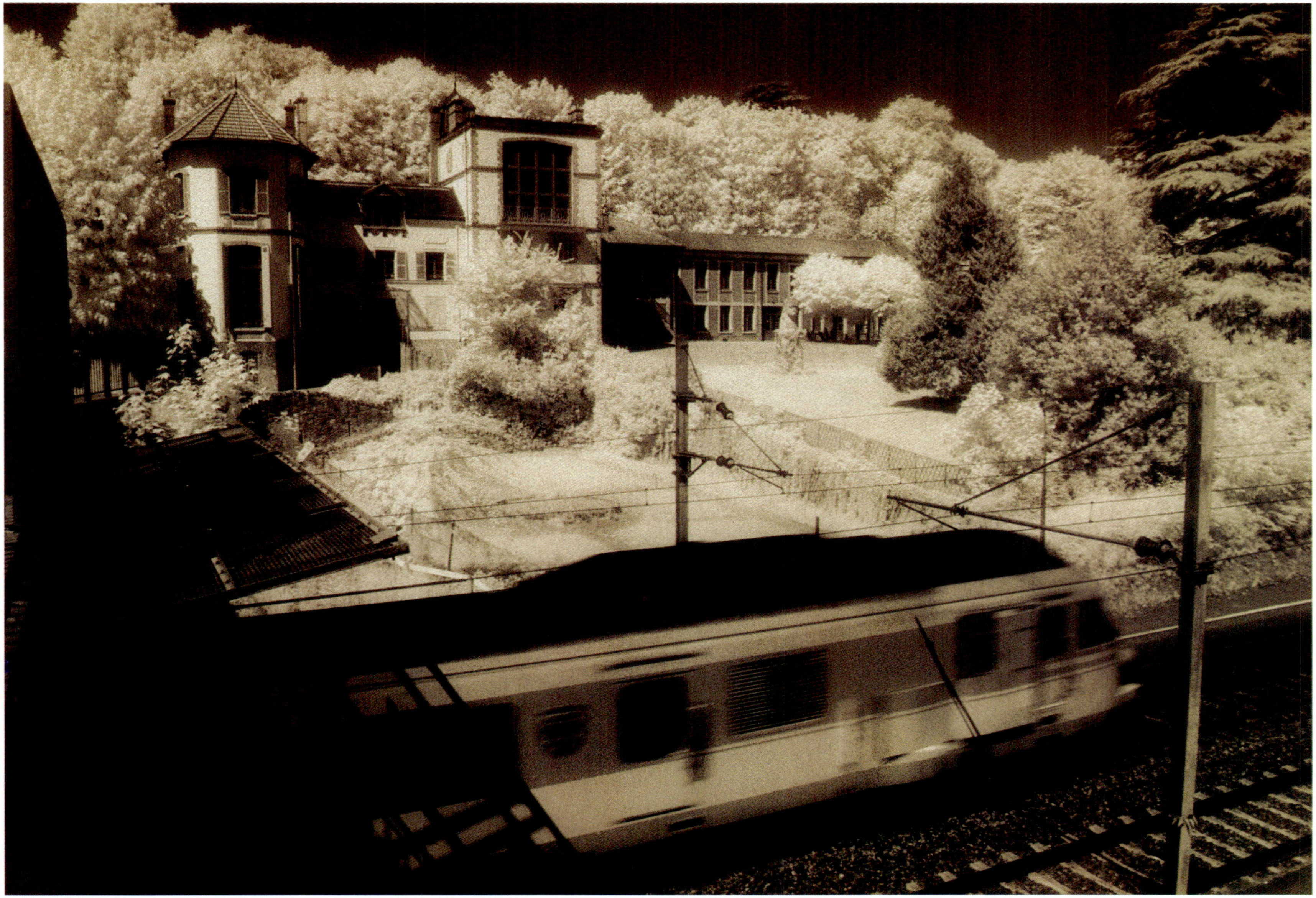

EMILE ZOLA'S HOUSE, MÉDAN

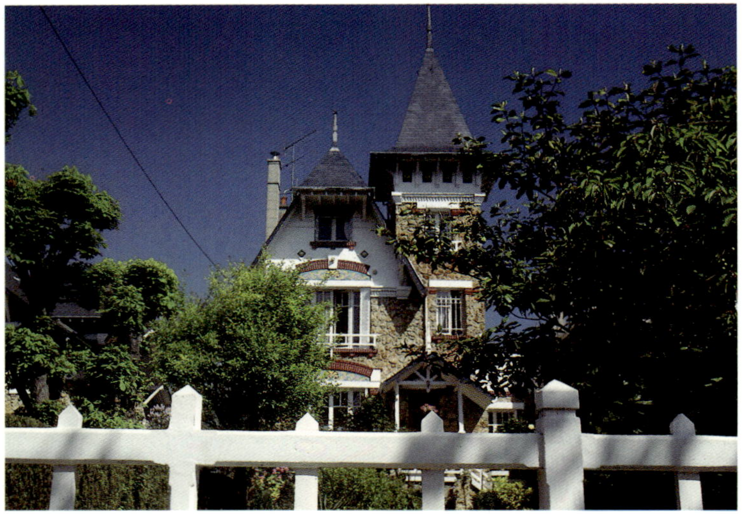

ILE DE MIGNEAUX

geraniums, shrubs and a giant blue watch hanging by the entrance. Time has stopped, as we eat our salmon in black butter.

Crazy half-timbered houses line Avenue Emile Zola, and Beverly Hills-style mansions adorn the Ile des Migneux. The Paris-Rouen railway weaves along the river bank beside us – to Médan, Zola's house by the railway station. What an inspiration for *La Bête Humaine*, whose deranged engine-driver speeds his train to catastrophe at its Paris terminal! A bust of Zola, brows beetled in concern for his Industrial Revolution victims, gazes sombrely beyond the railway to the tree-lined river below.

Inspiration, too, for another poetic realist – Barbizon painter Corot, forerunner of the Impressionists. At Mantes, two Seine-side masterpieces: the medieval collegiate church and the old Pont de Limay. I stand on the new bridge, and absorb the archetypal Seine view – a little different from Corot's painting. Of the 1750 bridge, where once mills and fisheries thrived, only the porter's lodge remains. An EDF power-station beyond the broken arches, a boy peddling a magenta kayak, and a barge-crêperie bridge the centuries.

At Vétheuil, idyllic rural countryside on a chalk-cliff bend inspired Monet – in fog, snow and sunshine during 1878–9. The river narrows, yellow mustard fields fringe the river banks and summer birds appear again, their voices no longer drowned by quayside traffic. Cuckoos, peewits and moorhens – and birds of a wilder feather in the village.

La Roche-Guyon, a little further downstream, inspired Zola. In *L'Oeuvre*, his Impressionist artist hero Claude (modelled not on Claude Monet but Zola's childhood friend Paul Cézanne) retreats from city pressures with his companion, Christine.

'. . . and they also had the river, taking to it like wild savages, living entire days there, sailing, discovering new lands, remaining hidden beneath weeping willows, in narrows dark with shade. Going with the stream, between a scattering of islands, there was a whole mysterious township in motion, alleys criss-crossing down which they gently ambled, lightly caressed by low branches, alone in a world of wood-pigeons and kingfishers . . .

. . . he often took a slow walk along the Seine, without ever straying further than a kilometre. Weary of the same old garden subjects, he now attempted some sketches at the water's edge; and on those days, she went looking for him with the child, and sat watching him paint, waiting for them all three to return, listlessly, beneath the subtle red glow of twilight. . . .'

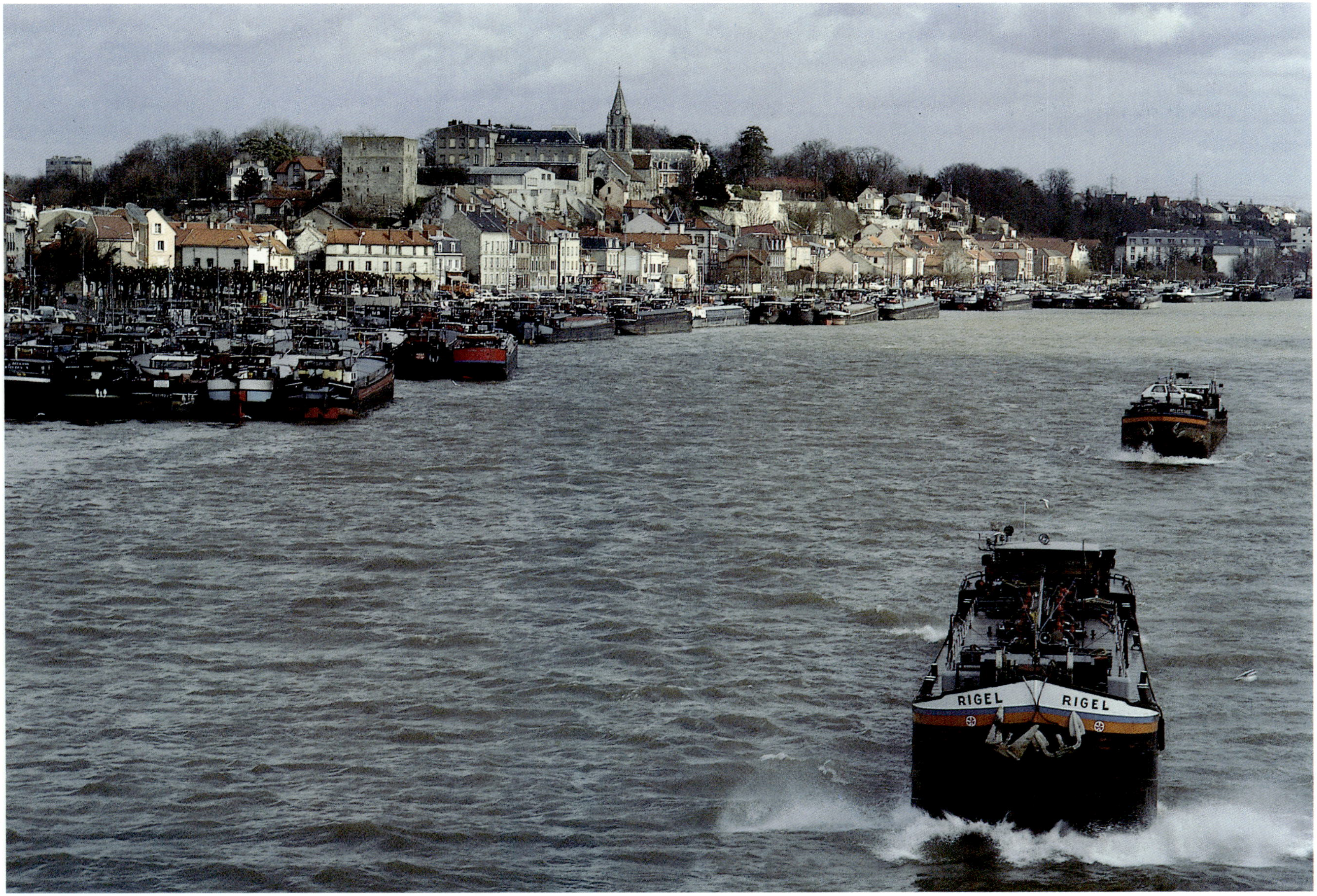

CONFLANS STE-HONORINE

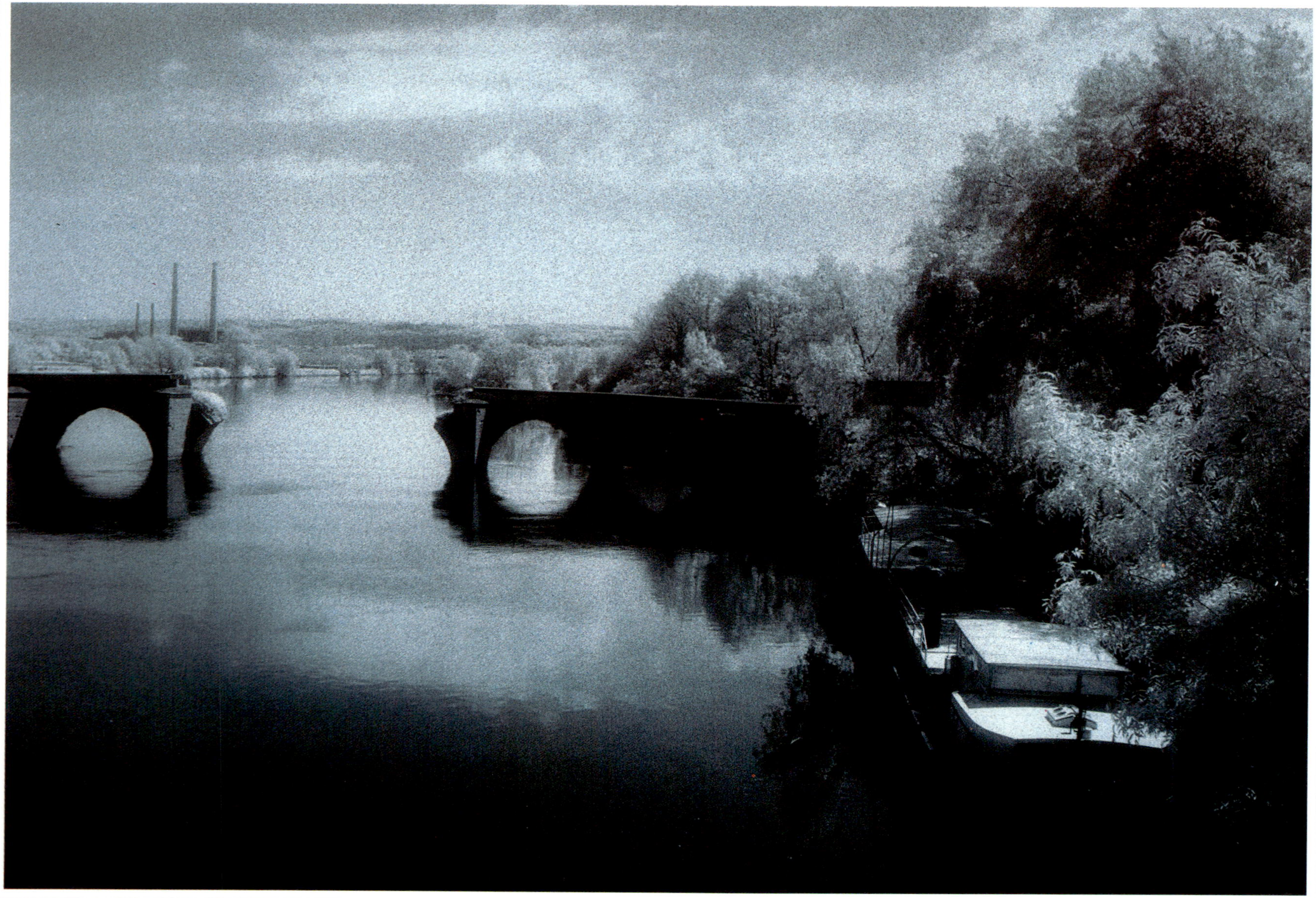

PONT DE LIMAY, MANTES-LA-JOLIE

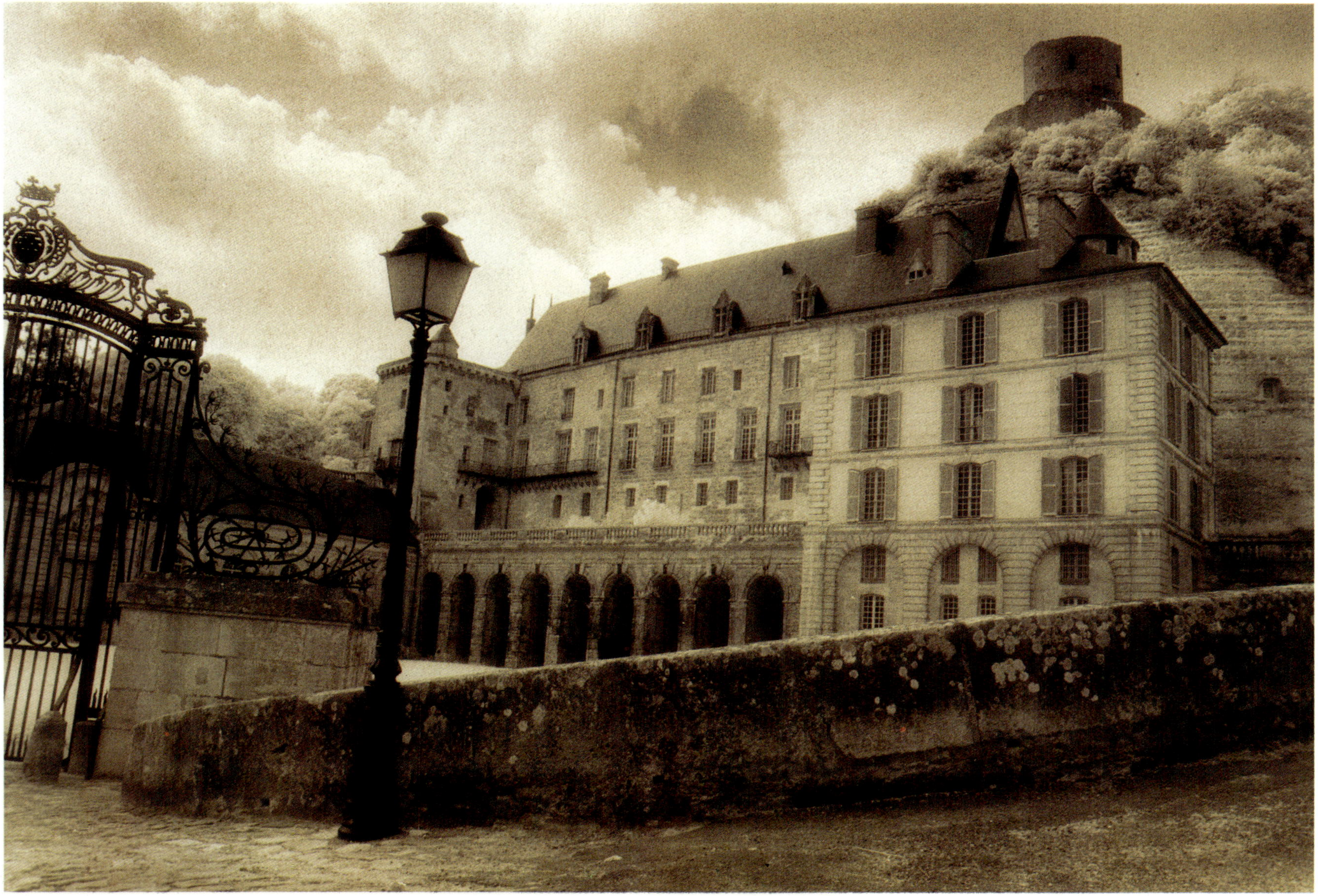

CHÂTEAU DE LA ROCHE-GUYON

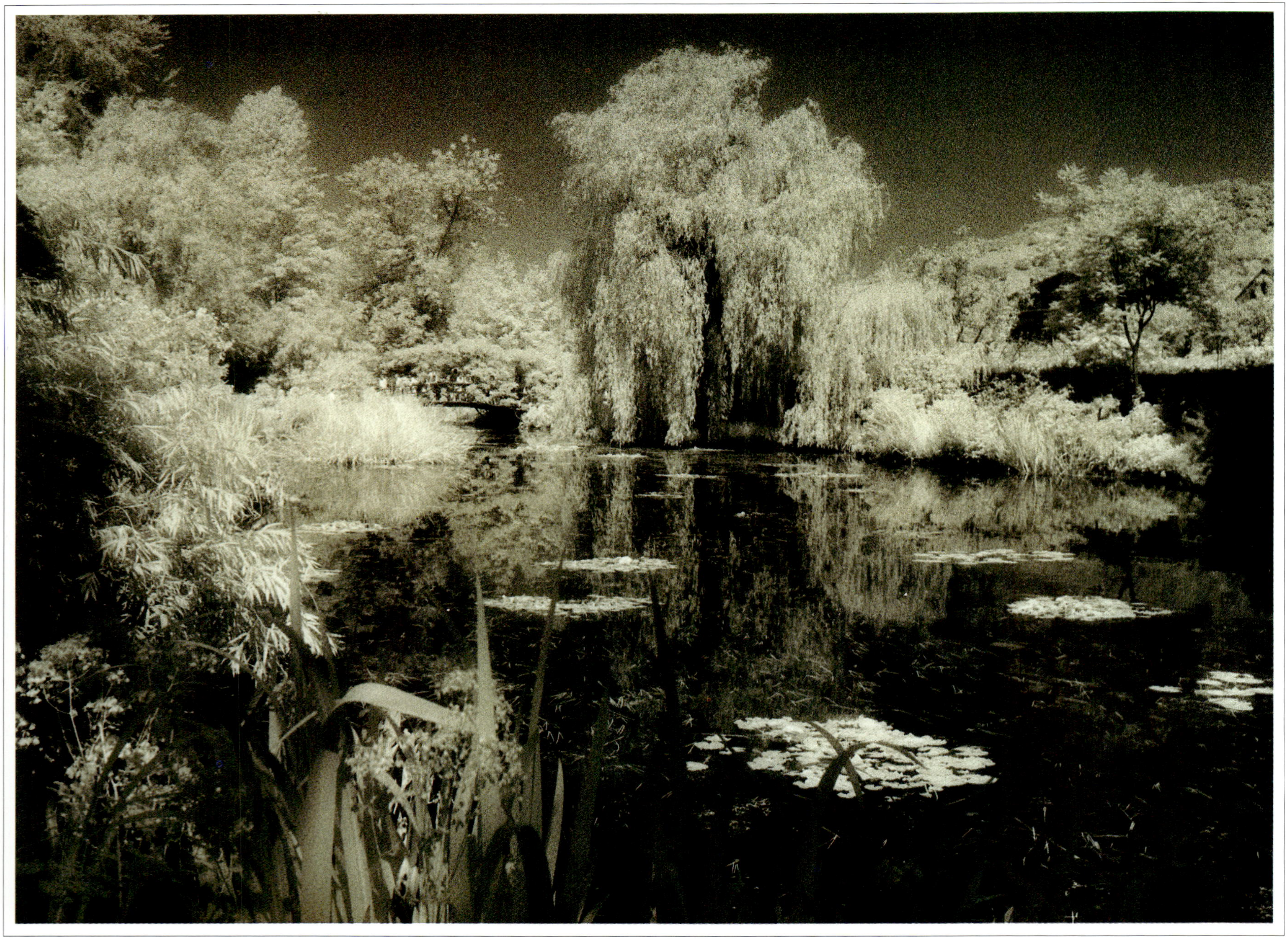

Water garden, Giverny

GARDEN WITH WATER-LILIES

Claude Monet presided over the Seine like a river-god, an all-seeing eye. 'Monet was only an eye,' said Cézanne, 'but my God, what an eye!'

And even the gods have homes.

Giverny was Monet's home from 1883 to 1926, the period of his great series paintings. He had moved from Le Havre, his childhood home, via Honfleur to Paris. And then came back downstream again, via Argenteuil, Poissy, and Vétheuil to the rose-pink country house with apple-green shutters and blue-and-white gingham curtains, where he stayed till his death.

Sunlight on water was Monet's life-work. And, at Giverny, he had water and its reflections in all shapes and sizes. The property was bounded by a brook, the Ru; a branch of the River Epte flowed through the meadows to join the Seine an easy walk away, near the reedy mooring where Monet kept his boats – his floating studio, two shining mahogany sculls, and a rowing skiff; and, finally, the famous water-lily pond he constructed with the help of his eight gardeners, Japanese bulb-senders, and Norman carpenters engaged to build a Japanese bridge.

On the day of our visit, Japanese pilgrims to the river-god's shrine were already pouring out of their coaches at nine in the morning. Giverny is Normandy's Notre-Dame. But birdsong mercifully prevailed over the din of tourists and, once in the *clos normand*, the walled garden that Monet made his horticultural laboratory of colour, the herd instinct kept groups together and people dissolved into the profusion of June flowers.

Apple-green hoops festooned with roses made an arbour for our peaceful progress. Salvia, tulips, lupins, poppies, convolvulus, freesias, dianthus and roses, roses all the way, gave the garden a haphazardly English ambiance. Monet fought with his head gardener, who wanted flower-beds arranged more formally *à la française*.

In the water-garden, crowds were denser. Fat ladies posed for photographs on the Japanese bridge. A screeching mother slapped her child for trying to pick a water-lily and nearly fell into the stagnant water. But a hazy light took the edge off the ugliness. A little girl in a straw hat looked just like the one in *The Artist's Garden at Vétheuil*, and her father had dressed the part, too, resembling to the life a Renoir oarsman.

Thanks to them, my misanthropy fled. Only the very crusty could resist this magical place. But, like Monet's canvases, it was not about people in the mass. It was about one person and his family. And we all seemed to intrude – except at the blatantly commercial Claude Monet Boutique selling Claude Monet sweatshirts, Claude Monet table-mats, calendars, gardening books, matches, and even an Eau-de-Toilette called 'Les Fleurs de Claude Monet'.

But at least I had seen Giverny, its house and garden. And, submerged as the true spirit of place might be, a reflection among the water-lilies seemed to show a long white beard, a brown felt hat and floppy jacket. And I could imagine Claude Monet's day at Giverny.

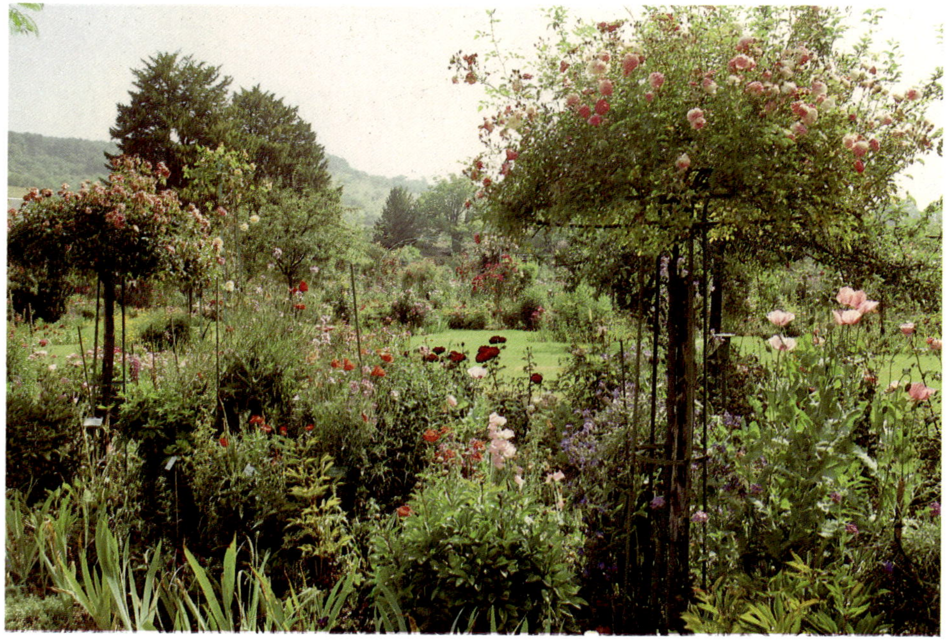

FLOWER GARDEN, GIVERNY

In June the dawns were early. First, a weather check. If the Normandy clouds glowered, so did Monet. His family avoided him on rainy days, which was not hard as he stayed in bed for much of them, tormenting himself about his work, which he never considered perfect.

But when the sky was still starry, and low mists hung over the river, and not a breath of wind blew, he'd be up at his hearty English breakfast. Off through the garden, the aroma of a fine cigar mingling with the dewy perfumes of early morning flowers. Through the garden gate, followed by a servant, carrying fourteen canvases to be worked on that day. Across the narrow-gauge railway and dusty road that then separated water-garden from house. Over a humpbacked Japanese bridge covered with sweet-smelling wisteria, and the little brook, and the damp-grassed meadows to the river bank shrouded in mists.

Then Monet rowed himself in the little skiff to his studio-boat. There, where the Seine met the Epte, little islands made peaceful, hidden lakes, tall trees were reflected on the ripples. Monet would work on a single motif for a series – *Poplars* or *The Seine at Giverny*; each of the canvases showed changes of hour, sunlight and clouds. And as the morning progressed, he would change the canvas accordingly; he had been known to paint the same stretch of river under eighteen different atmospheric conditions!

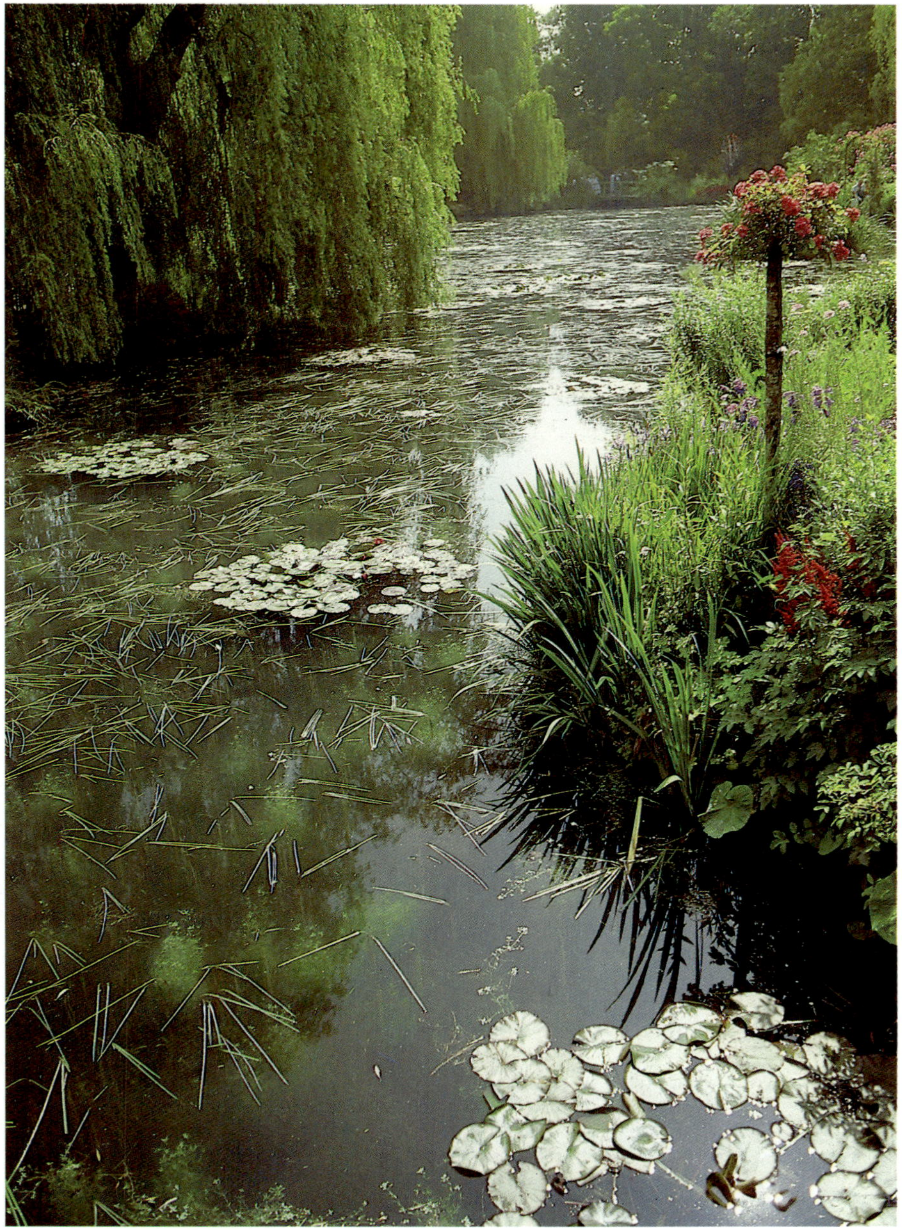

WATERLILIES, GIVERNY

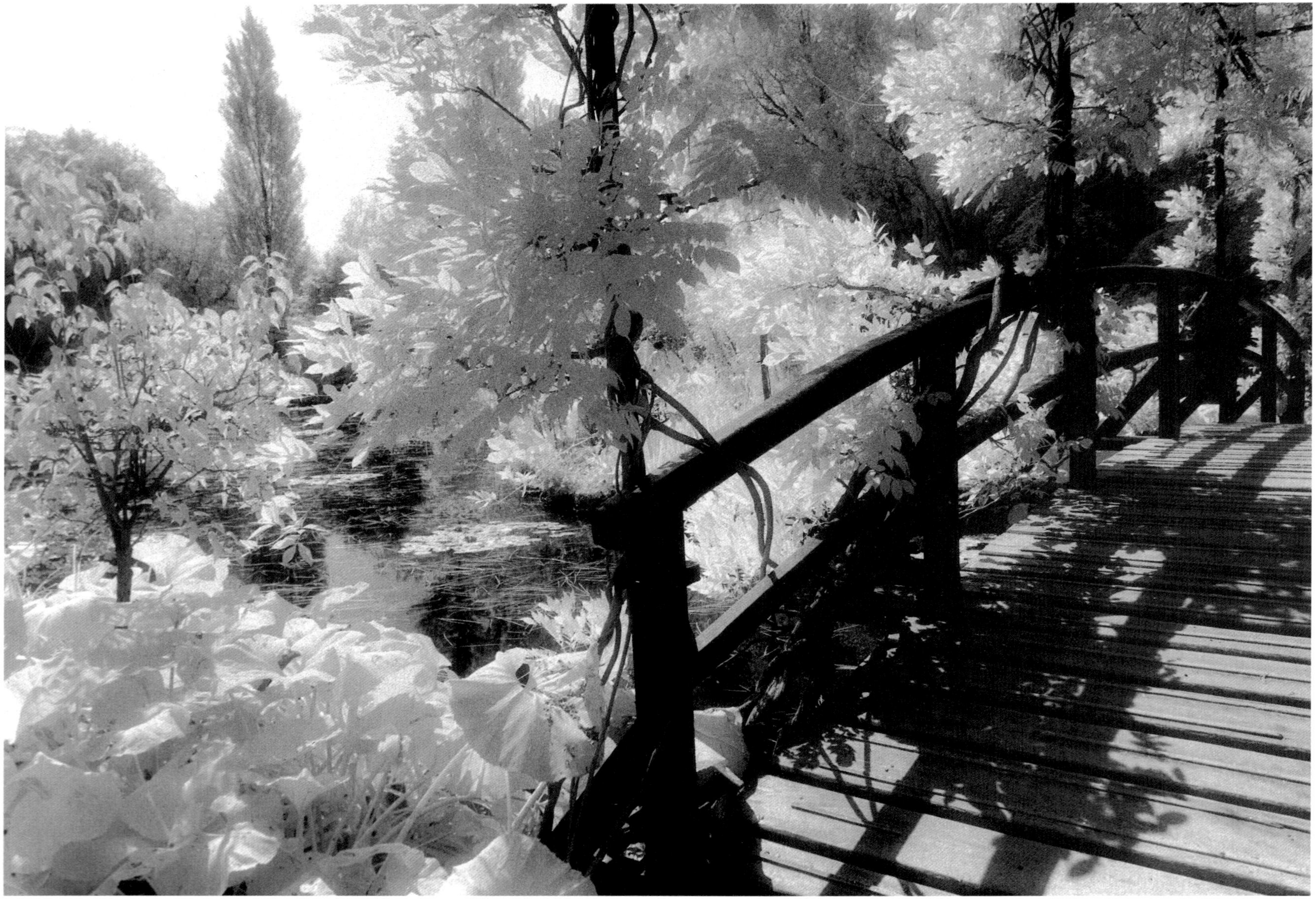

JAPANESE BRIDGE, GIVERNY

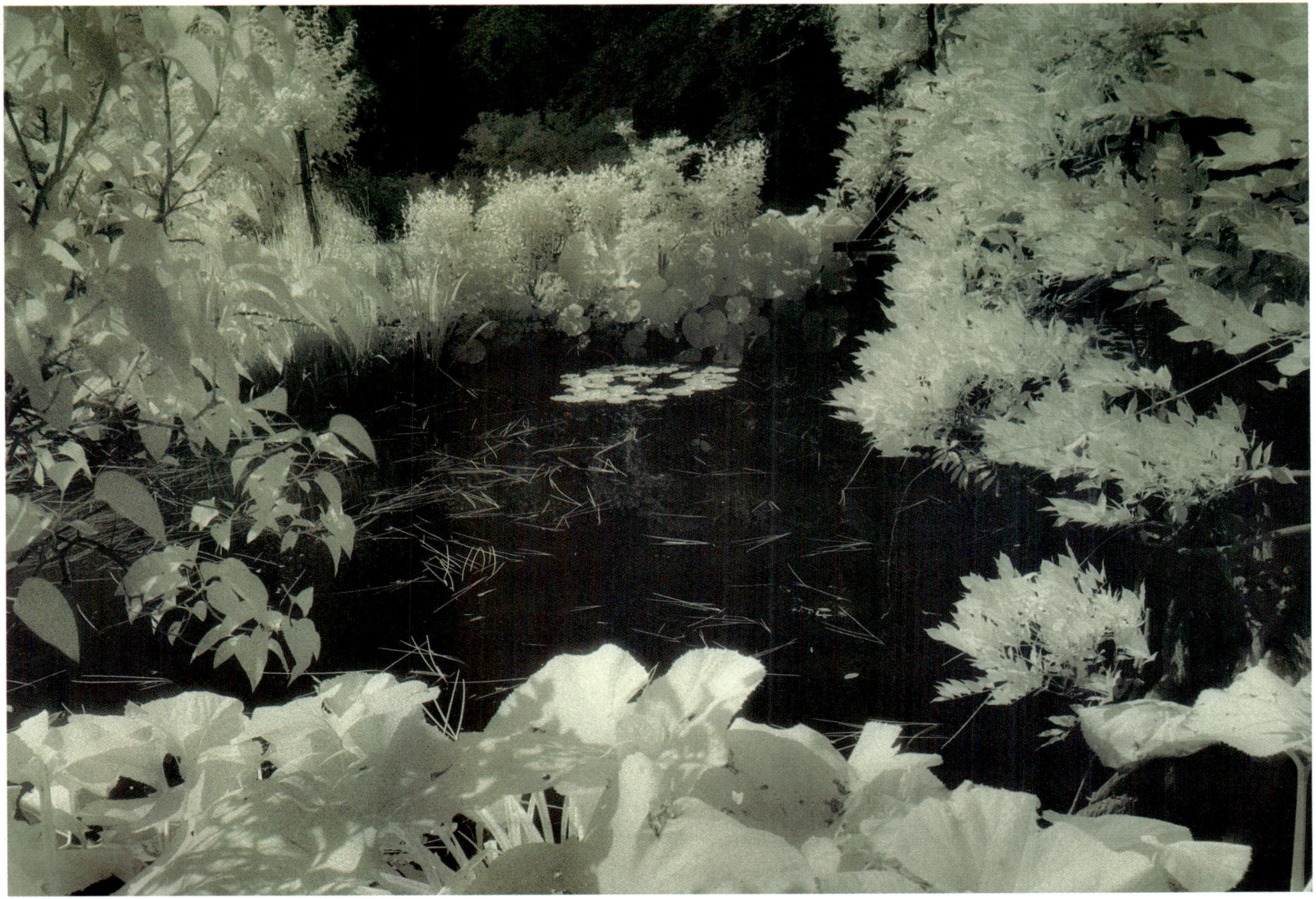

Waterlilies, Giverny

Back to lunch at eleven. A bell rang twice. God help a child who was late. The large family had to be sitting, all together, in the yellow wood-panelled dining-room with matching Limoges china and Japanese prints. Bourgeois? It happened to Monet, as it happens to the best of rebels in the time of their hard-earned prosperity.

But the ménage shocked the village. This rich artist who sometimes dressed like a peasant lived with a woman who was not his wife, and they had eight children. And two of the children married each other! What goings-on at the Maison du Pressoir! In fact, of course, some of the children were widower Monet's and some those of Alice Hoschedé, the woman he lived with, so the marriage was perfectly legitimate. But Giverny never approved or understood – until today, when Monet means big money to the village.

In the afternoon, if he was in a good mood, he would go on picnics with the children. And later, in 1901, he bought a Panhard, motoring with enthusiasm and as fast as possible all over Normandy, and even to Madrid to see the Prado – quite a drive in those days.

A man of routine and obsessive self-discipline, Monet was punctually in bed by nine-thirty, hopeful of another early start. The years of the Giverny series were prolific: besides those already mentioned, there were *The Haystacks*, *Rouen Cathedral*, and his final monumental work, *Water-lilies*, for which a special studio had to be built. Encouraged by Prime Minister Clemenceau, he worked there, with failing eyesight, from 1918 until near his death in 1926. And the result was this mysterious, grandiose evocation of the Giverny water-garden, a tribute to his last home.

'Paint, paint always,' his friend Clemenceau, told him, 'till the canvas explodes from it. My eyes have need of your colour, and my heart is happy with you.'

Vernon is the nearest town to Giverny.

With happy heart but eyes heavy from the dazzling images, I siesta gratefully on a grassy bank by the ruins of a half-timbered Norman bridge house. The silhouette of Vernon church, on the other side of the river, comes and goes as my eyelids rise and fall. I remember Monet's appreciation of 'the mists hanging on the irregular surfaces of the building . . . the stone that time had rendered golden'. And Monet's reflection of it in the water. And how he had used the façade of Rouen cathedral, its neutral grey like the river's non-colour, as a reflection for light at different times of day.

Awoken by piercing cries. Schoolgirls, rougher than those two languid ladies of the Monet family in *Boating on the Epte*, are having canoe lessons at the Ecole Française de Canoe-Kayak. Jeers from the boys as one turns turtle, slapped by the wash of a barge convoy so heavy that its pusher has its bows out of the water like a speedboat.

Lesson over, the instructor leaves. Mayhem. The boys start throwing the girls into the Seine. Wriggling, giggling, shouting and laughing. The water is warm, and they come out proud and hoydenish, showing off dripping bodies. One of the larger girls topples a boy off the jetty, and it all starts again.

A strange mix, this waterfront park: apart from the rowing school larkers, toddlers paddle at the beach and old people saunter along the strand. A nineteenth-century hunting lodge stands cheek by jowl with the twelfth-century Château de Tourelles, the latter a reminder that here begins, in earnest, Lower Seine Médiéval.

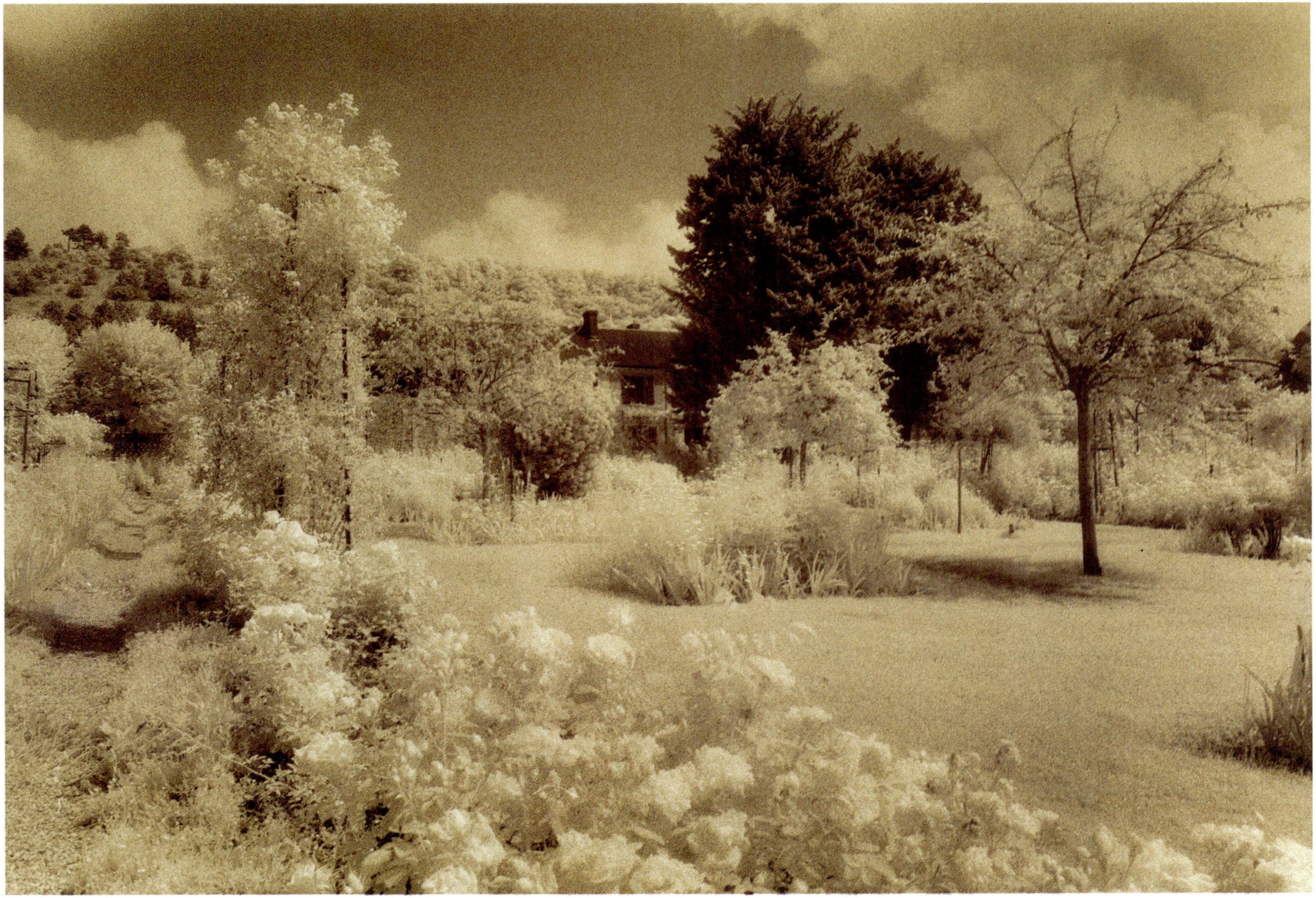

Monet's house and garden, Giverny

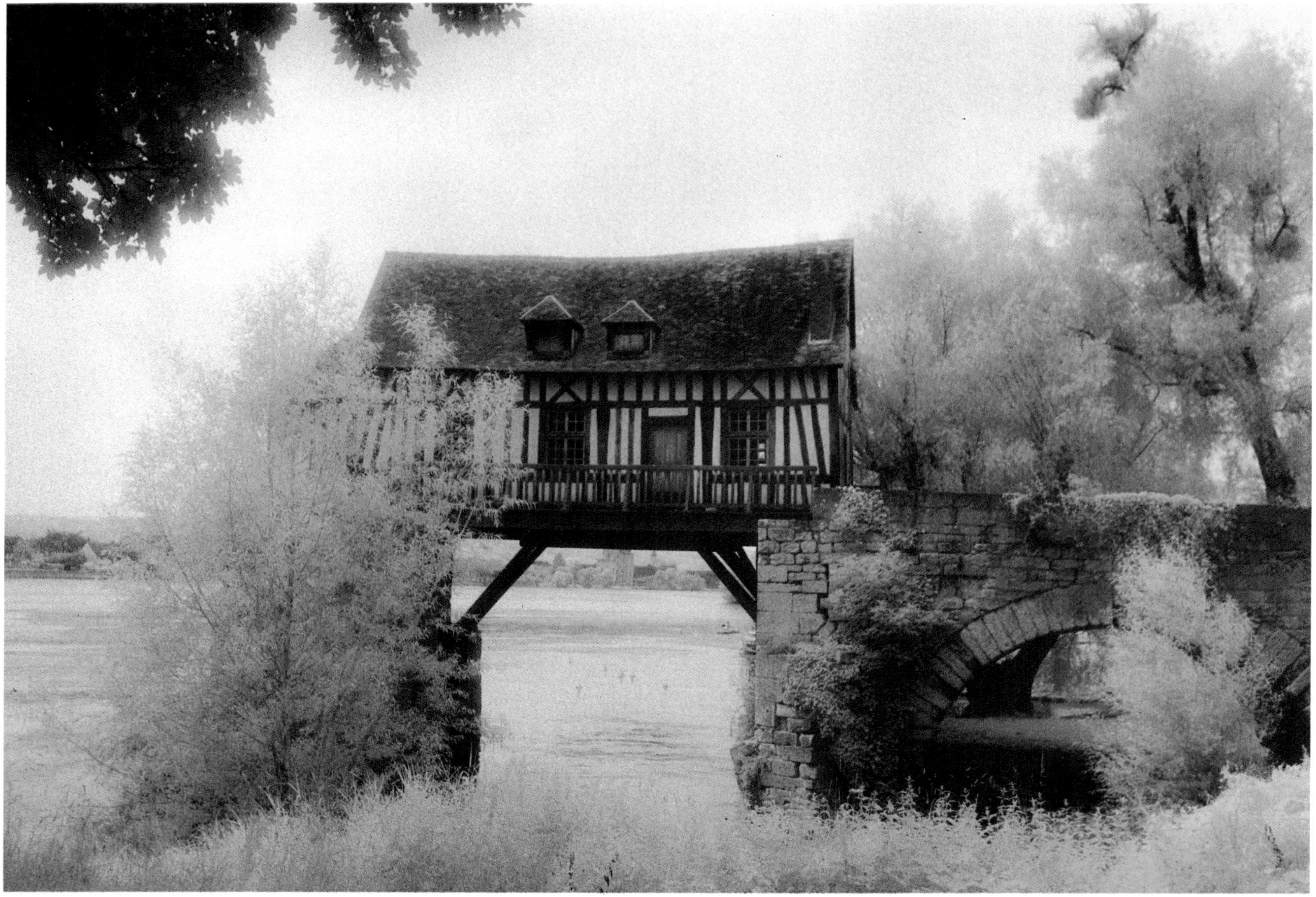

Norman bridge-house, Vernon

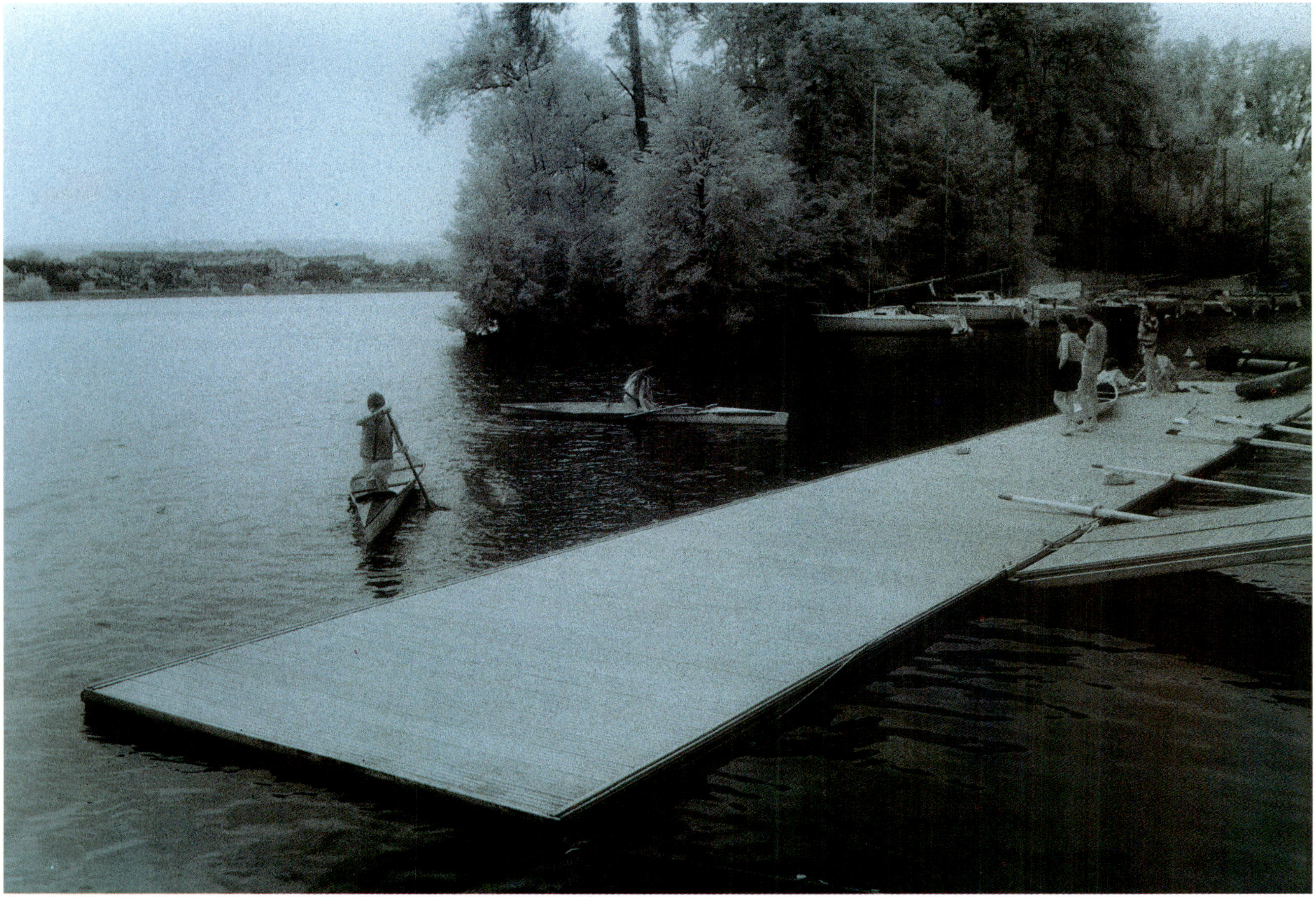

Kayak school, Vernon

Medieval Meandering

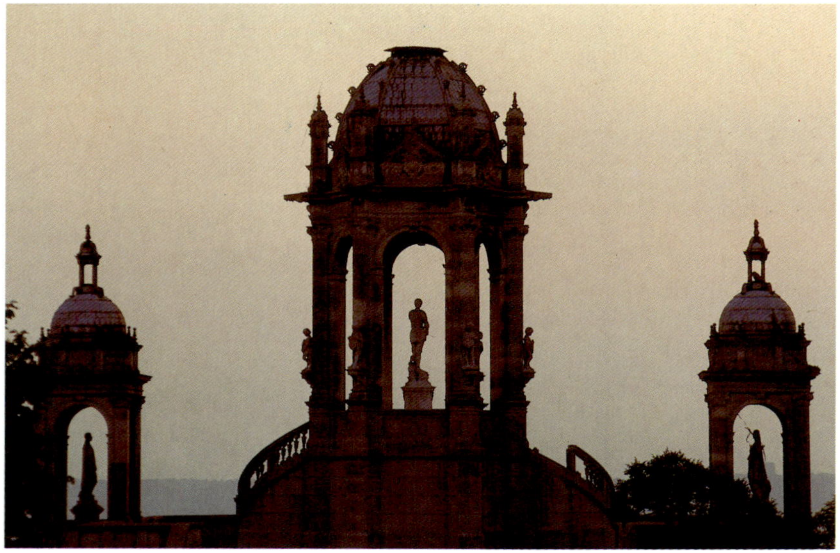

From the fifth century to the fifteenth, the Seine was alive with the clash of swords, the twang of bows, and the cantillation of plainsong. In the vicinity of Rouen, legends are legion in the fortresses and abbeys, which rise majestically from green woods and golden fields along the river bank.

At Les Andelys, on a spectacular bluff overlooking a sweeping bend of the river, stood the ruins of Château Gaillard, silhouetted against dark, menacing clouds rolling up river from the English Channel.

Richard the Lionheart, King of England and Duke of Normandy, built the fortress in 1196 to prevent the French King Philippe-Auguste reaching Rouen. Speed was of the essence, and after only twelve months, Richard could proudly pronounce: 'How beautiful she is, my one-year-old daughter!'

On Richard's death, however, his son Jean Sans Terre lived up to his weedy name, Landless Jean; after a five-month siege by the forces of Philippe-Auguste, the Normans capitulated. One story has it that French troops entered unexpectedly by the latrines, catching the Norman soldiery at a rare, unguarded moment.

Considered a masterpiece of military strategy, Château

Joan of Arc monument, Bonsecours

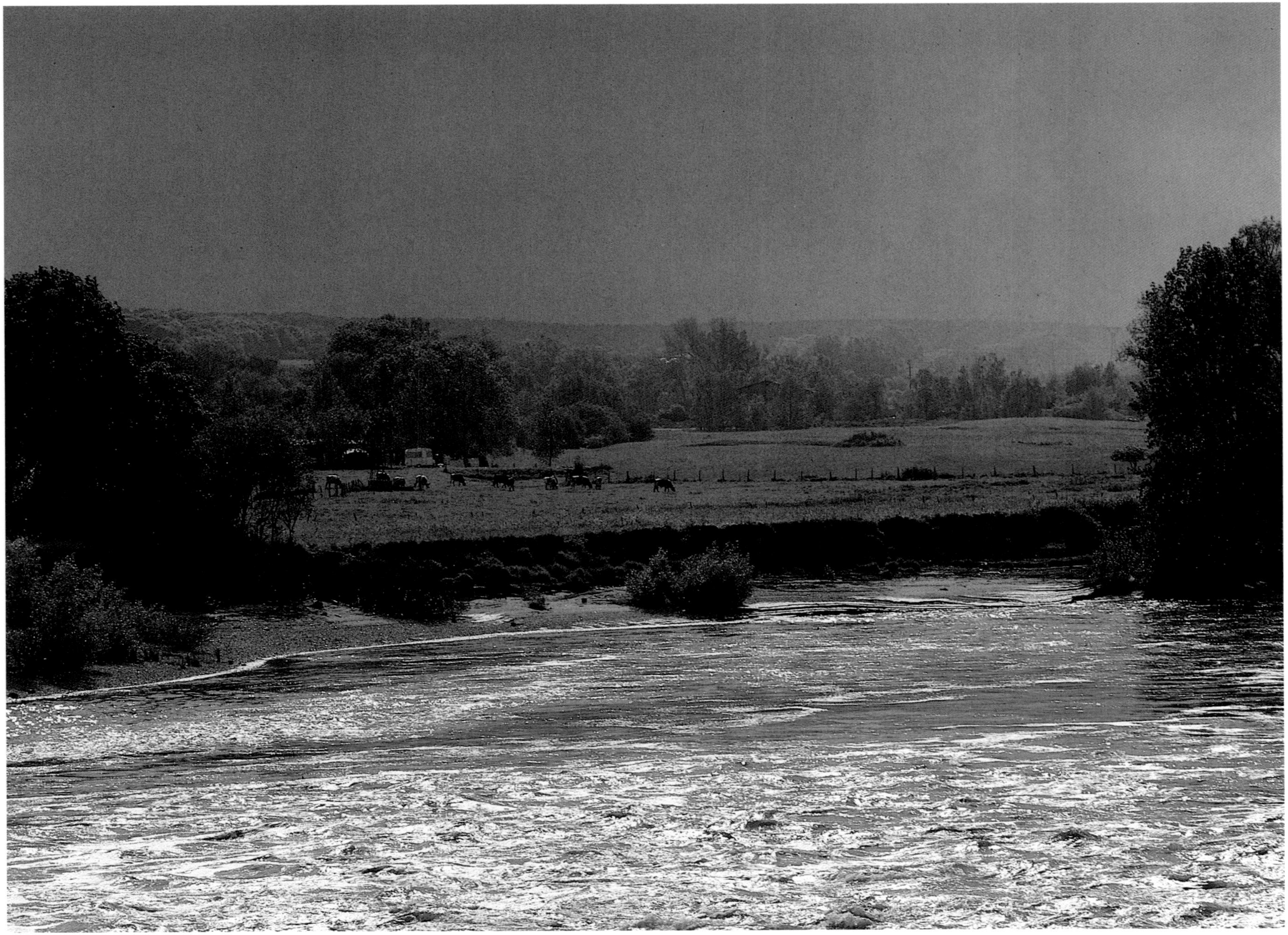

Meadow, Amfreville-sous-les-Monts

Gaillard still has one tower more or less intact. Like goats, we switchbacked along a narrow path round the fortress, now dipping into a deep ditch, now clambering to a spot where, panting, we exhaled the bracing air and marvelled at the view. Across a wooden bridge, a portcullis still loomed; a notice warned of the danger of falling masonry.

How could anyone have kept up a siege of such a place for five minutes, let alone months? Or, further downstream, how could a swain have run up 'Le Coteau des Deux Amants' with his beloved on his back?

By the time we reached this doom-laden hillside, high above the locks of Amfreville, I was feeling more and more unfit. Smaller they may have been in those days, but surely bigger in heart and wind.

Once upon a time, they say, in a castle dominating this grim, high cliff lived the wicked Baron Rulph and his beautiful daughter, Calixte. One fine hunting day, her swain Edmond saved Calixte from a wild boar. Baron Rulph wished to reward Edmond, but was not expecting the young varlet to ask for his daughter's hand in marriage. Furious, Baron Rulph imposed a terrible condition. Edmond must climb up the hill, three times, carrying Calixte on his back. Edmond nobly accepted the challenge. But, on arrival at the top for the third time, amid the cheers of the crowd, he dropped dead. Smitten with grief, Calixte picked up the dead Edmond and hurled herself and him off the nearby cliff. And Baron Rulph, his heart full of remorse, did penance by founding a monastery and joining a Crusade.

More truth than legend lay in the tragedy of Joan of Arc, and Rouen has done the Maid proud in simple, touching memorials. The first we came to, at sunset on Mont Thuringe, was near the drab nineteenth-century basilica of Bonsecours. Beneath an elaborate, sentimental rotunda, guarded by cherubs, a statue of Joan looked out over the city where she was burned at the stake. It was hard not to be moved by the quiet dignity and expression of forgiveness on the face of the statue, for all its lack of artistic merit. Below us, in a golden, smoggy haze deepening over the Old Town, lay the cathedral, the Seine, and the Place du Vieux-Marché, all of which played their part in her final hours.

At the cathedral, where magnificent floodlighting made the Gothic spire resemble an eerie green space-rocket about to lift off to Heaven, was a small chapel dedicated to Saint Joan. She was canonized as late as 1926 after an unbelievable five centuries spent clearing her name of the heresy for which she was burned.

In the Place du Vieux-Marché, the Joan of Arc museum could be forgiven its lifeless waxworks and corny, multiple-language commentary (genre: 'Oh, buck up, my liege,' says Joan to the Dauphin in her humorous peasant manner. 'I will see thee crowned in Rheims Cathedral, that I will!'). The story was clearly recounted: starting with the voices which told her she would unite the French against the English; her dressing as a male soldier (for which the Church condemned her); her victories, defeats and trials; her abjuration and relapse; until, not yet twenty, she was put in a cart by the English soldiers and made to wear a mitre with the words: 'Heretic – Apostate – Relapse – Idolatress.'

On the very place to which the cart took her in 1431 rises a fine modern church with a roof shaped to symbolize the flames of Joan's stake. There are Joan of Arc jokes just as there are Concentration Camp jokes. But time does not heal some wounds; her agony is unimaginable.

According to legend her heart and entrails would not burn. And, lest they became relics and symbols of resistance, the English soldiers hurled them into the Seine; each year flowers are

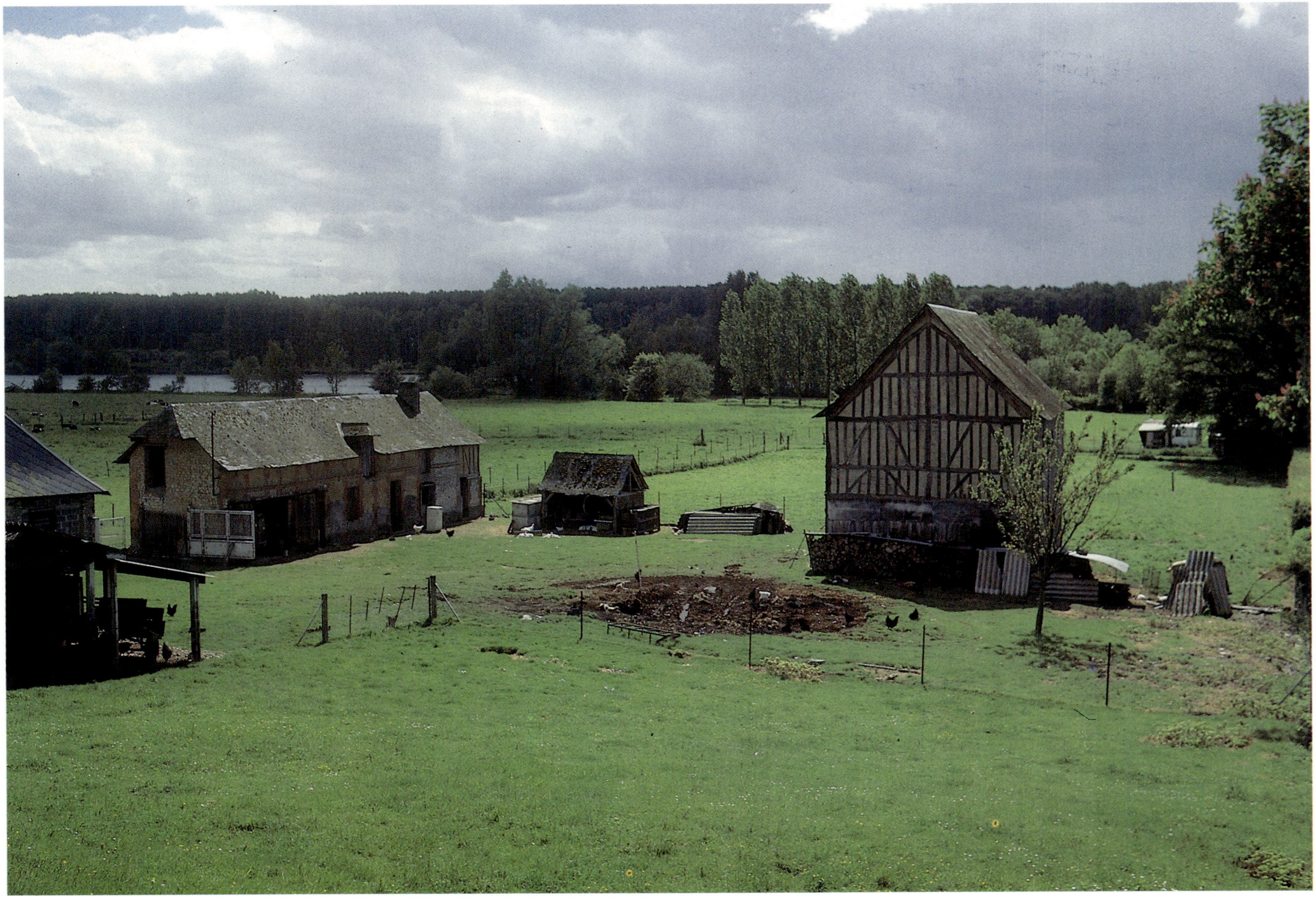

Farm, Amfreville-sous-les-Monts

scattered at this place in a ceremony of remembrance for the young girl who had helped bring peace to a united France after the debilitating horrors of the Hundred Years War.

Our medieval meandering, dictated by the river's flow, took no account of chronological order. And back we went to 1066 and earlier for the next stronghold downstream. William the Conqueror's father was known as Robert le Magnifique or Robert le Diable (Devil) – presumably according to whose side you were on in a battle. Proud of the fear he put into the enemy, he called this fort, now a romantic ruin overlooking the western outskirts of Rouen and its port, '*Le Château de Robert Le Diable*'. His famous son William, who brought England under the control of Normandy, was in its sixth Duke, and a descendant of the Vikings. And these ruins, perched strategically on a steep, wooded hill, now contain a Viking museum.

I felt numbed by the very idea of man taking on the capricious river Seine so long ago. In 841, the Vikings sailed from their misty fjords, across stormy northern waters, and down the English Channel in '*drakkars*', hefty wooden galleys rowed by forty to eighty men. At Amfreville-sous-les-Monts, we had met a Vexin farmer with the fair-haired beefiness of his Norse antecedents; his were looks we saw more and more, but never with quite his openness. In no time, he began telling us where best to photograph the church where he was married, describing the procession from church to farm, the wedding feast, the bridal gown, and how much cider was consumed.

Medieval times, he assured us, were not all rape and pillage. Besides the endless conquering and regaining of land, the Seine, since the seventh century, had seen the flowering of Benedictine abbeys along its banks.

On the edge of the forest of Roumare, a field with cows. The

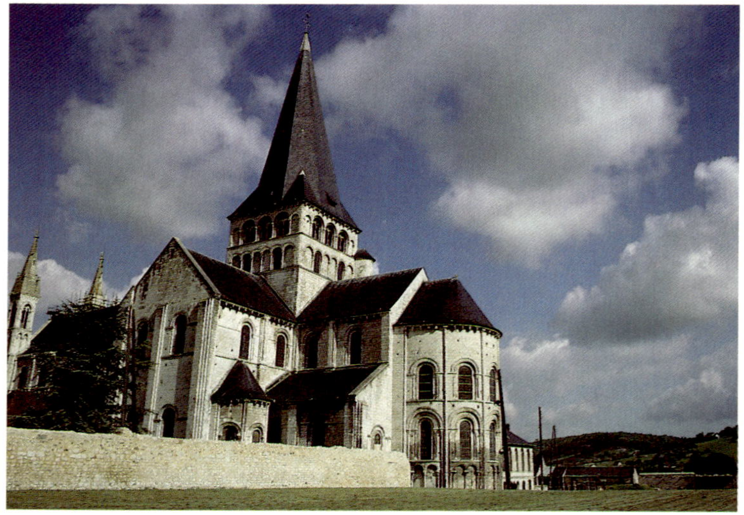

ST-MARTIN-DE-BOSCHERVILLE

cows placidly munched rich grass that made the cream that made the sauce that made the *moules à la marinière* and the *escalope normande* with calvados and apples. We turned from this meditation upon the staple of Norman cooking to an even richer vision: the Abbey at St-Martin-de-Boscherville. Norman Romanesque fitted perfectly into the rural scene, and one could imagine monks milking similar cows in the twelfth century.

At Jumièges Abbey, further downstream, the monks were also keen fishermen, catching a species of whale which provided tallow for their lamps. The monastic tradition of Saint Philibert, the abbey's founder in 654, was divided between prayer, work and study. The combination of manual work by the river and copying manuscripts in the library gave the austere life an increasing richness; and the eight hundred monks eventually

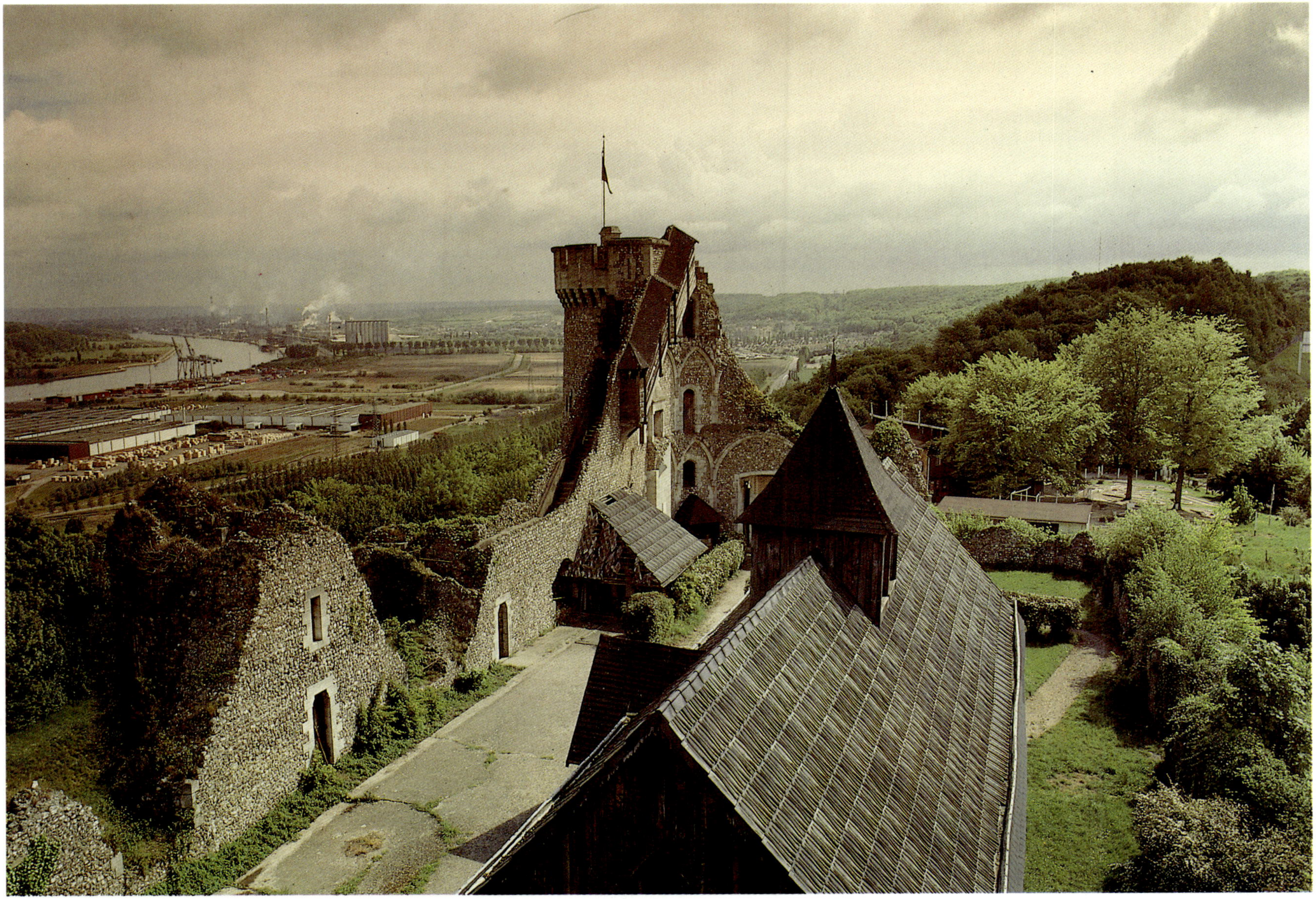

CHÂTEAU DE ROBERT LE DIABLE, NEAR ROUEN

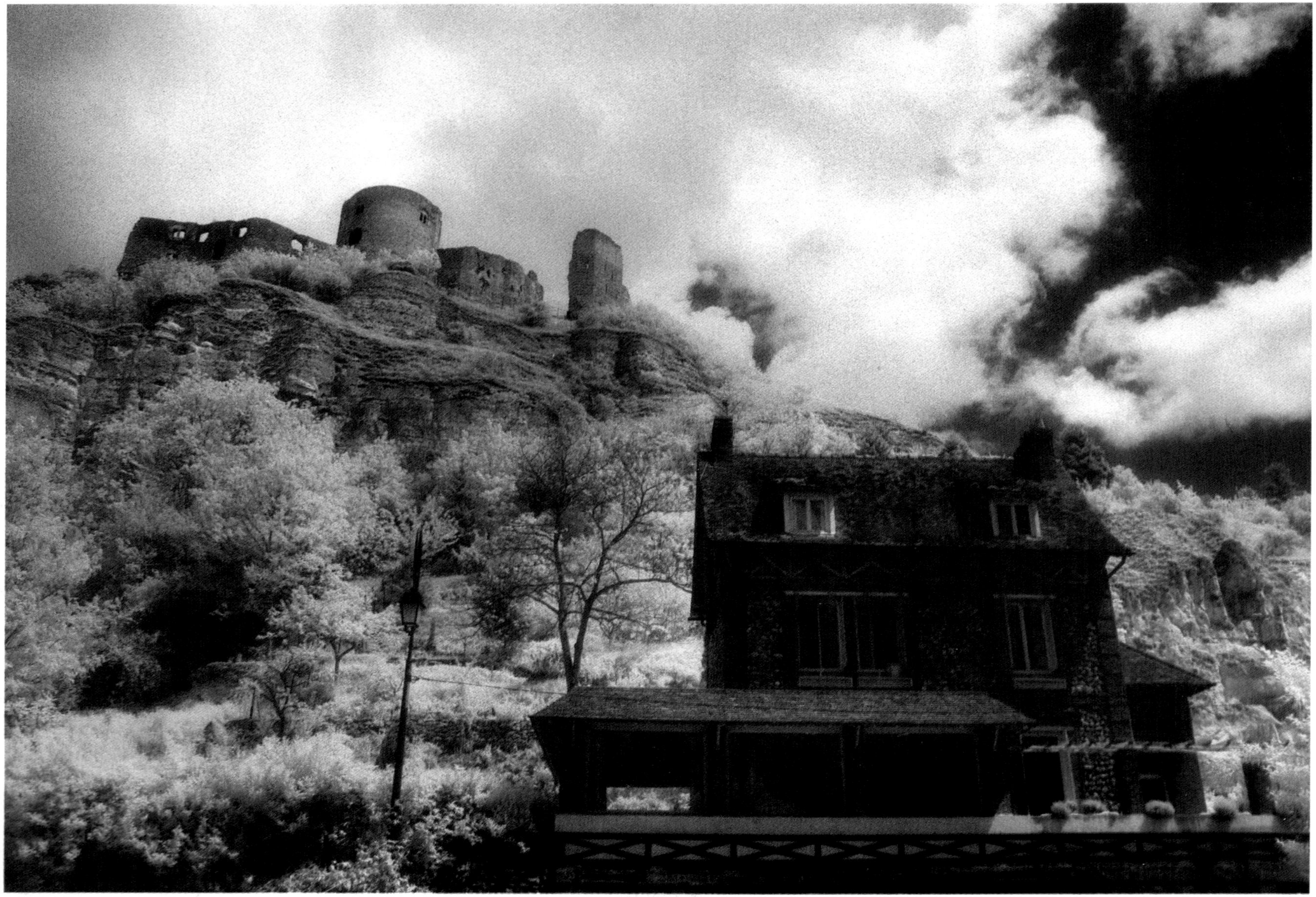

CHÂTEAU GAILLARD, LES ANDELYS

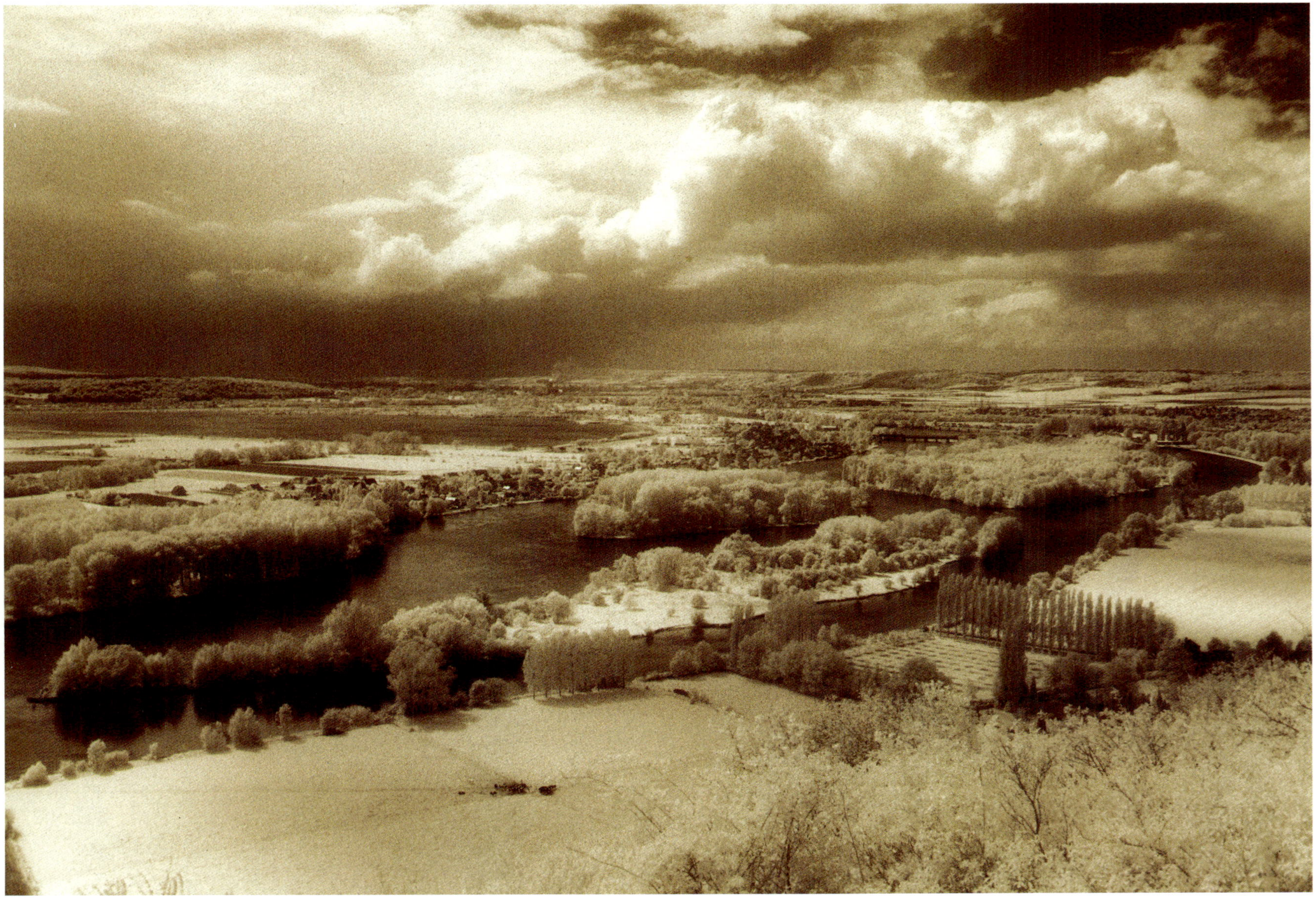

The Seine from Le Coteau des Deux Amants

had their own servants and silver, their comfort outdoing that of many a squire.

Jumièges is now a magnificent ruin. Of the three churches, Notre-Dame's twin towers rose to greet us above the trees, spectral and enchanting, like a Romanesque apparition. Its skeletal, stage-set transept and lantern-tower had rooks fluttering and swooping above us. Over to L'Eglise de St-Pierre they flew, to nest among the branches of trees now forming a roof above the ogival arches of its later Gothic additions.

We lay among the buttercups of a lush meadow behind the abbey. A bell was tolling. Bees hummed their own canticle in the lime-trees and the scent was stronger than incense. It was the perfect place to contemplate Jumièges, justly described as 'one of the most admirable ruins that exists in France'.

Not long after the abbey, down to sixteen monks, had been confiscated by the State during the Revolution, a timber merchant from Canteleu bought it and blew up the chancel in order to sell its stone. The abbey was turned into a quarry.

The fate of St-Wandrille Abbey, also founded by Saint Philibert, was a little better. But its fourteenth-century ruins are sparse, and the present monastery building is eighteenth-century. To take photographs, Carey meandered through its massive gates, which inadvertently slammed behind her. A Benedictine father remarked gleefully: '*Zut*, now she's shut in with the monks!'

Before the sound of the Gregorian chant returned in 1931, St-Wandrille had become a private house. Maurice Maeterlinck, Belgian author of *The Blue Bird*, lived there. So did Lord Stacpoole, who added a nineteenth-century front gate of hideous pomposity. May Saint Philibert forgive him.

Where did we begin this medieval meandering? Not far upstream of the locks of Amfreville. We return. Dramatic change in the river here. Upstream, a system of seven locks raises the boats to Paris; downstream, the river becomes tidal and the channel and river walls built since the Second World War mean cargo ships of up to 60,000 tons, fully loaded, can reach the port of Rouen. Rouen is the fifth largest sea-port of France – over sixty miles from the sea.

From the narrow iron footbridge beyond the locks, we look down on the Barrage de Poses, the last of the Seine's mighty, rushing weirs and quite the most awe-inspiring. The footbridge trembles under us with the force of the race, but the noise does not seem to bother a fisherman, his line cast into the water beyond detritus of driftwood and plastic bottles at the weir's edge. The fish, dazed by their rough passage, are easy prey.

Elsewhere, everything is spit-clean and ship-shape, the locks operated from a central, modern control tower equipped with closed-circuit television. An efficient lockside Bar-Restaurant serves Pelforth beer to mariners, and cream with everything.

We hurry from the bridge. A dark rainstorm is approaching upstream from Elbeuf, where the fast-running Eure joins the Seine to confuse her waters. A sinister industrial area looms from the blackness with ghostly white smoke pouring from Impressionist chimneys.

And then we are at Rouen, city of high technology, where Eurocrats dine at Dufour and Bernard Warin. Long gone are the diligences for lovers' trysts; contemporary Madame Bovarys make do with the back of an executive Renault 25, parked on a moonlit night on the Corniche, with the lights of the port and illuminated churches reflected in the river below.

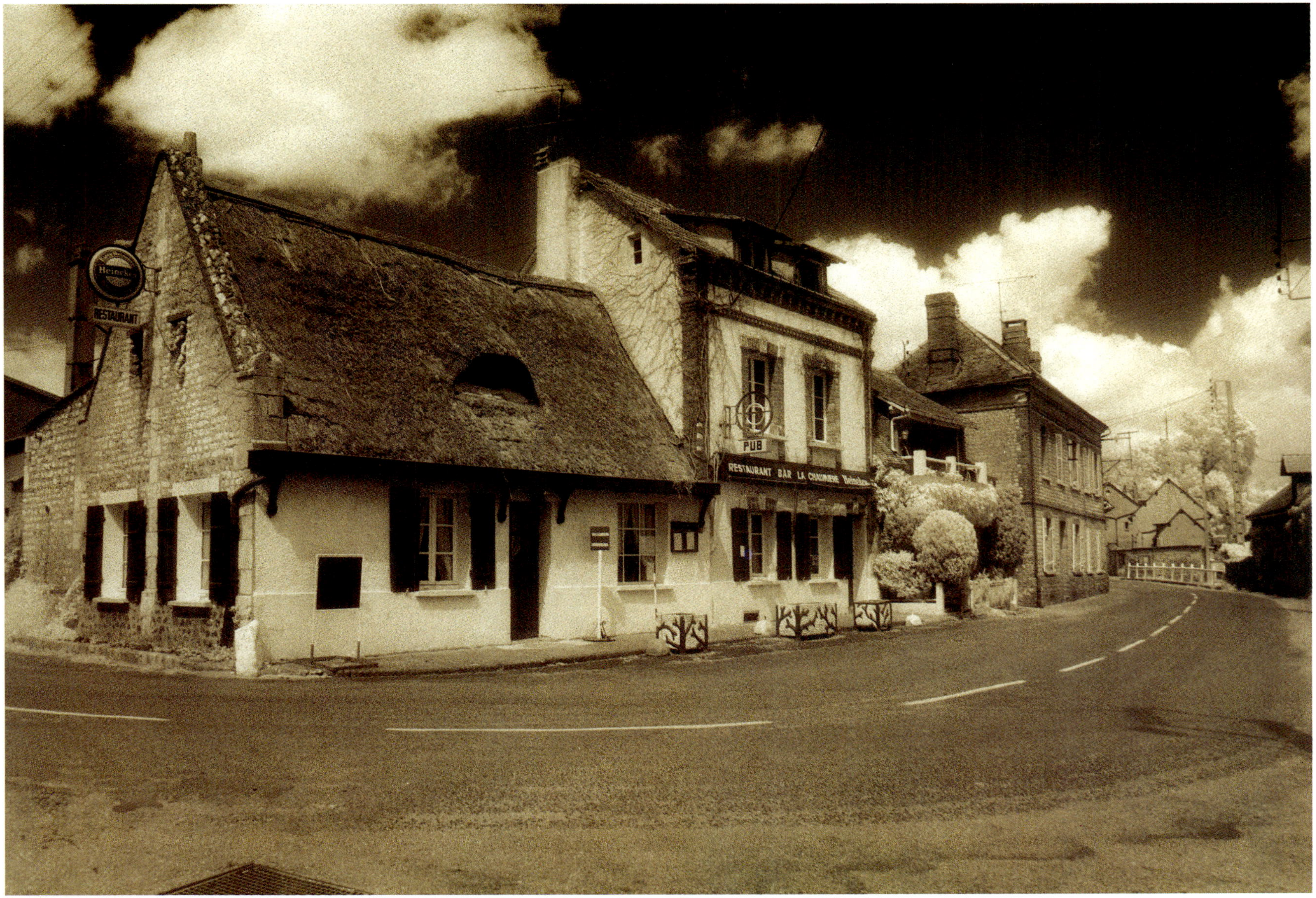

Restaurant-bar, Muids

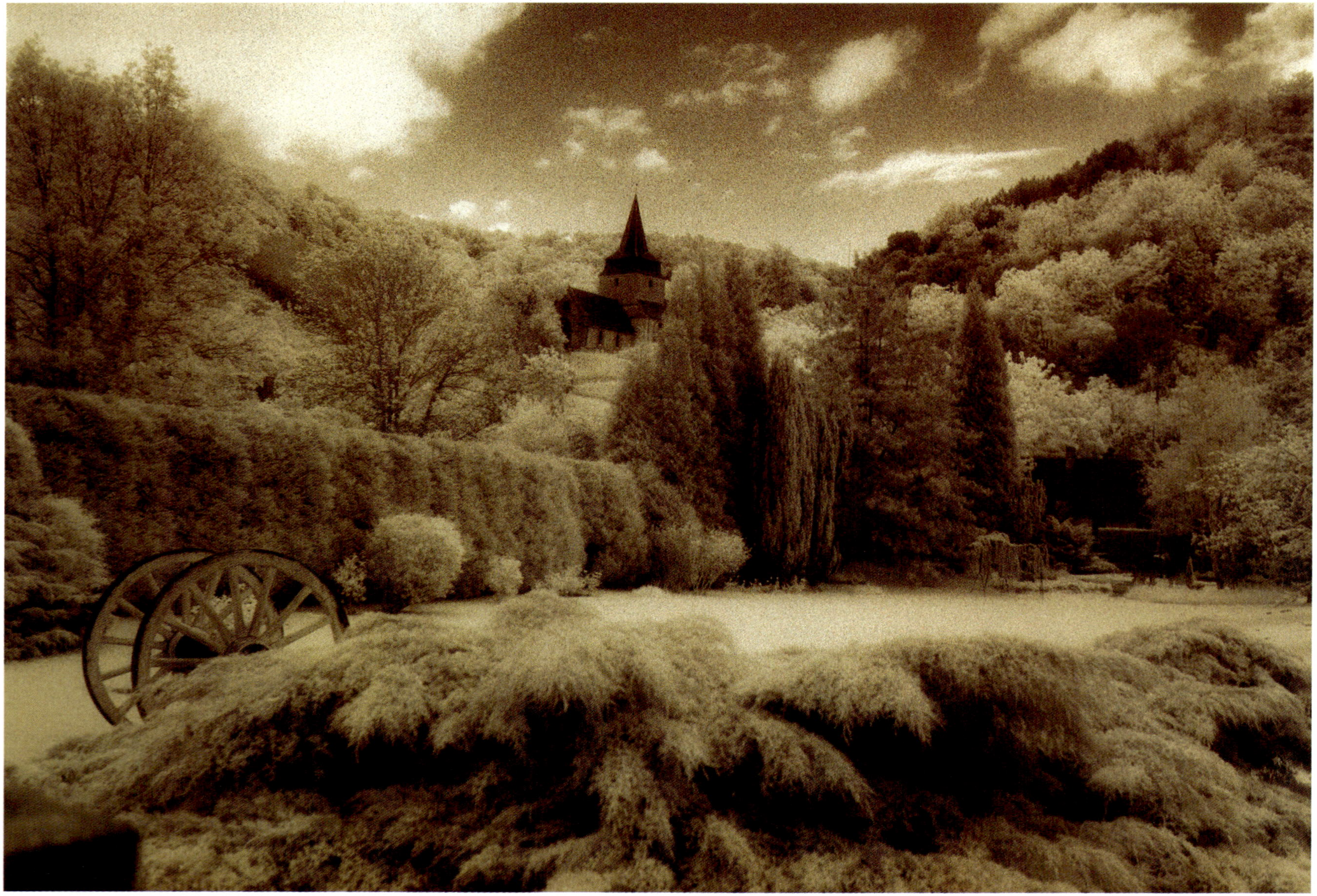

CHURCH, AMFREVILLE-SOUS-LES-MONTS

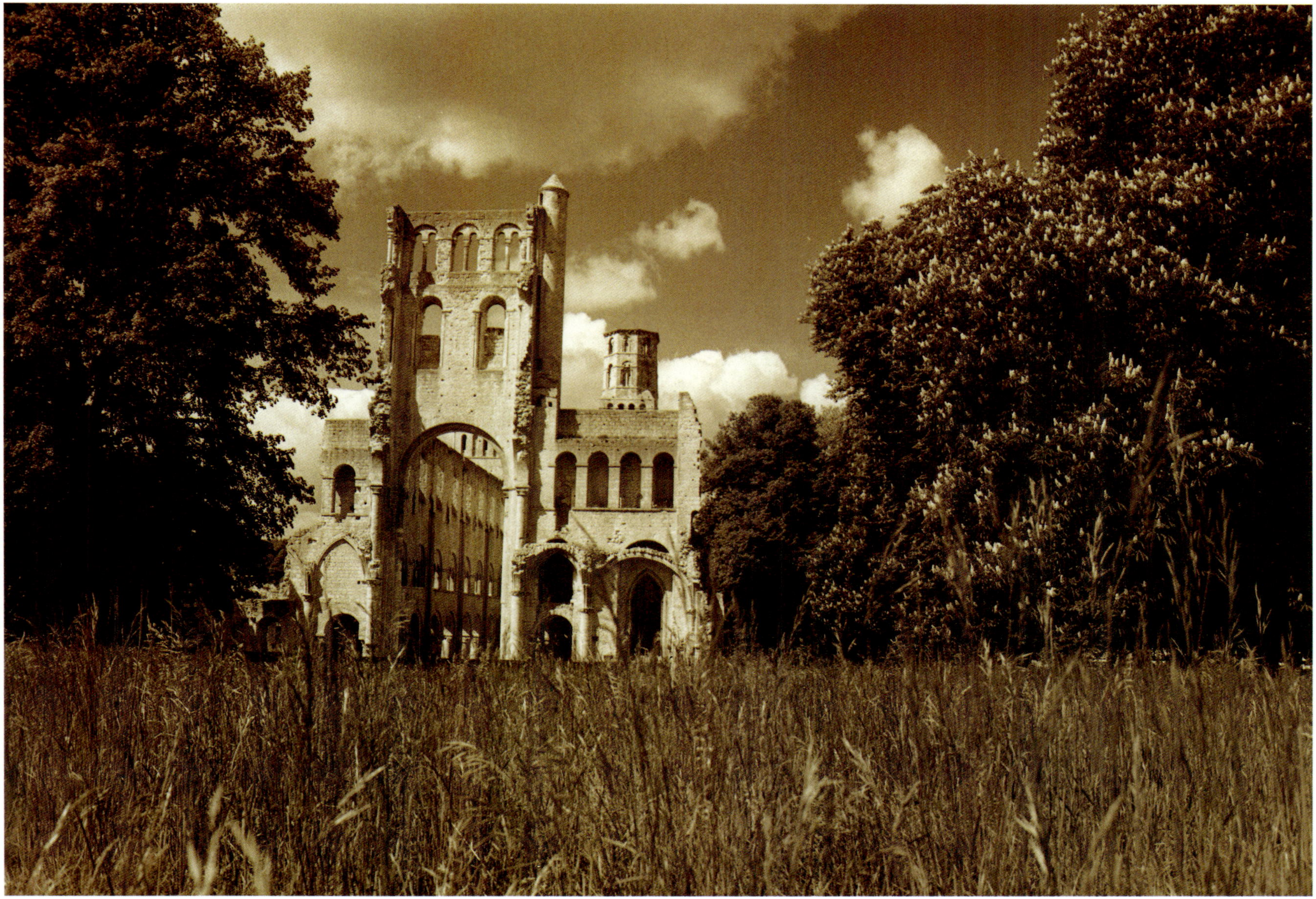

Benedictine abbey, Jumièges

WRITERS' ROUEN

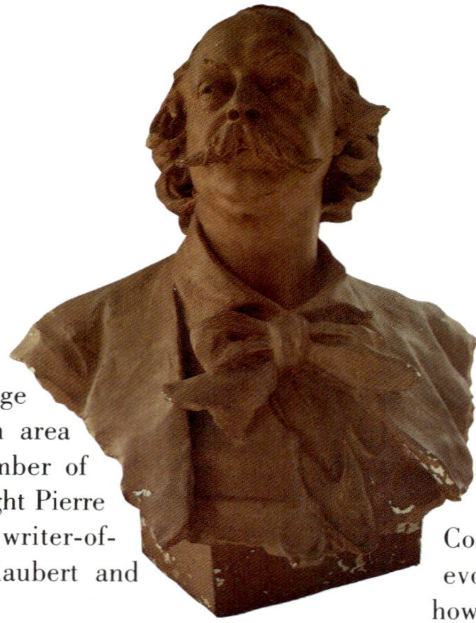

GUSTAVE FLAUBERT

Despite its industrious Seine-side image and bourgeois richesse, the Rouen area has spawned and hosted an unusual number of writers – from seventeenth-century playwright Pierre Corneille to twentieth-century Anglophile writer-of-all-work André Maurois, via Gustave Flaubert and Guy de Maupassant.

Corneille, Flaubert and Maupassant, linked by one incident, were the source of our quest.

It was a Norman summer's day. As the rain slatted into us, a dapper Vietnamese *gardien* in a smart blue suit ushered us across the garden from the gatehouse of the Manoir Pierre Corneille, near the riverside Shell Refinery at Petit-Couronne. He seemed impervious to the downpour and dreary surroundings. Quietly, he showed us the fifteenth-century, half-timbered country house, its manorial façade and original furnishings in fine order. With impeccably discreet commentary, he talked about the ennoblement of Corneille's lawyer father after the success of *Le Cid*, written by his son in the family town house off the Place du Vieux-Marché; how a menu for the bicentenary of Corneille's birth had amused diners with dishes evoking his plays – *ragoût Medée* and *bombe Cinna*; how Corneille's sitting for hours at that very chair and writing table, his spirit wracked by Jesuitical self-torment, had never altered his belief that with God's help the Will could conquer all; how his classical inspiration was still honoured by the occasional performance of a play at the manor's grassy Greek amphitheatre. The cathartic rain outside was well timed.

But, good though our guide might be, my mind was elsewhere, obsessed with another image: Flaubert and Maupassant, those two equally introverted Normans, together at this same house more than a century ago, paying homage to Corneille. By an old pond with a stone in the middle, the authors felt a kinship with

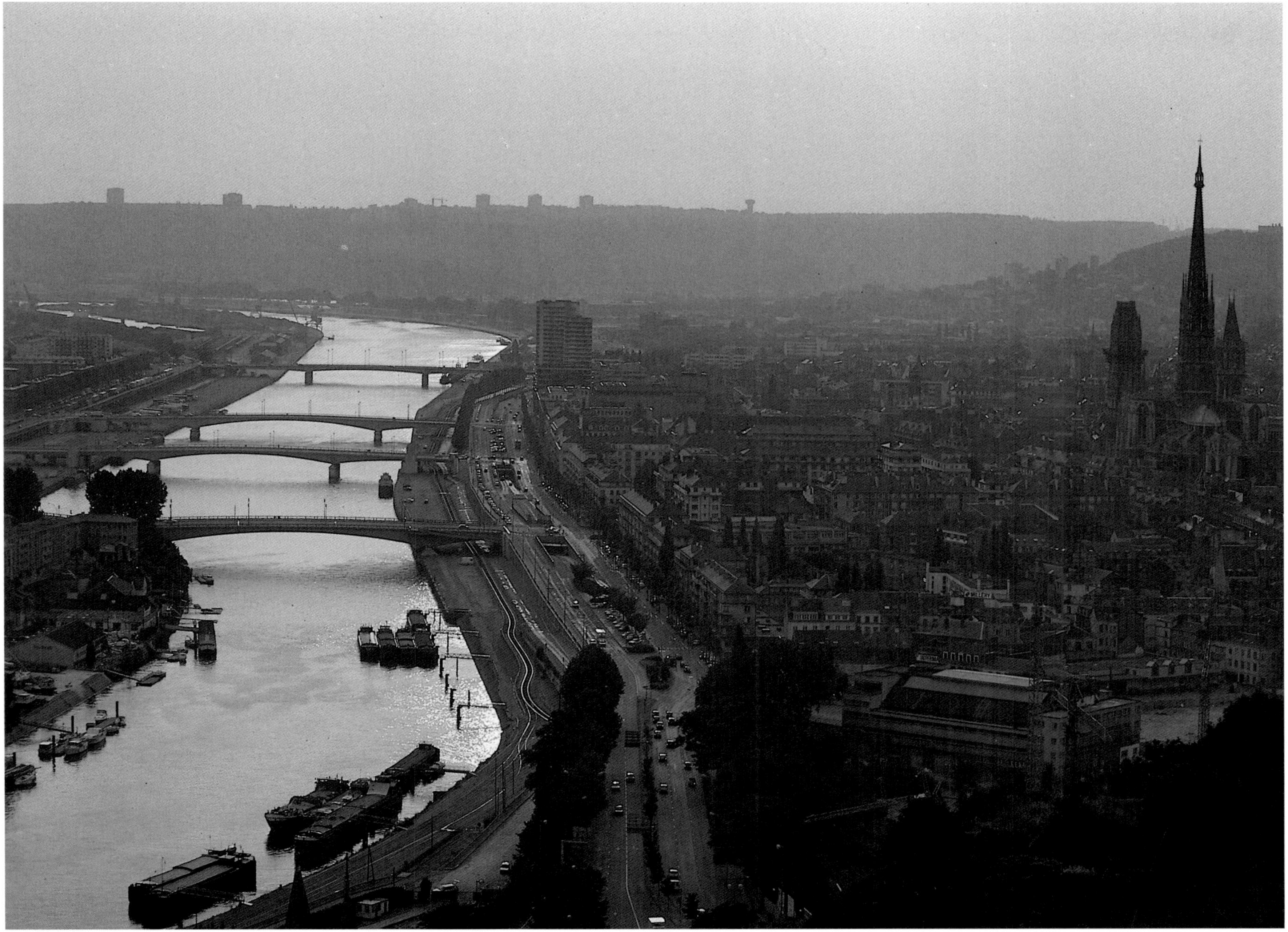

Rouen from the Corniche, sunset

their illustrious predecessor; being Norman, he must, they agreed, have spent hours contemplating that stone in stagnant water. To fix his eye on something hard and concrete amid the dead liquid of the world around it.

Flaubert and Maupassant shared Corneille's Norman need for water, stagnant or in motion, and in particular a closeness to the Seine. Like Corneille, Flaubert was born (1821) into the *professions libérales*: his father was a Rouen surgeon, and the present Musée Flaubert at L'Hôtel-Dieu hospital celebrates both father and son.

Rouen seemed to specialize in exotic guides: this time, we were shown round by a jovial man in a white coat with a distinct bedside manner. A retired medic? With hearty quips, he showed off gruesome nineteenth-century medical instruments – and I immediately thought of Flaubert *fils*, dissecting bourgeois society with a sharp and merciless scalpel. Among the exhibits was one of Flaubert's famous parrots. 'The real one, of course,' said the guide.

Julian Barnes' biographical novel *Flaubert's Parrot* is a must for anyone travelling the Seine, and I was glad to see a copy in French had been given pride of place in the Pavillon Flaubert at Croisset, a suburb of Rouen. Here we found yet another parrot. The real one, of course. They were everywhere, according to Barnes. The *fil conducteur* of his erudite and funny literary quest is: will the 'real parrot' please perk up and be recognized? The real parrot is the one borrowed by Flaubert from the city museum as a model for Loulou, the pet in his story 'A Simple Heart'.

The *pavillon* was all that remained of Flaubert's home – a little riverside box of a place with bits and pieces of memorabilia. Here, the female guide told us, Monsieur Flaubert would come to rest, exhausted by love affairs, epilepsy, and the *Madame Bovary* trial. As she spoke, beyond the windows a freighter loomed large on its way to the sea. In the writer's day there had been a white, eighteenth-century house with a terrace overlooking the river; one could imagine Flaubert, the observer, watching through sharply-focused binoculars the rich bourgeoisie on their Sunday boat trips. From Croisset, he could take the paddle-steamer up to Rouen, as his hero Frédéric had done to Nogent, watching the city's approach with jaundiced eye. There was no love lost between him and his birthplace, and no fitting monument remains to him – except his own words. To the Rouen of his time, Flaubert, son of the good doctor, was a dissolute pornographer; the curé of Canteleu, next village downstream from Croisset, forbade his parishioners to read that shocking *Madame Bovary*. And Flaubert himself admitted: 'All of us Normans have a little cider in our veins: it's a bitter, fermented drink which sometimes bursts the bung.'

Guy de Maupassant was rumoured to be Flaubert's son and it was often remarked how benevolently Flaubert treated him. Flaubert spent time encouraging him in his writing, understanding the mordant Norman temperament.

After schooling in Rouen, Maupassant escaped joining the Naval Ministry to write and sail dinghies on the Seine. And, in 1880, following in his master's footsteps, he wrote to Flaubert: 'I am definitely being prosecuted for outrage to manners and public morality!!! All because of "By the Water's Side".' In French the title of Maupassant's poem was not so innocent – *'Au Bord de L'Eau'* hid the word *bordel*; brothels were, in those days, situated by a river, so that neither the girls nor their clients need ever go short of water. But it was not the sort of thing the curé of Canteleu would like his parishioners to know, let alone read in a poem.

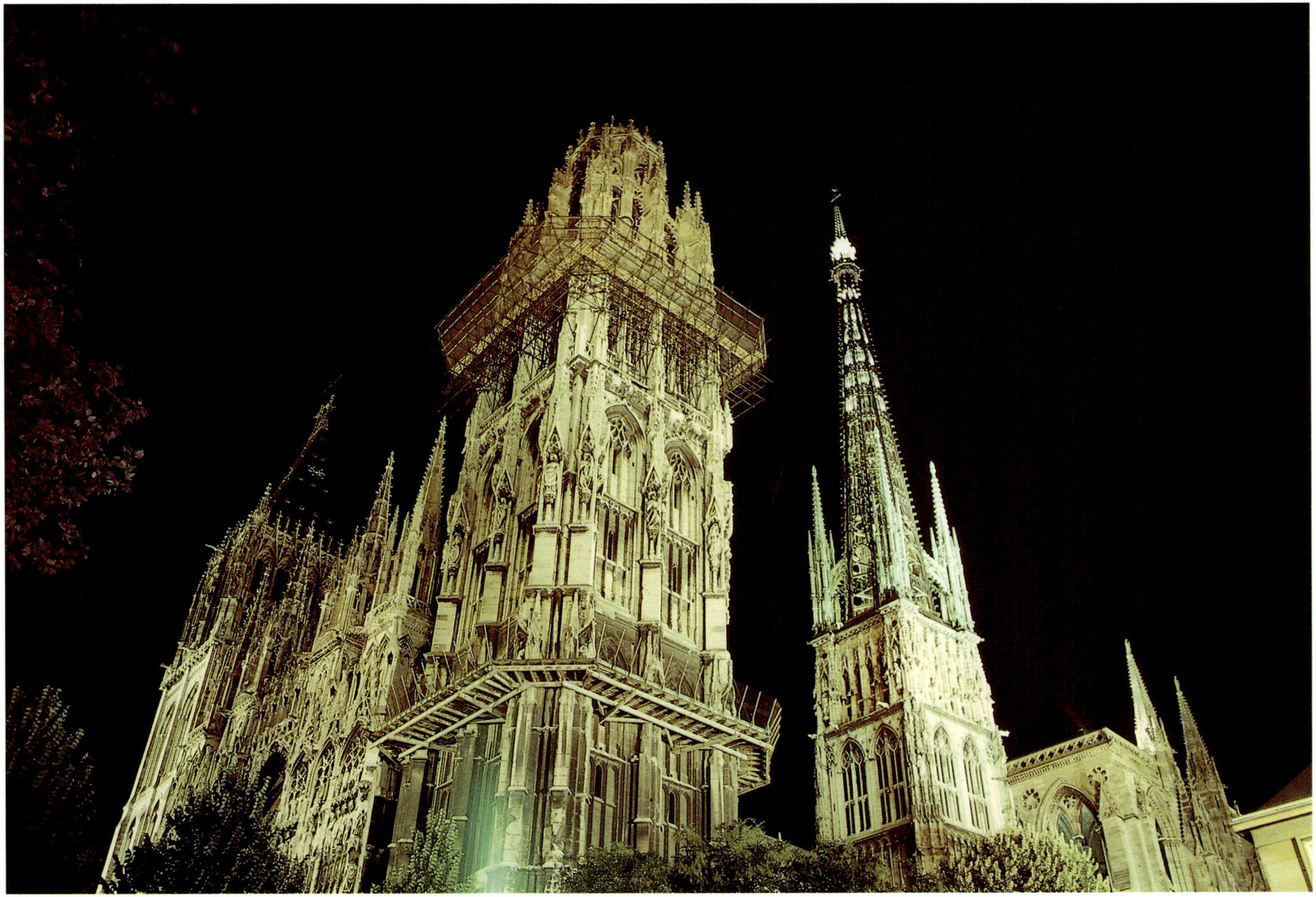

ROUEN CATHEDRAL, FLOODLIT

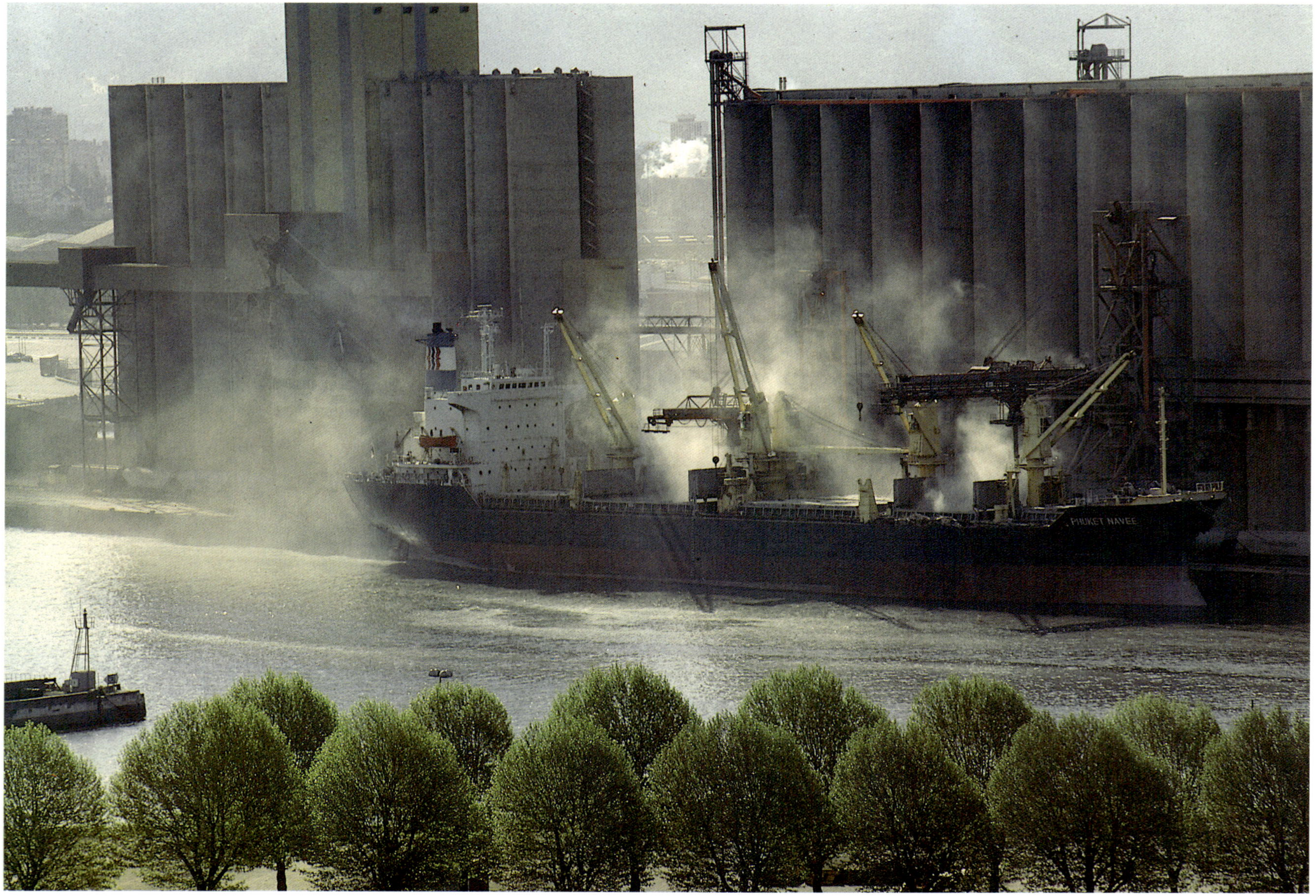

Port of Rouen

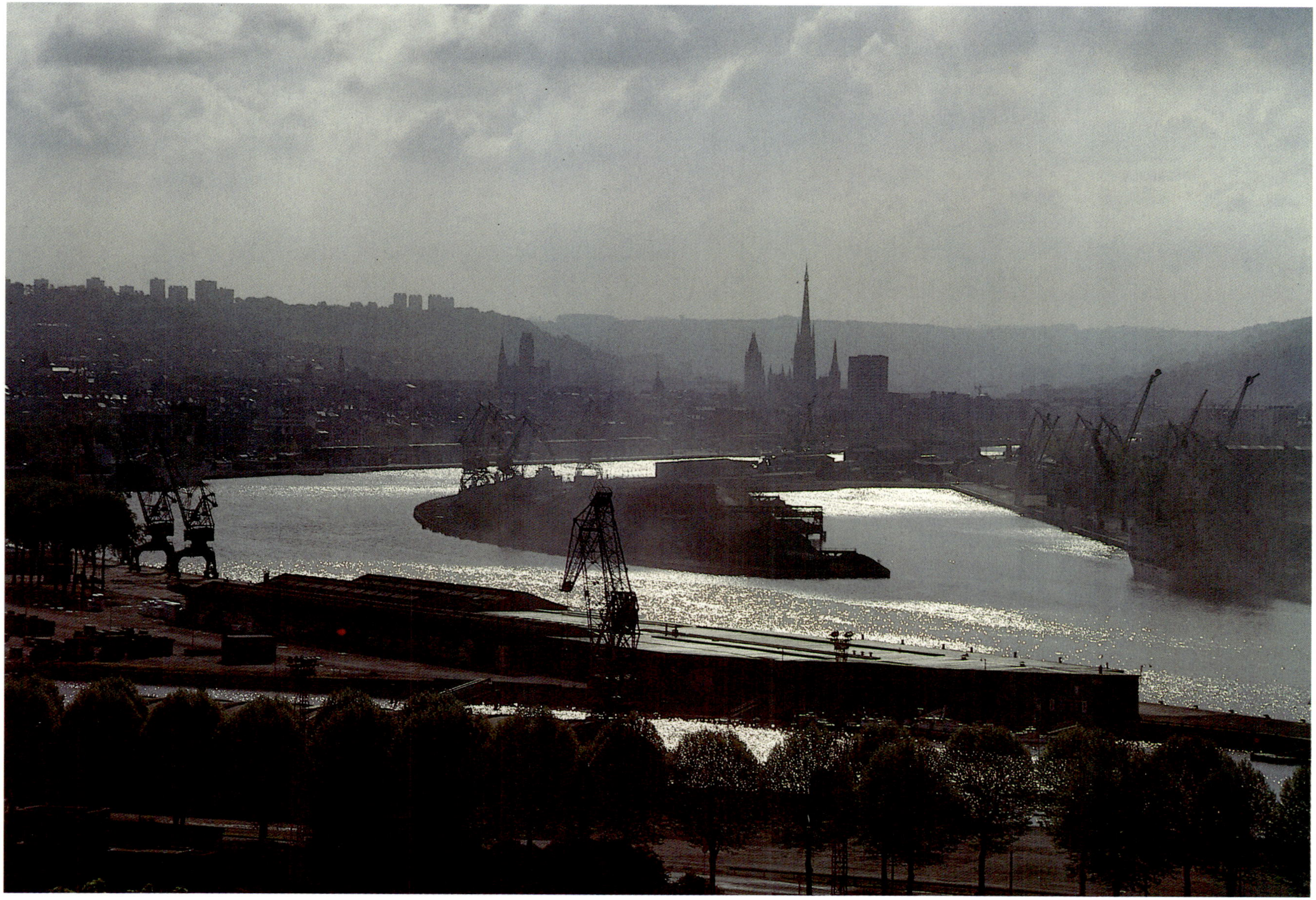

Rouen from Canteleu

Maupassant, seeing life as a constant conflict of extremes, loved the paradoxical nature of the Seine. In 'Springtime' the intoxication of a country cruise on a *bateau-mouche* whetted the sexual appetites of lovers; but the heroes of 'Paul's Girl' and 'Simon's Father' both drowned themselves. For the fisherman in 'On The Water', the Seine was '. . . the land of mirages and strange visions . . .', a tombless cemetery where the dead return, wearing their death-masks to haunt their lovers.

In the lagoons along the river, water was as stagnant as the motionless, limited lives of Norman country folk, fixed in their ways. But the river was also wide, long and winding, with the sails of boats catching the wind, filling the heart with a sense of freedom and escape. For Maupassant, the Seine was a bitch goddess, destroyer and liberator – and, above all, deeply seductive.

A real-life literary tragedy surrounds the premature death of the eldest daughter of Victor-Hugo. In 1843, six months after their marriage, Léopoldine and her husband Charles had come by boat to visit their lawyer in Caudebec-en-Caux. On the return voyage, the weather worsened, and capsized the boat. They were both drowned. Ironically, Charles's family were descended from river pilots; their house at Villequier, with its fine Empire furniture, is now a charming small museum by the river, full of Victor-Hugo memorabilia, and fresh flowers in every room. The poet, inconsolable, wrote one of his most moving poems about setting out at dawn to visit his daughter's grave.

A vast national park fills the concave meander across the river from Caudebec. Le Parc Naturel Régional de Brotonne has acres of forest, villages where dying trades are practised, and a thirteenth-century windmill, Le Moulin de Hauville. The name

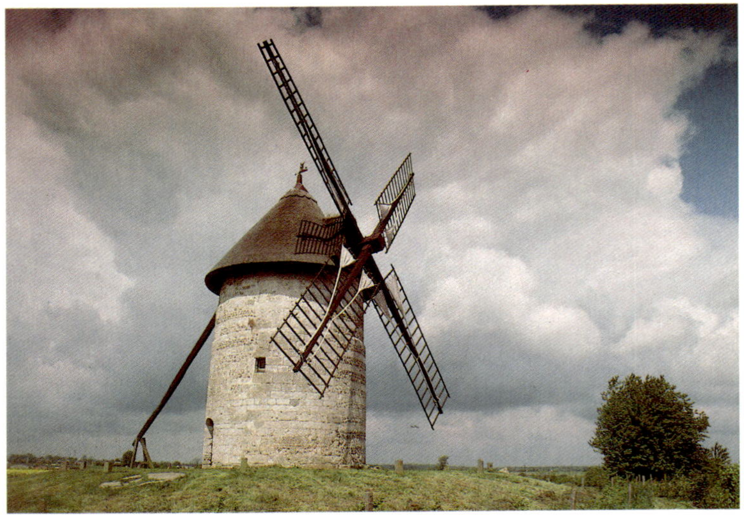

Moulin de Hauville

Brotonne means Breton; monks from Brittany were the first to christianize the lower Seine.

There is a stunning view of the forest from the terrace of the Château d'Etelan, owned by a couple called Boudier, one from Le Havre, the other from Rouen, their Renaissance home conveniently placed between the two. Madame Boudier gives us a warm welcome, although it's Sunday and the house is not open to the public in May. Children are playing in the shadows of the flamboyant Gothic roof.

From the terrace, the Seine, its waters hidden by the lie of the land, is a presence felt rather than seen. A cargo ship appears to be floating majestically across distant fields between us and the forest – a dreamlike amphibian as out of place as a Rolls-Royce encountered in mid-Atlantic.

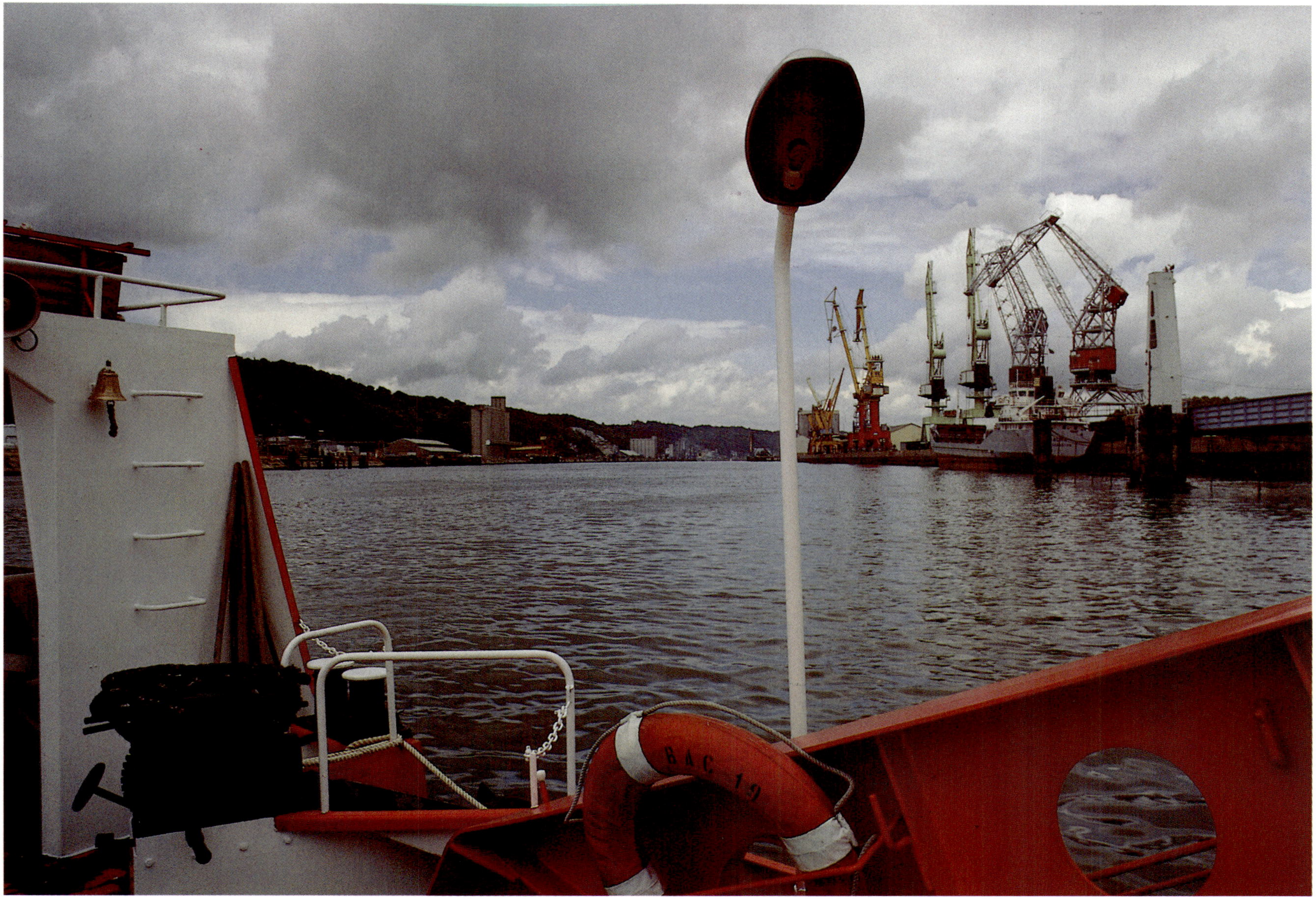

FERRY, PETIT COURONNE

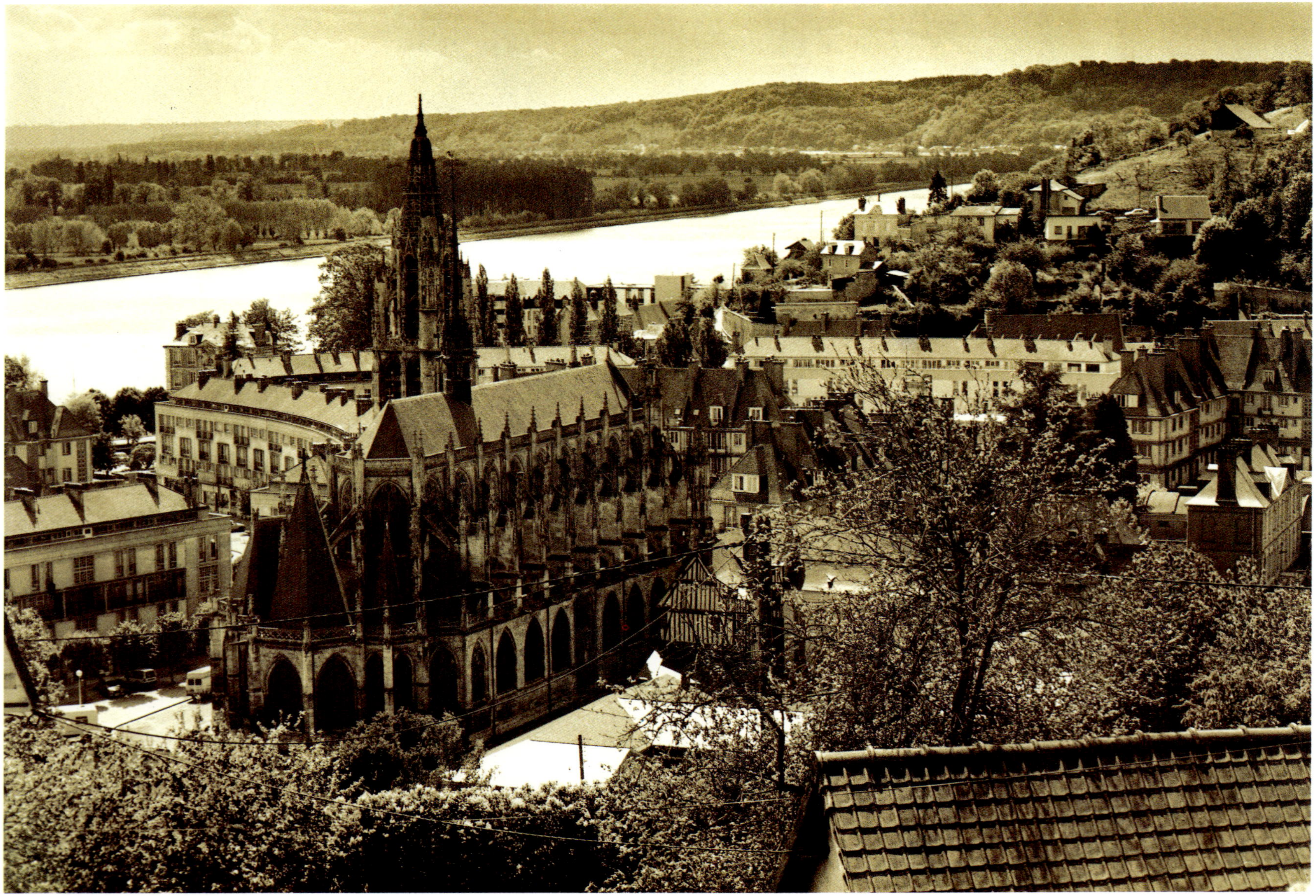

NOTRE DAME, CAUDEBEC-EN-CAUX

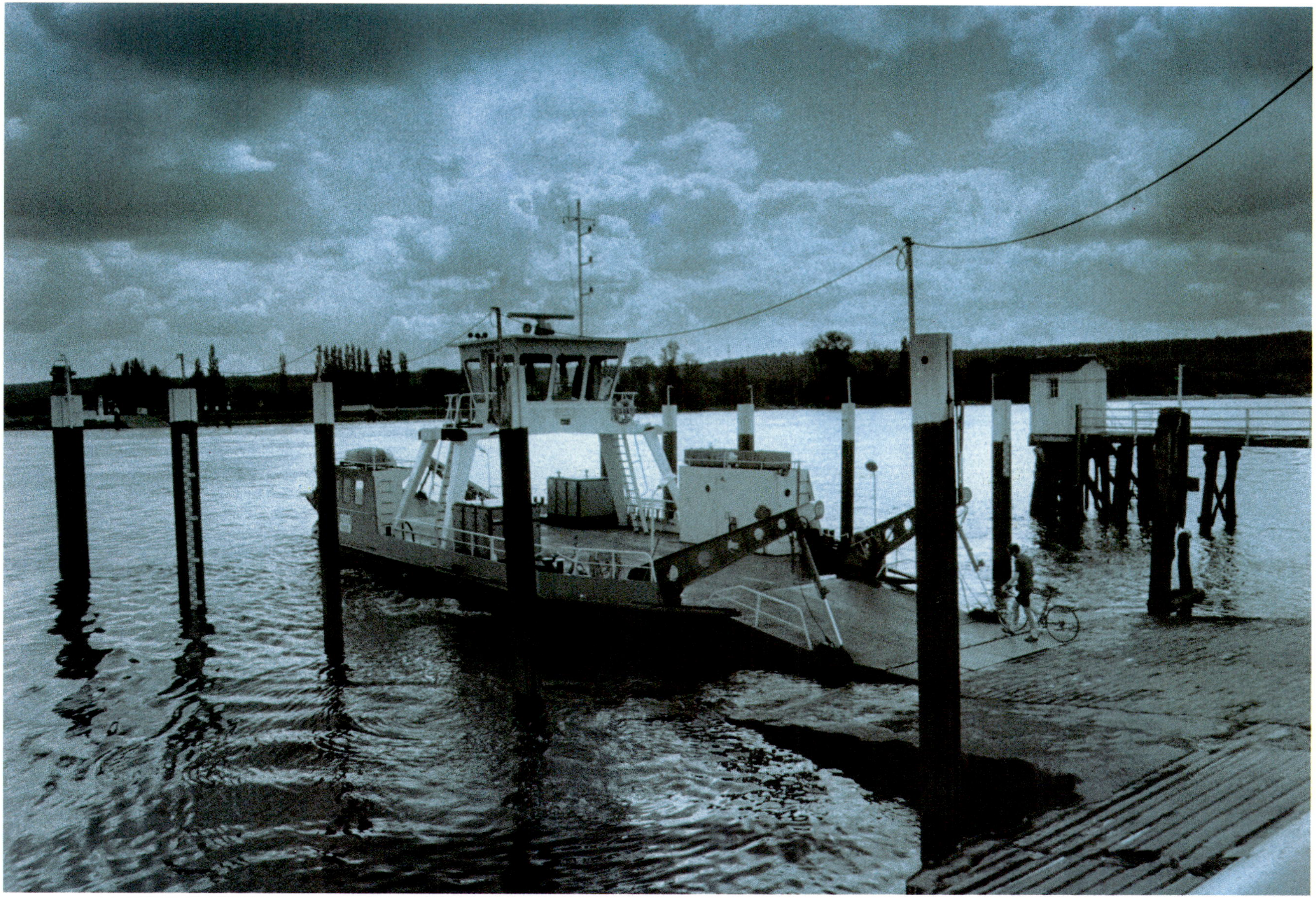

FERRY, LE MESNIL-SOUS-JUMIÈGES

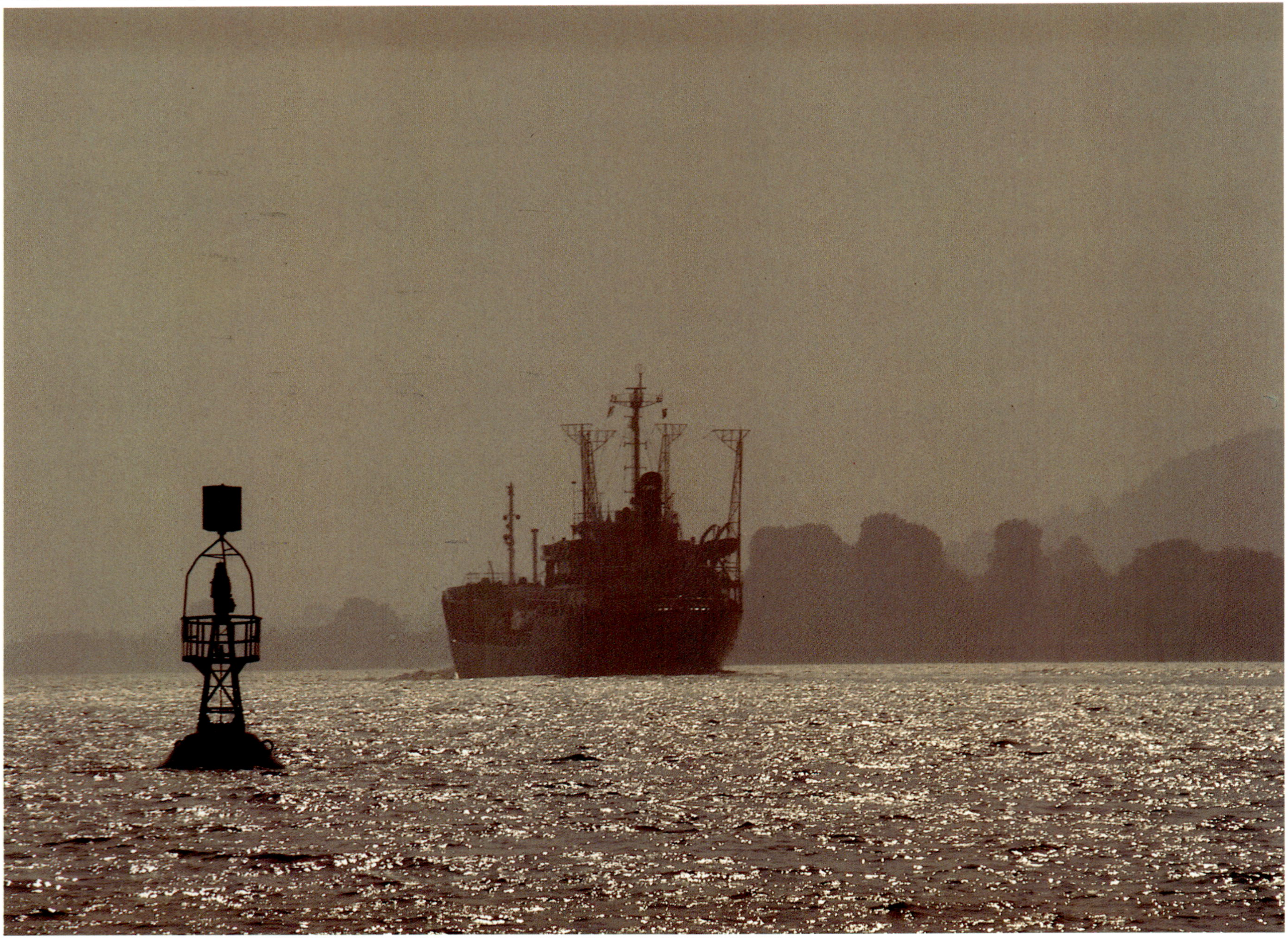

Cargo ship, Pointe de la Roque

A Norman Corrida

At the western end of the forest of Brotonne, I became aware of the sea's comparative closeness. Though we were still twenty-five miles from the English Channel, valley began to widen into estuary, the steep escarpments on the concave side of the bends giving way to gentler slopes of woodland. An intense, painter's light bathed the rich, flat marshlands ahead of us. And the farming villages grew more frequent.

Vieux-Port, at low tide, had gulls lounging on the sandbanks. It was a village almost too perfect: on the thatched roofs of cottages, irises grew and blossomed; apple orchards were everywhere; and I sensed the nearby presence of potters potting, weavers weaving, and cider presses crushing, and seemed to hear, above the squawk of seabirds, a rhythmic clang from the blacksmith's anvil.

It was hallucinatory countryside. And in that clear, shimmering light, I could be forgiven a mirage or two. Was that a *drakkar* ploughing upstream between the fields? Or a *gribane*, that sturdy wooden Seine barge of the last century? We were approaching the Marais Vernier. Longhorn Scottish cattle grazed on its marshy pastures, tossing the flies from their fringes. White horses galloped, manes flying in the west wind. And sheep grazed on the saltings. Down there, below the lighthouse at St-Samson-de-la-Roque, they chomped the rich grass along the river bank and achieved their *pré salé* (salt-meadow) status. But, that day, it was another animal's turn to steal the Marais Vernier show.

In the stillness of a country lane near the ferry village of Quillebeuf, I thought I was hearing things again. This time, it seemed like a befuddled football commentary – in what language it was impossible to tell. But there was not a car in sight, no GB with a holiday home in Normandy, its radio tuned in to Liverpool versus Huddersfield United. A gusty breeze off the river didn't help. I listened harder, and traced the now-you-hear-me-now-you-don't voice across a meadow to the edge of St-Aubin-sur-Quillebeuf.

We approached. Parked cars now lined the hedgerows. And at the entrance to a field, local farmers and their families bought tickets or, being notables, were waved through without paying. The commentary, loud and rasping now, came over the PA system as unintelligibly as a train announcement. What could it be? Bear-baiting? Cock-fighting? There was a small ring, round which haycarts had been placed to make a grandstand. We climbed up on one, inserting ourselves among the spectators.

Nothing, at that moment, was going on. A large rubber pool of water in the centre of the ring told us little. Swimming races? Water polo? Not deep enough. But there was an air of expectancy. Tension mounted. Five local lads and one lusty girl assembled in the ring, to the cheers of the crowd. Suddenly, with no trumpets or alarums, what should appear in the ring but ten baby wild boar, hurtling like Gadarene swine to a fate much less final. With fearsome yells, the five lads and the girl hurled themselves upon their protagonists, which were as slippery as giant eels.

In a few seconds, the ring was a mayhem of human bodies flying this way and that, falling, grabbing at wild boar run amok. The contest was more than equal. Each 'matador' had to grab the tail or back legs of his 'bull' (or any other grabable part) and drag him to the water. The whole wild boar, and nothing but the wild boar, had to be immersed. But, of course, many times his opponent got a thorough drenching, too. The brave 'Senorita Matador' rolled over and over in the water with her equally brave wild boar, splashing about as though in passionate embrace. Even the *aficionados* in the crowd cheered and laughed.

The winner was the one who immersed the most wild boar, during a timed bout that seemed endless. I was too enthralled to check its exact duration, say three minutes. And keeping the score, in the chaos of tumbling bodies, human and porcine, was well nigh impossible. In any case, the day was not really about winners or losers. Neither got hurt. It was a good laugh. And at St-Aubin-sur-Quillebeuf, that breezy Sunday, the cider barrels emptied as fast as that pool slopped out its water.

Well, Spain was in the Common Market – and many nations before Spain had passed along that stretch of the Seine.

Viva los bravos Normanes!

Opposite the Marais Vernier, the right bank of the Seine is equally international – but how different! Plonked in the middle of this dream countryside, Port-Jérome. And the dream becomes something of a nightmare. A short mile across the river from wild boar corridas and apple orchards and lowing cattle, a vast petro-chemical complex covers the waterfront.

In our boat, we drift past a windowless biscuit box of a building, marked Esso. Along the endless wharfs, huge bursts of graffiti indicate the loading bays of regular tankers – one in Cyrillic characters for a Russian ship. A wreck of a Thirties building, glimpsed between derricks, bears witness to Port-Jérome's beginnings. Deceptive, because all else is a contemporary, high-tech art show of gaily-coloured pipes and funnels and cranes. Nightmare is an exaggeration, perhaps. Just a culture shock, as one's nose adjusts from warm hay to petro-chemical fumes. A red fire-fighting gun looks like a child's space toy, and security men in plastic helmets eye us with interest and wave, like children to a passing train.

Ahead, more high-tech art. The Tancarville suspension bridge, an H with supporting wires languidly festooned, nearly a mile of spare elegance, spans the river from marsh to limestone cliffs. Above us, 157 feet up, heavy freight trucks creep across, bound for Le Havre or the autoroute to Paris; and higher still a tiny maintenance trolley, like a toy funicular, travels the suspension wires. Looking upwards, a vertiginous twinge goes from head to vitals as we pass beneath.

Completed in 1958, with not a single mortal accident, the Pont de Tancarville and the Pont de Brotonne (1977) are the only two bridges across the river between the sea and Rouen; they combine the best of French engineering and architecture, practical, spare, with respect for the surrounding countryside.

Just beyond the bridge begins the Canal de Tancarville. Spanning the centuries are two twentieth-century locks and a tenth-century château, near where William the Conqueror assembled his barons for the invasion of England. The canal was built in 1887 so that inland waterways transport, between there and Le Havre, could avoid the estuary's variable tides, shifting sandbanks and submerged wrecks. The Seine estuary was once known as The Ship's Graveyard. We are just about to enter it. It looks as peaceful as Père-Lachaise.

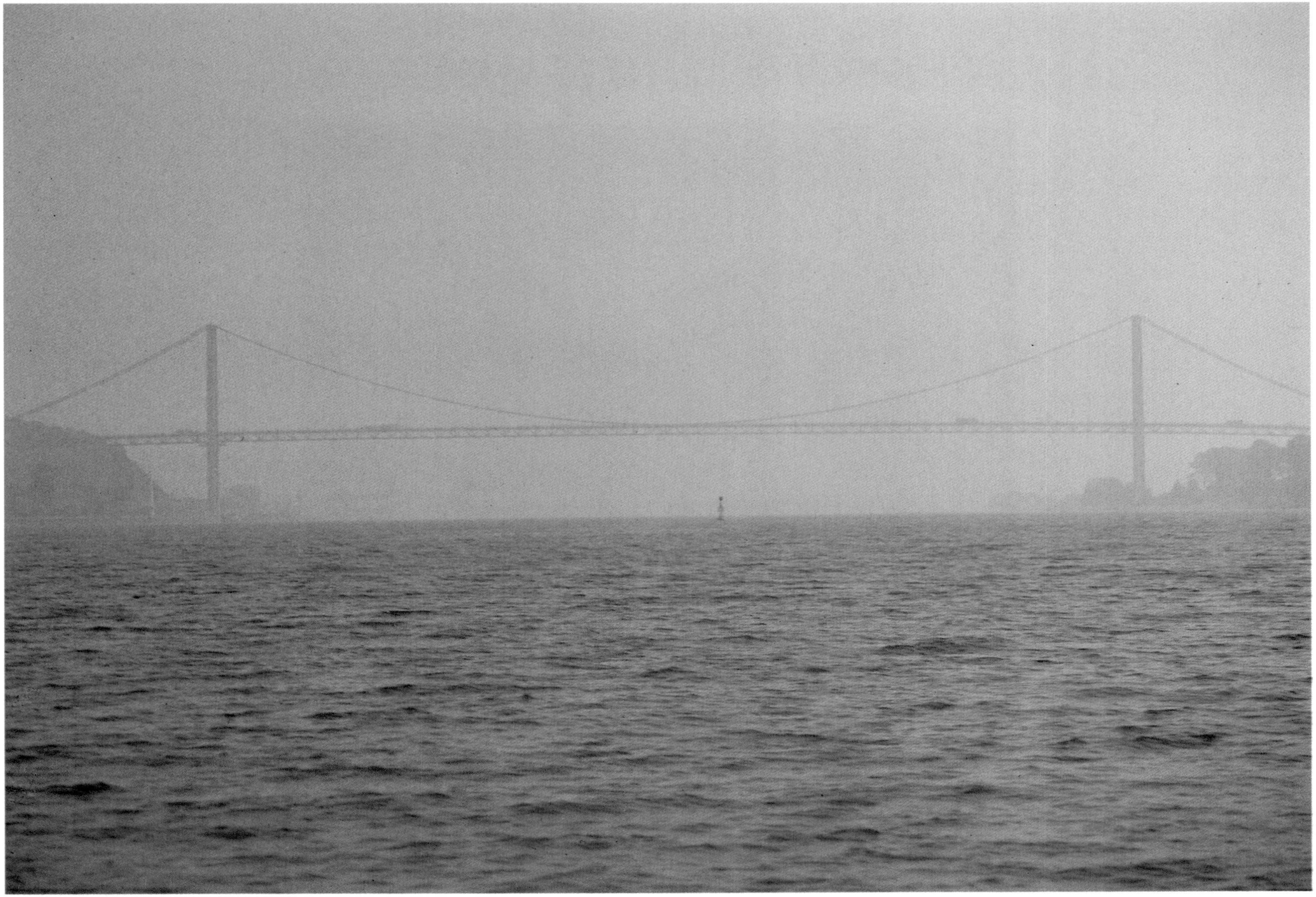

PONT DE TANCARVILLE

A Fair Wind to Honfleur

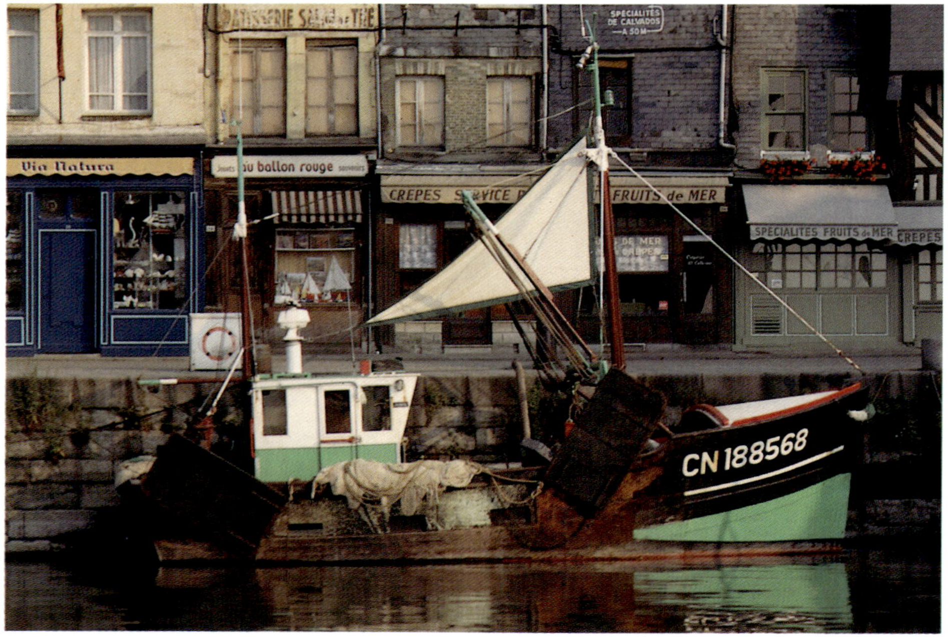

For the last reach of the river, from Quillebeuf to Le Havre, we had bummed a ride on an old friend's yacht.

'How much water have we got, Leslie?' asked Dick, the *Persona Grata's* owner, constantly sounding depths and studying charts. Leslie, his co-yachtsman, inspecting the depth-sounder, kept us off the sandbanks.

Dick and Leslie, though in their late sixties, were ocean yachtsman, and unfazed by the Seine's treacherous waters. But the trip from Rouen, beautiful scenically, could be hard going. A cargo ship took six hours, private pleasure boats much longer.

Pleasure gives way to cargo. And now, once again, Dick had to navigate us out of the deep water channel to let a tanker past. Yet another bound for Esso-Saf at Port-Jérome. Priority to petro-chemicals was the order of the day and night.

QUAI-STE-CATHERINE, HONFLEUR

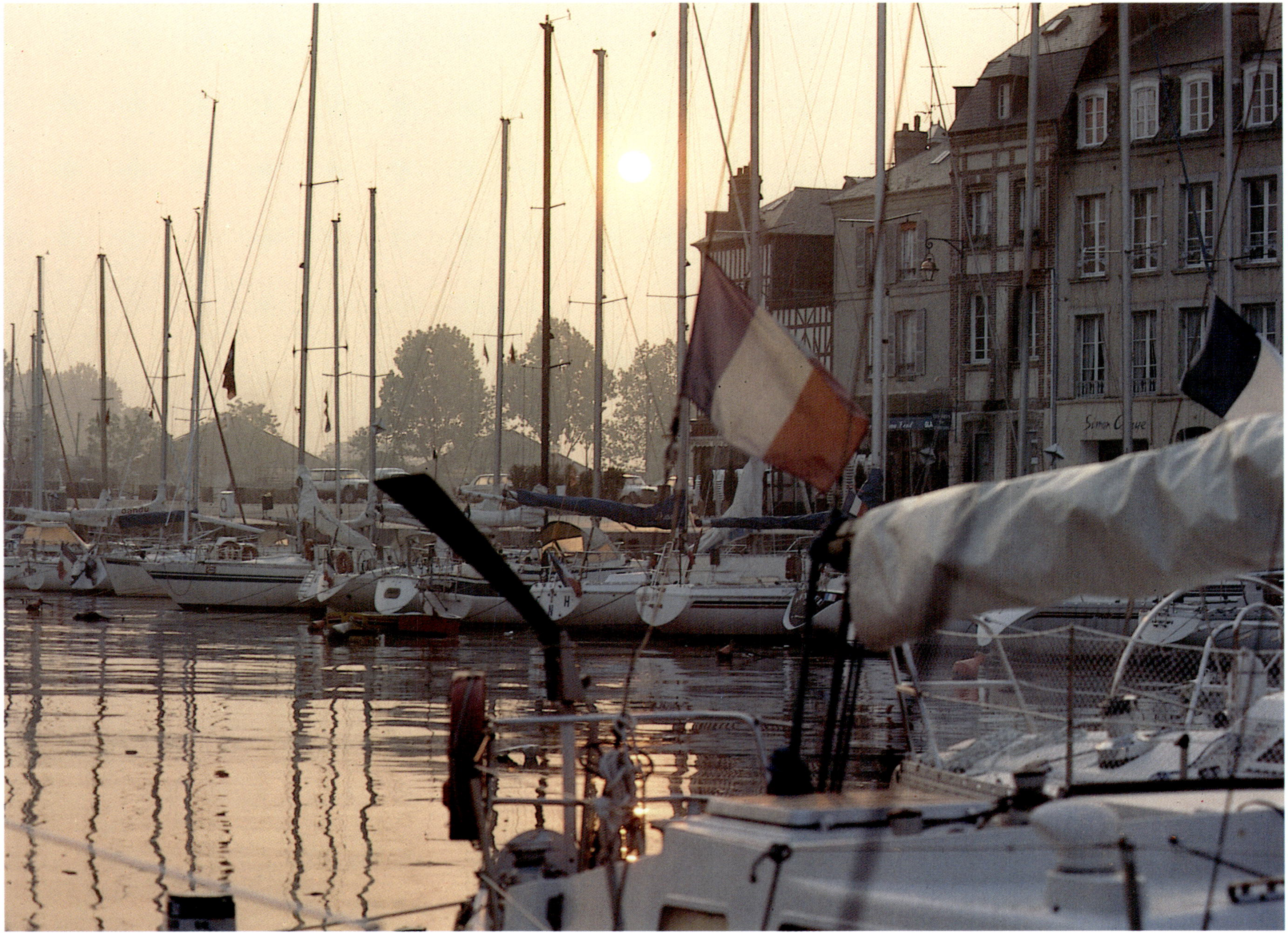

Yacht Marina, Honfleur

To save us from a good rock-and-rolling, he swung us over, bows into the tanker's wash. Still we pitched and tossed, and waves broke against the river walls. That wash could be dangerous, Dick said, if you moored to the bank for the night – and not exactly conducive to a good night's rest.

But now the river was widening. Dick hoisted the mainsail for the following wind which had blown up. The diesel engine cut, and the only sound was lapping of water and flapping of wings as tern dived for fish. On the left bank, cows grazed. The lighthouse at the Point de la Roque stood out on its cliff. And the tributary of La Risle – last of the many since La Douix at Châtillon – wound away between reedy banks into rich, alluvial farming country.

Ahead, Le Havre to starboard – a city of gleaming petroleum storage tanks, catching the light of the evening sun. Across a Boudin panorama brought up to date, a few timeless, wispy clouds hung over the Channel's choppy aspect. And, on the south side of the river's mouth, the Radar Control Tower of Honfleur, that mariner's landmark, beckoned encouragingly.

Dick and Leslie, in yachtspeak, were deep into high water times. 'Honfleur is minus twenty-five . . .' 'But you said minus —!' 'That was Deauville.' 'Well, we should make it by six.' 'Six is pushing it.' 'Six-ten, then.' 'Six-five.'

At six-seven precisely, we were entering the Vieux-Bassin, Honfleur. The road-bridge was raised, and a veritable flotilla of yachts, bow to stern, poured into the dock for the night. How would we all fit in? There were yachts of all shapes and sizes, from family tubs to an impressive British racer, *Zulu*, all spit and polish and pretty sailors busying about in a most seamanlike manner. Genuine ocean-goers here. French and British yachtsmen, mooring side by side when the quays had no more room, exchanged *politesses* in each others' languages. The French, bearded, intellectual-looking, were the more nonchalant, throwing their boats about in the confined space with a certain insouciance – or perhaps better knowledge of the dock; Dick, very English in his white sun-hat, spry, calm despite the near-misses and potential chaos of the berth-finding, took us in with only mild tetchiness.

'Bloody unseamanlike mooring,' he muttered, observing that there was no line from the quay to the last boat – we were now ten deep – to stop one row of boats crashing into another. 'Could be dodgy if a storm blew up.'

The kind of storm Courbet knew about, when he painted a sunset on the Seine estuary. As the sun goes, dark clouds menace the rocks and shadows black and grey envelop the water. There's a mere glow on the horizon, as Coubert describes it, 'sparing the orange, leaving it late to good effect'.

On such an evening, this could have been the view through the vast plate-glass windows on the top floor of the Musée Eugène Boudin – out over Honfleur's approach canal, tree-lined, with its low-tide mudbanks and boatyard slipways, and, beyond, across the estuary to Le Havre. Boudin, too, knew those storms – the great waves that broke over the jetties at Le Havre in the stormy winter of 1895.

Boudin, a great influence on the Impressionists, had the estuary in his blood. Cabin boy on a cider-transporter from Le Havre, he grew up at Honfleur and, apart from his own talent, had the distinction of persuading Monet to paint. In Boudin's paintings, his sailboats scud across the canvas against an almost abstract background of green, blue and grey. On a Normandy beach, a small, Proustian group, dressed in Sunday clothes, sit on chairs, conversing. Near his woods on the road to Trouville,

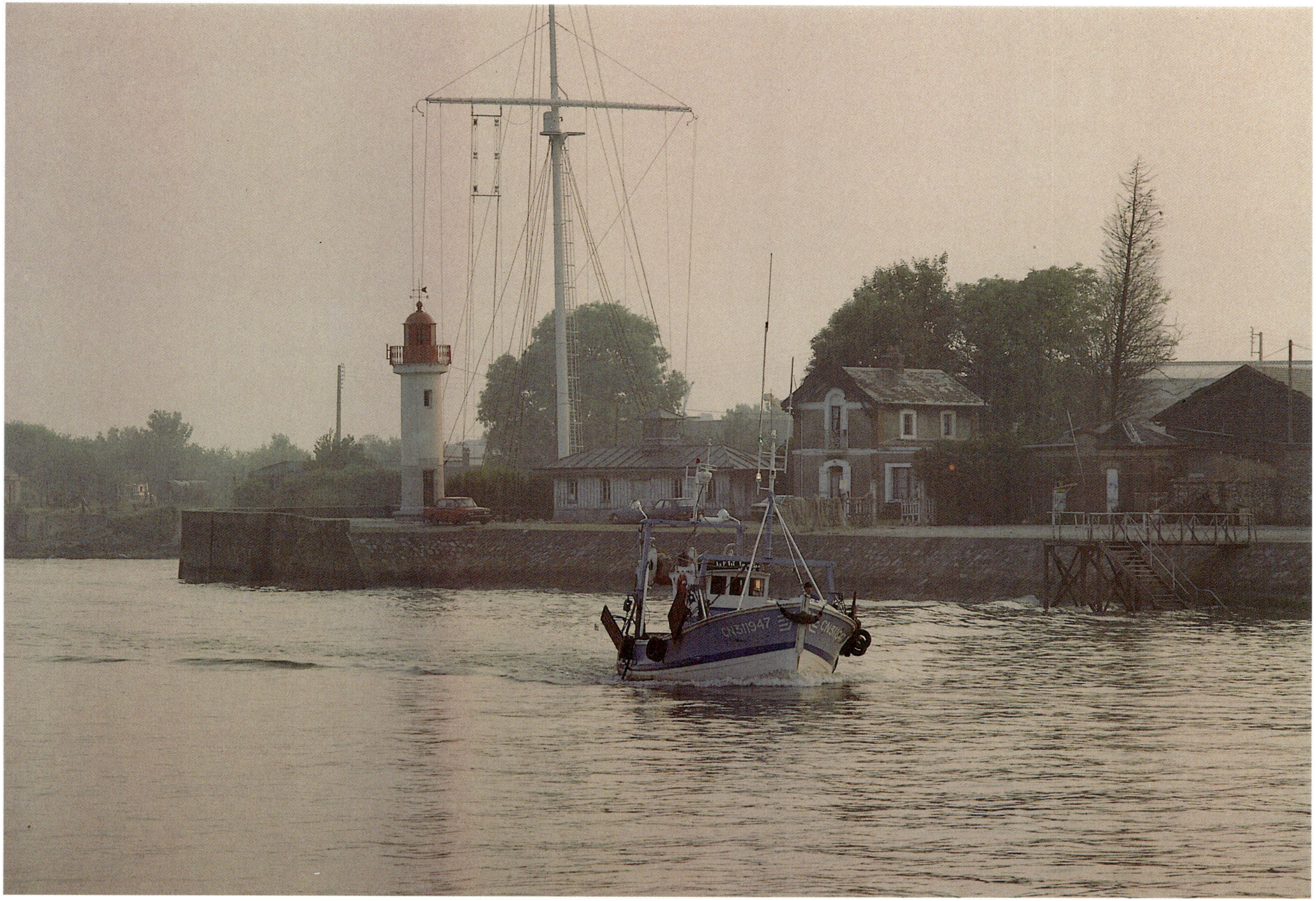

Fishing boat returning home

we found a beautiful Norman barn overlooking a sandy beach, and watched the tide speeding in over the sandbanks; we felt like figures in a Boudin landscape.

Even more so at the Ferme Saint-Siméon, the hillside inn which was the haunt of Boudin and other artists between 1825 and 1865. Monsieur and Madame Toutain were lucky if they had their cider bills paid by the artists who emptied barrels of it beneath the apple trees. Dubourg, who founded the museum with Boudin, painted its gardens; Jongkind and Monet played dominoes there, Boudin skittles; and Courbet, the serious drinker, led gargantuan piss-ups around town, for which many apologies had to be made next day.

Today, the Ferme is more sober. British property hounds on a Normandy buying spree were not even singing as they left the lunch table at 4.30. Now a £100-plus luxury stopover, the Ferme Saint-Siméon's rustic restaurant for rich peasants serves *beignets* of mussels and scampi with ginger, little stews of shellfish with Calvados and larger ones of lobster.

The bedrooms, I'm told by friends, are a delight, with a cliff-top view and therapeutic bathrooms. No marble baths on Dick's yacht – my only complaint.

For dinner, we headed uptown, avoiding the tourist traps on the waterfront. In a narrow street, Rue de l'Homme-de-Bois, was 'La Tortue', intimate, crammed with people (always a good sign), and promising good local cuisine at sensible prices beneath its gabled roof. For once, Norman food was pleasantly light. Chicken cooked in cider, fish brochettes done with bacon, apple tart flamed in Calvados.

'. . . Isle of Wight, German Bight, Heligoland, Finisterre. . . .' Dick was already listening to the BBC shipping forecast, when I joined him on deck next morning. Limpid, hazy sun hung over the Vieux-Port and the sixteenth-century Lieutenance, the harbourmaster's house. Seven-storey buildings along the Quai Ste-Catherine housed galleries galore, and British influence extended to a boutique called 'Twiggy'. Swifts and martins swooped from the high eaves down through the yacht masts, as I set out for the breakfast croissants.

We were out of butter. Too early for the food shops, but the kind woman at the *boulangerie* sold me a kilo destined for tomorrow's croissants. On the way back, I took a detour past a modest back-street house, the birthplace of late-nineteenth-century composer Erik Satie, whose witty, anti-romantic music matched the rebellion of the Impressionists.

But today it was the turn of the brass bands. Honfleur was *en fête* – the Fishermen's Festival. Honfleur fishermen, skilful at navigating that treacherous estuary of shifting sands and heavy seas blowing up out of nowhere, provided some of France's pioneer sailors. From Honfleur, Quebec was colonized in 1608; four thousand Normans from the Honfleur area were the first French settlers in Canada; and Honfleur fishermen were the first to trawl the Dogger Bank.

It was fitting, then, that Whit Sunday should commemorate the exploits of its seafaring ancestors, themselves descended from the Vikings. The tradition continued. Fishing boats in the East Dock were gaily festooned with bunting and paper flowers. *Squatina* won my vote for the most colourful – a startling combination of purple and white. Its skipper, like the others, welcomed aboard anyone prepared for a tight squeeze, as his boat filled up for the flotilla. The skipper wore yachting cap, tailored jeans and Honfleur tee-shirt. Strangely, though – no wine, no cider or beer on board. The puritan north? Imagine a fishermen's festival at Marseilles without pastis!

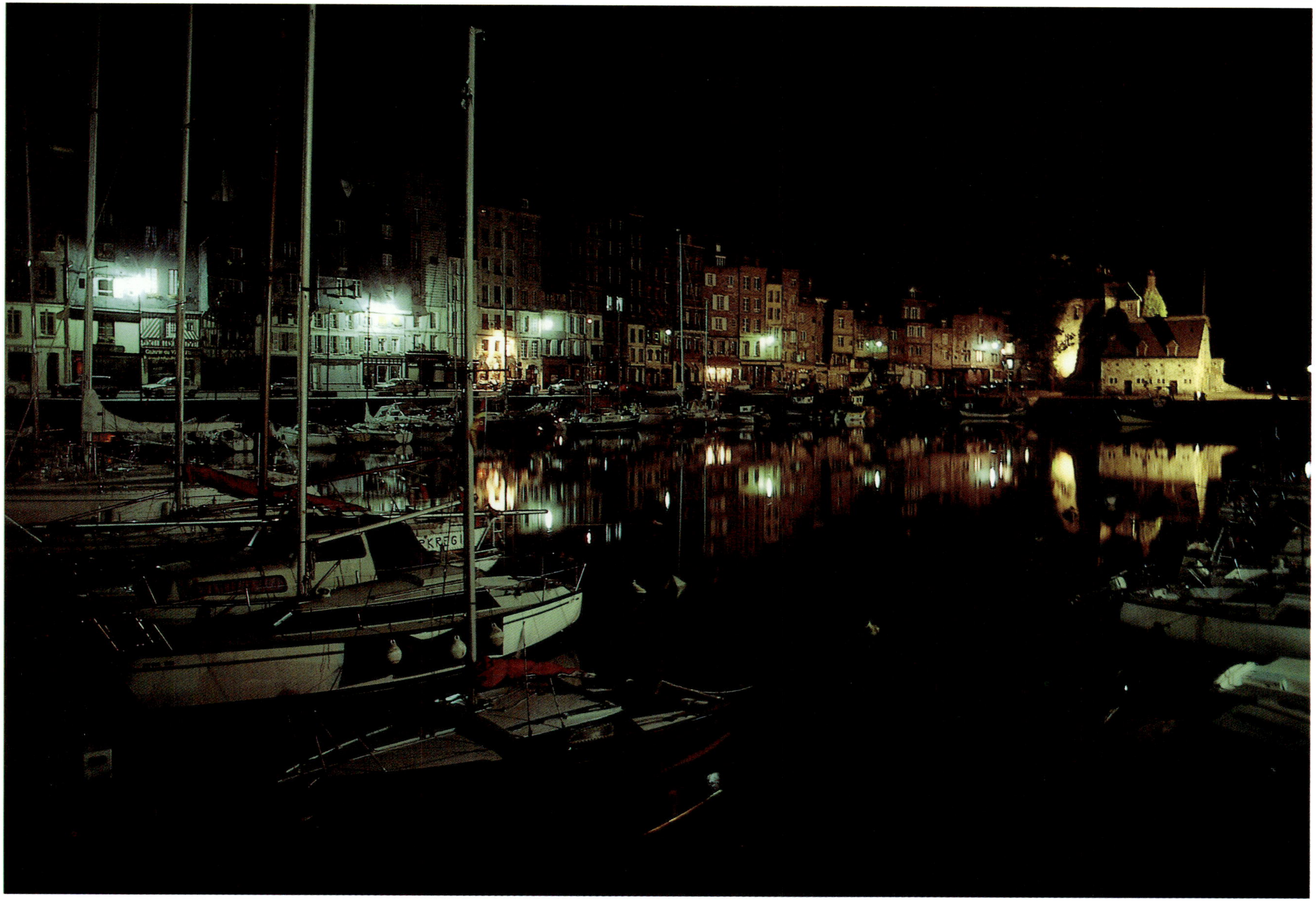

VIEUX PORT, NIGHT

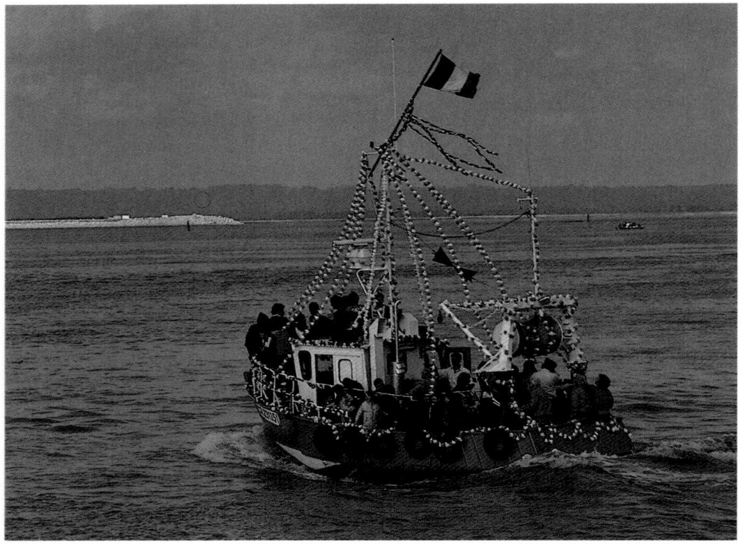

FESTIVAL FISHING BOAT

But the bars near the Lieutenance were doing brisk business. A boy sold pisciform balloons – seahorses and sexy-looking, big-eyed fishettes. On their strings, they lollopped over the heads of the crowd and occasionally, when a child let go his string, went flying away over the fishing boats, to a great wail of tears from its loser.

The water cavalcade was on. Out from the harbour and into the canal came the fishing boats, yachts, dinghies, even a naval sloop showing the French flag. One fishing boat was decked out in Revolutionary red, white and blue. A brass band on board played a march, which was carried out to sea on the off-shore breeze. Some of the boats looked perilously overloaded. But at least today's passengers were not headed for Quebec – nor even for Le Havre, which, though only seven miles across the estuary, could be quite a crossing in a heavy sea.

Popply with flukey airs. In other words, roughish because we had a gusty, Force 6 wind over tide in shallow water. Invigorating spray breaks over our bows, as Dick coolly tacks across a giant tanker headed upstream. Seems impossible we won't be struck amidships.

Missed! Dick knows his speed – and it's fast with this wind. Astern, patches of sunlight dapple the vivid greens of the Côte Fleurie. Rolling meadows and woods fringe the coastline between Honfleur and Trouville with, here and there, the turrets of a seaside home like some whacky fairy castle.

Ahead, dirtier weather. The chimneys and petroleum tanks of Le Havre loom from the misty gloom. I take the tiller, while Dick and Leslie study charts keenly, in the dryness of the keeled-over cabin. Apparently we're too close for comfort to a dangerous hidden sea wall, below the water's surface, marking the limits of the deep water channel. Hit that and we'd be in serious trouble. Dick plays Mozart good and loud to keep our spirits up.

A fisherman, putting on yellow dungarees, makes a rude gesture as we pass his bobbing boat. The rolling gets worse nearer Le Havre, the grey blacker, the waves flecked with white spray higher. This is nothing, Dick assures Carey, who is apprehensive of losing a camera, or herself, overboard. We're right over now, fairly whipping along. All hands are on Carey, as she shoots away, to steady her and protect the camera's lens from spray with a sou'wester. And suddenly the water calms. Between the sea-walls of Le Havre we sail, more upright now. We celebrate with pink gins. The crossing of the estuary has taken 3 hours 25 minutes. A good sail, Dick reckons.

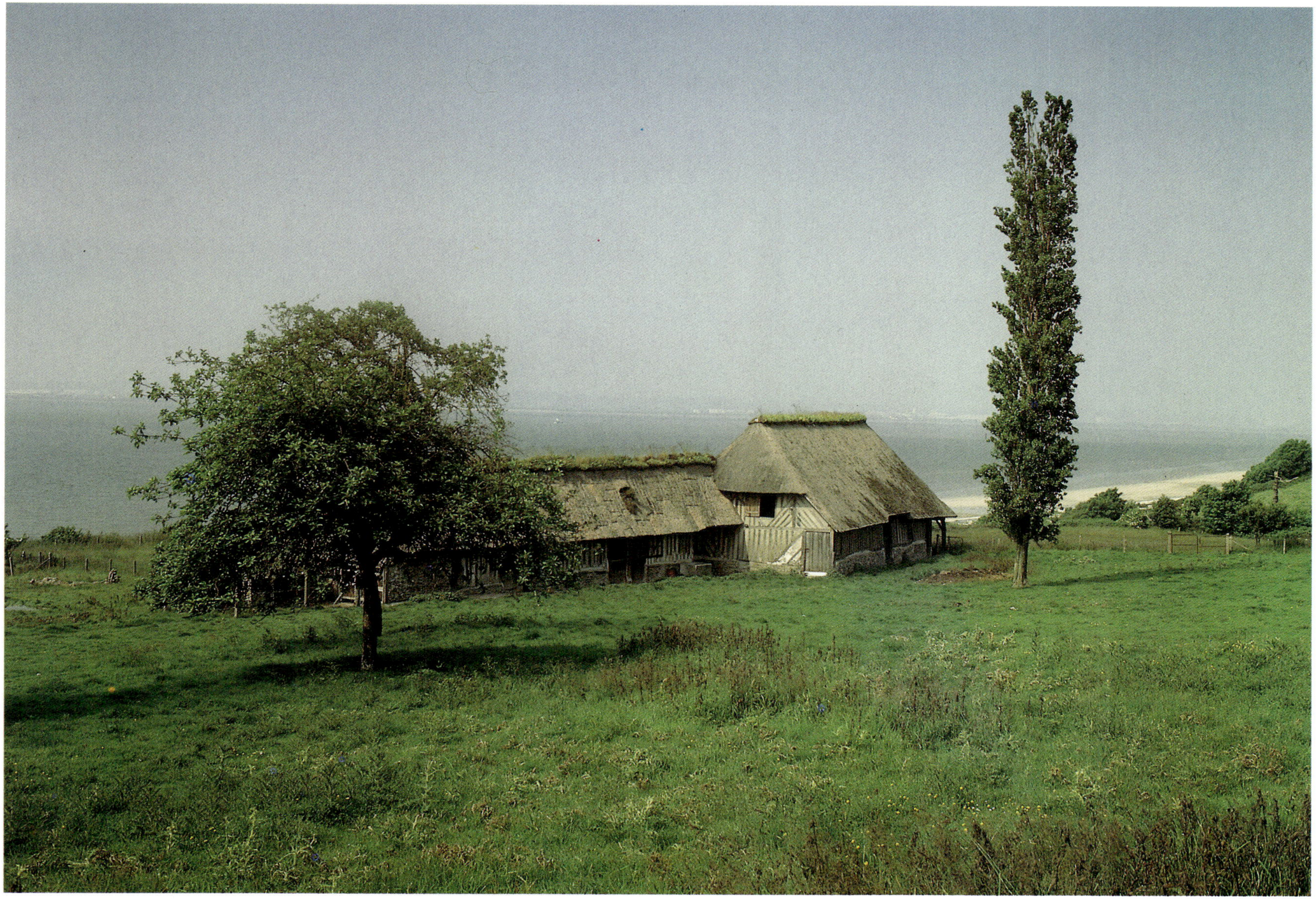

Norman barns, Côte-de-Grâce

AND SO TO SEA

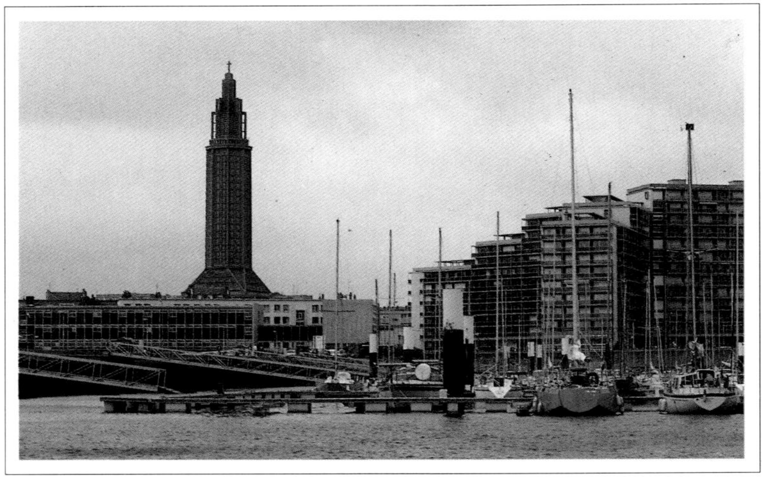

The Haven of Grace – that's how François I, the ubiquitous monarch, named his port. A poet once called it the Constantinople of the North. But over the years, Le Havre developed commercially and often far from gracefully into France's first transatlantic port: in 1850, the *Franklin*, a packet-boat powered by sail and paddle, made New York in fifteen days. During the American Civil War, because Le Havre was trading cotton for arms with the Confederate States, a rare naval battle took place off the coast between the Confederate ship *Alabama* and the Union ship *Kearsage*. The painter Manet, like a one-man television news crew, dashed to Le Havre, hired a fishing-boat and recorded the event on canvas.

All along the Seine since Troyes, we had encountered a staggering number of images of the river and its former life by innumerable artists. Often a museum had highlighted the work of a particular artist, associated with the place – Boudin at Honfleur, Monet at Giverny, and now Raoul Dufy at the Beaux-Arts André Malraux. Le Havre had also spawned Georges Braques and Otto Friesz, and Monet's childhood was spent there. But Dufy, the Fauve, was the one who seemed to evoke its recent, rapidly changing past with most youthful abandon.

In 1905 Dufy was part of the Matisse revolution, '. . . the miracle of imagination introduced into drawing and colour'. His *Port of Le Havre* showed an orange boat and mauve roofs; his

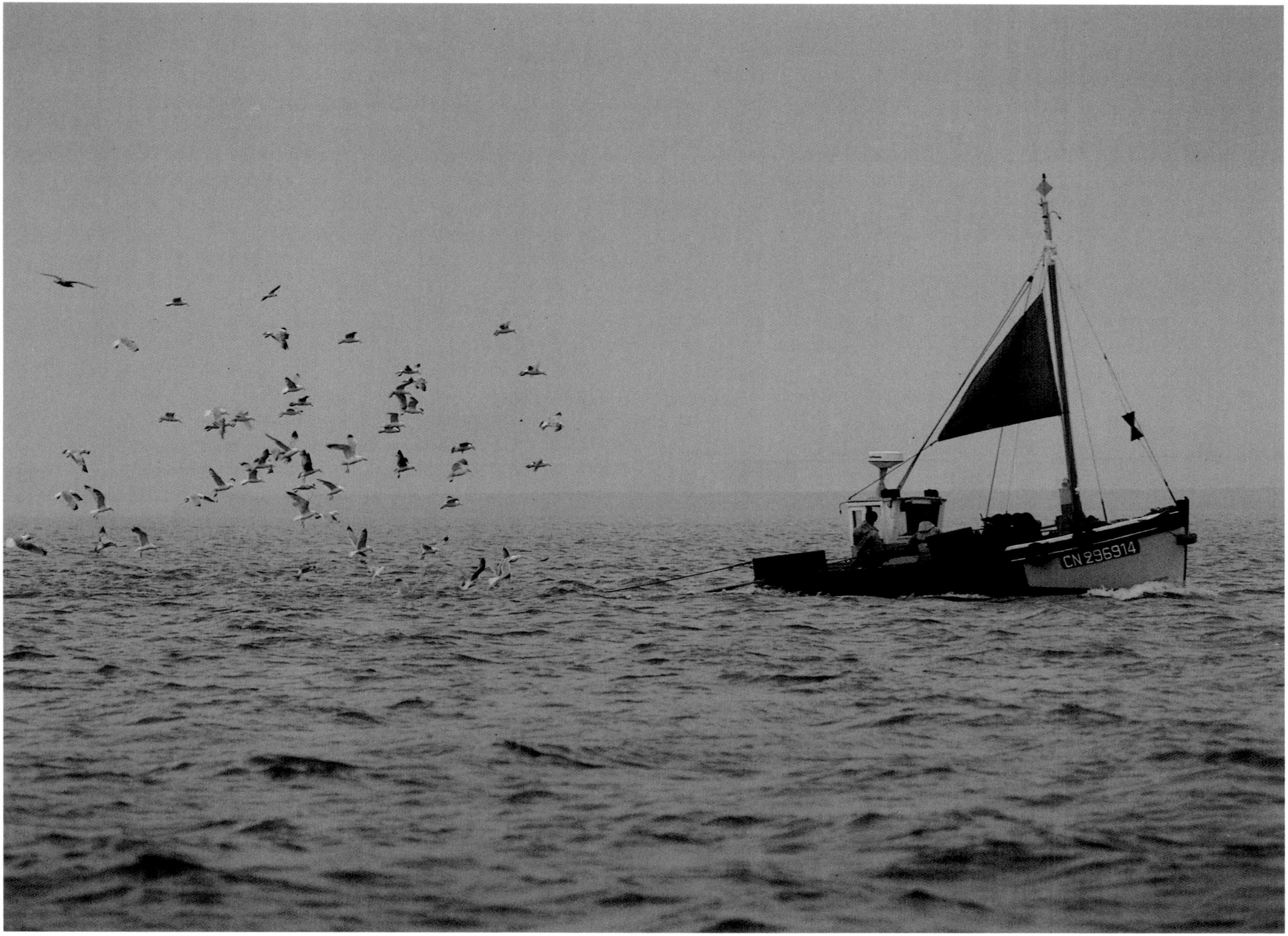

FISHING BOAT AND SEAGULLS, MOUTH OF THE SEINE.

Fourteenth of July concentrated not on the people but the effect of midsummer sun on a variety of bright banners of lively design; *Memory of Le Havre* showed three scalloped shells, the liner *Normandie* and a scroll; *Maritime Festival and Official Visit to Le Havre* was almost a toytown vision of little boats with flags, sailors with oars horizontal and a paddle steamer.

The Havre museum, built in 1961 on the Corniche, was all steel, glass and concrete, spacious and airy, its works of Monet, Friesz, Boudin, Sisley and Pissarro appropriately lit by the sea light. Typical of Le Havre, the museum had salty energy. It felt good to be there – a fine modern building in a city risen from the ashes. In 1945, Le Havre had the doubtful privilege of being Europe's most damaged port; today, it is the second biggest port in France and the third biggest in Europe. Nothing much survives, however, of its images depicted by the Impressionists and Fauves – regattas, transatlantic liners, fishing boats, balls, festivals, bathing beaches, old town, a vital combination of business and pleasure.

But who could not admire the work of Auguste Perret, known as 'the magician of reinforced concrete'? Under this imaginative, practical architect's aegis, the town was completely rebuilt in the 1950s. Utilitarian maybe. But I loved the austere beauty of L'Eglise St-Joseph, its hollow tower with rectangular, stained-glass lozenges in single, primary colours. And the Espace Oscar Niemeyer, the Brazilian architect's cultural centre like a sawn-off nuclear cooling tower.

That Saturday afternoon, the port was quiet. Locks, tugs and dredgers were all resting; and, in the Bassin du Roy, a few little craft lay up on the mud. At the P & O Terminal, however, it was a different story. Cars were boarding the ferry to Southampton. And everywhere around emanated the British Connection: Quai Southampton; Terminal de Grande Bretagne; restaurants called Le Channel, Le Ferry Boat, Le May Flower. The famous Toulouse-Lautrec painting must have been inspired somewhere around here – *The English Girl at The Star in Le Havre*.

Today, in the yacht marina, English seemed to be spoken more than French. After crossing the Channel, Le Havre is the first port of call before heading up the Seine to the canals of France. Masts have to be taken down for bridges, and last-minute preparations made with chandlers and suppliers. We met a young English couple – computer programmer and ballet dancer – who had given it all up, bought an old tub with their savings, and were about to venture through the French canals and across the Mediterranean to Corsica. Their boat didn't look all that seaworthy, nor did they have much experience. But they looked so happy together, as they tinkered and mucked about, that you couldn't believe that anything could mar their dream. The world was their St-Vaast oyster, and they would probably end up going round it.

So, in spite of the petro-chemicals, there was still romance at Le Havre. I scanned the panorama of bobbing masts and high-rise buildings against the grey, bleak sky. And closed my eyes. The tintinnabulation of metal rigging became another sound: a ship's band playing '*Je Reviendrai*'.

Long, long ago, the *Normandie* was sailing for New York. Gaily-coloured streamers festooned the Quai de L'Atlantique. The last siren blew. And, as the departing passengers watched the tugs pulling the great liner out to sea, some shed a tear for the Seine at Bougival, and the Paris quays, and a winding stream in the depths of Burgundy.

Paris, sunset

ACKNOWLEDGEMENTS

We are grateful to the following for their help:

Freddie Archer, Madame Boudier, Duncan Caldwell, Madame Cuny,
François Gouhier, Bernard Higton, Sheila More,
Richard Odgers, Monsieur Pasquier, Port Autonome de Paris, Pierre Richard,
Jacques Rougerie, Pierre Stefan, Abner Stein and Colin Webb.

BIBLIOGRAPHY

La Vie des Bords de Seine by Jean Aubert
Paris et La Batellerie by François Beaudouin
La Batellerie et Confians Sainte Honorine by François Beaudouin
River of Light by Douglas Skeggs
Le Fauvisme by Jean Leymaire
La Peinture de L'Impressionisme by M. and G. Blunden
Flaubert's Parrot by Julian Barnes
L'Oeuvre by Emile Zola
L'Education Sentimentale by Gustave Flaubert
La Femme de Paul, *Souvenir*, and *Sur L'Eau* by Guy de Maupassant